moving on up

Edited by Sarah Brown

EBURY PRESS

First published in Great Britain in 2003

10 9 8 7 6 5 4 3 2 1

© PiggyBankKids Projects Limited, 2003

Each contributor has asserted their right to be identified as the author of their
individual contribution to this work under the Copyright, Designs and
Patents Act 1988.

First published by
Ebury Press
Random House,
20 Vauxhall Bridge Road, London SW1V 2SA

Random House Australia (Pty) Limited
20 Alfred Street, Milsons Point, Sydney, New South Wales 2061, Australia

Random House New Zealand Limited
18 Poland Road, Glenfield, Auckland 10, New Zealand

Random House South Africa (Ptd) Limited
Endulini, 5A Jubilee Road, Parktown 2193, South Africa

The Random House Group Limited Reg. No. 954009

A CIP catalogue record for this book is available from the British Library.

Cover Design by the Senate
Text design and typesetting by Textype

ISBN 0091889685

Papers used by Ebury Press are natural, recycable products made from wood
grown in sustainable forests

Printed and bound in Great Britain by Cox and Wyman Ltd, Reading, Berks.

PiggyBankKids Projects Limited is the trading subsidiary of PiggyBankKids,
UK registered charity number 1092312

contents

foreword

This special edition of *Moving On Up* has been printed as a gift to secondary schools and other education centres in the United Kingdom for students to borrow from their libraries.

This edition has been funded by charitable donation to PiggyBankKids and generously printed by the publisher, Ebury Press, at cost.

We hope that you find people of interest to you in this book and that their stories serve as an inspiration to your own goals. We wish you every success as you start to plan your own career. May you find the inspiration to fulfill your own dreams and ambitions whatever they are.

Sarah Brown   Jim O'Neill

PiggyBankKids

introduction

by Sarah Brown

Most people are fascinated by glimpses into the lives of successful people. Through pictures of the latest celebrity-studded première, coverage of a major political event or telling an individual's heartfelt story, the media reflects our appetite to know more about the people behind the headlines. But as we watch how people succeed in their chosen fields, most of us want to know how it all came about: it can't be just me who is endlessly nosy. We all have our heroes and role models, especially in our chosen fields, both figureheads we have never met and those closer to home, and even as we achieve our own successes, we hope to find people along the way who will encourage, nurture and support our own career dreams.

When you're starting out it can seem very daunting to fathom what the secrets of success are. When you face exam choices at school how exactly are you supposed to decide what you want to be when you grow up: and answer those awkward questions of kindly relatives at seasonal holiday gatherings. And how, once you have that first toe on the bottom rung of your career ladder, do you move on up to reach your goal?

I have always believed that no one moves forward without the practical help, advice or inspiration of others. *Moving On Up* is a collection of personal accounts by people from many walks of life who have achieved enormous success in their work. Everyone in this book was invited to submit their contribution and asked to explain who were their most inspiring people, how this made a difference, and what their own advice is now for someone just starting out.

The contributions range from leaders in business and public service to the arts, entertainment and sport. I have tried to cover the widest range of professions and to find a balance of all sorts of people. I have approached friends, presumed on people I've only met once, and cheekily written to people I haven't met at all, and all of them have kindly supported the project for no fee and to a very tight deadline. I know there are gaps, but I hope that the mix here offers a fair representation, and it certainly makes for fascinating reading whatever stage of life you are at.

The generosity of all those involved shows how ready even the most stratospheric high-flyers are to acknowledge and thank their teachers, bosses, colleagues and other role models who have inspired or mentored them. They have been more than generous in offering their own advice, and in their frank admissions of their own struggles and setbacks along the way. Somehow I think I believed that successful people always had a glittering confidence and self-belief right from the start. But it turns out that many of them were shy, failed exams, and were unsure of their own worth at school or university. Some changed tack once or twice, or failed to find that vital first break for a long time. Drawing on the common themes, it seems that hard work and self-belief are important as well as learning to overcome the fear of failure, and, best of all, to enjoy what we do. There are also unusual and unexpected words of wisdom that make for some surprises in the book too. Clearly the pathways to success are not always easy ones, but no one here complains that it was not worth the effort.

It is fascinating to see that even after many years, a special teacher, boss or friend's words are remembered vividly and act as guiding watchwords. This book is full of amazing stories of the dedication, energy, patience and skill shown by people, often working quietly behind the scenes, devoting their time to teach and pass on their expertise, advice and encouragement. Anyone in a position of mentoring a young person in the classroom or the workspace can take heart that all good teaching is lasting and worthwhile.

Some of the most important lessons are not the most obvious ones. I learnt lasting lessons from my art teacher at school. I was determined that while I could happily appreciate art, I was no good at it myself; looking at my own efforts at drawing it was easy to reach that conclusion. I have never really changed the view about my drawing skills, but I did learn from my art teacher, Joe Kusner, that if I just stayed focused on academic subjects I was missing out on a lot. I can still remember his quiet words, and the feeling of humility at my arrogance in dismissing something simply because I was not good at it. The art room was literally the heart of the school, it had warmth and energy and many of us finished our maths homework there so that we could stay on for the youth club after school. Then we could have fun with paint and clay and – I remember it well – plaster of Paris and chickenwire. We learned to open our eyes to enjoying art, drama, music and dance. Now, even though I work in business, my expertise lies in promoting the arts. My school went on to achieve specialist status in art – and I'll bet every student there learns to enjoy art and culture and that not everyone can draw either!

In receiving all the entries for this book, I was fascinated to see how my experiences compared to others – it was a real thrill for me to discover that similar lessons to my own had a lasting effect on the UK's Astronomer Royal, Sir Martin Rees – he can't draw either but is our most pre-eminent reacher for the stars!

I tracked down Joe Kusner, now retired and recognised for his achievements with an MBE, and invited him to write an entry to *Moving On Up*. I was amazed to see the journey he'd travelled to bring all that he had learned in his life to bear on his classrooms over the years. Now when I work with younger people, I try to find time to pass on what I've learned, and to encourage self-confidence in others and a belief in their own potential.

I imagine we all acknowledge that parenting has the greatest influence – and some of our contributors, despite my asking for the inspiration of other people, couldn't help but come back to the enduring impact of parents, grandparents, uncles and aunts, brothers and sisters. But what happens if your parents can't provide the time and support they would ideally want to? What happens when poverty or other events overtake stable family life? It is very hard for any child growing up without this support to gain the self-confidence they need. Or to learn about all the options and choices for careers available. Our contributors show that the influence of other adults who took the time to teach, encourage and advise them has also had a lifetime's influence.

The power of mentoring is clearly lasting and rewarding. Many more adults are finding time each week to devote to meeting with a young person to talk, go out, have fun – and more parents are finding, when things are pretty stretched, that an adult mentor for their child can bring valuable friendship and support at a critical time. There is no doubt that mentoring plays a powerful role in contributing to the confidence, development and success of a young person. And it can make the mentor feel pretty special too.

There have always been mentors throughout history: Charles Darwin said of his friendship with the clergyman-scientist, Professor Henslaw, that he 'influenced my whole career more than any other'. We all take for granted the theory of gravity, but Sir Isaac Newton was actually in difficulty at school until his headmaster, Henry Stokes, saw his talent and went on to encourage him to go to university. And Charles Dickens, after years of struggle, got his first break in publishing from John Macrone who commissioned a volume of his writing sketches bringing him universal acclaim at the age of only 24, and from that winning a new contract with a bigger publishing house for *The Pickwick Papers*. For women, education was so discouraged in the past, that Florence Nightingale would never have lit a candle without her friend, Sidney Herbert, telling her 'nursing needs people like you' and giving her books to study in secret. Sidney Herbert's mentoring role lasted a lifetime as he later arranged, against opposition, for Florence Nightingale to run the hospital in Scutari in the Crimea where she changed nursing practice for the better. Even people in powerful and privileged positions today are happy to build on their experience and knowledge to work more effectively. HRH Princes Charles is the first to acknowledge his good fortune in having the esteemed writer, traveller and philosopher, Laurens Van der Post, as his mentor in his early life.

PiggyBankKids works to support opportunities for children and young people through a range of partnerships with other charities and individuals. Having seen this book, first published in April 2003, meet with success in the bookshops, I am delighted that this edition will now be sent free of charge to all state and independent secondary schools in the United Kingdom. This has been made possible through generous donation to PiggyBankKids to cover the costs of printing and posting the books to the schools. Thanks are also due to Jim O'Neill for championing this new edition for free copies to go to UK schools and to Gail Rebuck at Random House and Fiona Macintyre at Ebury Press for arranging a big discount to print the books. Together with all the contributors (and their helpful PAs and agents), my deepest gratitude is also due to Hugo Tagholm for all his hard work as Programme Director of PiggyBankKids in making this book happen. And to Gil McNeil, PiggyBankKids Publishing Director and the charity's trustees, Lord Paul of Marylebone, Baroness Goudie of Roundwood and David Boutcher for their unfailing support for *Moving On Up*.

In the UK, mentoring projects are available in many parts of the country and more information about the mentoring charity, Big Brothers & Sisters UK and how to get involved are available at the back of this book.

You can dip into this book anywhere – there is no official starting point. All the entries are grouped loosely within professional areas running alphabetically, and each section has an opening introduction by a well-known leader in the field sharing their own story. Whether you are reading this book to find out the secrets of success as you start out, to add to your own knowledge, or to guide someone else – or you are just plain inquisitive about people, I hope you enjoy it and thank you for your support.

sport

Sir Alex Ferguson CBE
Manager, Manchester United Football Club

When you try to analyse your life, you invariably go back to the beginning. What part of your upbringing still exists in you, and what were those pieces of advice which made the difference.

I can think of many things that my parents instilled in me which have lasted forever, and those precious moments with my grandmother who always seemed to extract the best out of me, and my brother Martin, yes wonderful memories. Do you know one of the great disciplines my father instilled in me was time keeping? Every morning around 6.15am my brother and I would get the old shake of the foot from my dad, no words were needed: the shake told us it was time to get up and go to work. After a few minutes' extra respite from the exposure to those awful cold Glasgow mornings we'd hear those well-learnt words, 'Are those two up yet?', followed by the thunder of his feet making their way up to our bedroom. Did we move? You bet we did, like greyhounds out of a trap, grabbing at anything resembling clothes. Goodness, that was the hardest bit of the day and yet the most rewarding; this simple discipline of my dad's regarding time-keeping has stayed with me all my life. I was never late for work in six years as a toolmaker and I have tried to instil this in my own sons, as basically you are to a degree what your parents wanted you to be. But as you grow into adulthood you develop your own character and personality, and I have noticed this clearly with my own sons.

People keep asking me what has made me successful. At first I was often flummoxed by the question because I always felt to appraise yourself is very difficult unless you have a good amount of vanity, which, I can say without hesitation, I don't.

However, as years pass I think it is important to at least find some particular reason for what you think is most important, and went for the most sensational discovery – hard work, yes plain old hard work. Now, there are some people who may say, 'is that all?' Well I can say without equivocation that the ability to work hard all your life is firstly not easy and secondly an inspiration to those who work under or with you. I could write a list of the 100 most successful people in the world and 90 per cent have made it through the ability to work hard, persevere and be determined. Of course, no one should write off naturally talented people, but they also need the application of hard work to be successful, whereas hard-working people can survive without natural talent. In a sporting context the great examples are all there and will always be there because they never ignore the essentials of their sport. And yes, in a funny way they enjoy being able to come off the field tired because they know how much the balance of hard work applied to their skill has made them a winner.

When you witness a great piece of skill, by a sports star like David Beckham, you must realise it is not an accident, it is by pure hard work on the practice field, perfecting his free kicks and corner kicks which has helped to make him a star. I remember reading an article about the great golfer Gary Player when he was explaining why he practised for hours playing shots out of the sand traps on the golf course. He said, 'I practise those shots because I know that at one point in a championship I am going to land in that bunker and if I don't hole out I may lose that championship.' That is quite a revealing comment as most golfers would be just glad to get out of the bunker and get on to the green, but not Gary. He is talking about holing out from the sand!

I think that closes all the debates about hard work and hope all young aspiring readers of this take the advice to heart. Be proud of the fact that you work hard.

* * *

Kriss Akabusi MBE
400-metre athlete, Olympic medallist and British record-breaker

I began my international athletic career in 1983 as a member of the 4 x 400-metre relay squad and helped Britain clinch the gold in Tokyo in 1991. In 1990 I won the gold medal for athletics in the European Championships, breaking the British record. Today, I run my own public relations company, undertake a lot of public speaking engagements and still play lots of sport including golf and basketball. As a Christian I regularly attend my local church with my family.

The first person that really believed in me was Sergeant Ian MacKenzie when I joined the army at 16. I had come from a children's home and had never been a high achiever at school. Up to this point no one had tried to bring out my true skills. Sergeant Ian MacKenzie was the army's 400-metres champion, so naturally I was drawn into a sport that proved to be my forte! My rewards came early – Sergeant MacKenzie would never forget to put my name up on the Orders – the daily achievements board where performances would be displayed. He saw my potential, nurtured it and gave me the essential self-esteem to succeed.

After a year with this regiment I was posted to Germany where Hansi Boheme took me under his wing. He instilled in me the concept of a regular, focused training programme. He fixed my mind on one discipline, athletics, and taught me a systematic training technique, looking at the basic necessities to get the best performance. This is where I truly developed as an athlete and laid the foundations to become a world-class 400-metre runner.

Turning professional, one of my tasks was to be a mentor to new athletes. These included Roger Black, a formidable natural talent. Through the experience and knowledge I had gained over the years I helped guide and nurture him, which was a privilege and a two-way learning process. Roger has certainly proved his talent since, and it was a fantastic experience to help him on his way.

MY ADVICE: *Everyone needs a teacher and an inspiration in life, but never forget that you are also teaching and setting an example on your route to* *success. The struggle to succeed will always make you stronger, and remember, success comes in many guises.*

Roger Black MBE
Former athlete, TV sports presenter and motivational speaker

For 14 years, I represented Great Britain at the highest level in the world of athletics; both as an individual 400-metres runner and a member of the 4 x 400-metres relay team. I won 15 championship medals including European, Commonwealth and World Championship gold medals.

I now use my individual and team experiences in my work as a motivational speaker adding value to corporate conferences by motivating, inspiring and entertaining audiences from many organisations. I teach people to understand the dynamics of becoming a champion, how to live a dream, set goals and take the necessary steps to fulfil their potential. I also present athletics for BBC Sport and the live BBC flagship programme *Tomorrow's World*.

Many people inspired me throughout my athletic career including training partners, Kriss Akabusi and Daley Thompson, as well as coaches.

In 1995 I began to speak regularly to an ex-athlete called David Jenkins who had an enormous effect on me. He was my mentor and taught me to be proactive and focus on everything I could control instead of worrying about things out of my control. I learnt from the mistakes he made during his career and my self-belief grew and grew. In the end I won an Olympic silver medal over 400 metres in Atlanta.

MY ADVICE: *Train hard, dream of what's possible, set goals and find somebody to share your dreams with. Learn as much from your mistakes as your successes and always ask for advice from people who have succeeded (and failed) before you.*

David Davies
Acting Chief Executive & Director of International Strategy, the Football Association

After 24 years as a presenter and correspondent for BBC Television with programme credits ranging from *National News* to *Grandstand* and *Match of the Day,* from *Songs of Praise* to *Children in Need*, I joined the Football Association in 1994. My job titles there have been Director of Public Affairs (1994 to 1998), Executive Director (1998 to 2002), Director of International Strategy (2002 to date) and most recently Acting Chief Executive. People tell me my main attributes are persistence, resilience and an ability to evaluate priorities.

My father died shortly after I was born. I was brought up by my mum and aunt in central London. I was sent away to school aged eight, and by fifteen was sure education was not for me. Certainly, teachers, obsessed with strict discipline and learning everything parrot-fashion, were not for me. Richard Dilley was very different. He was a teacher at my senior school and he convinced me that education mattered. He communicated; he listened as well as talked. Unlike too many teachers I'd encountered, he hated corporal punishment. From being shy and withdrawn, I developed a new confidence. Perhaps he has a lot to answer for!

MY ADVICE: *Firstly ensure you know everything possible about your chosen profession and its impact on your life. Do you mind a job that effectively takes over your life or are you deep down a nine-to-five person? Look for role models. Look for and learn from those who've made a difference already in the organisation you join. Don't be afraid to admit mistakes. Constantly question and criticise yourself.*

Sharron Davies MBE
Former swimmer; now TV presenter

After a lot of training I eventually won many sporting honours in my swimming career, starting with bronze medals at the 1977 European Games, followed by gold medals a year later at the Commonwealth Games. I won a silver medal at the 1980 Moscow Olympic Games, and actually competed in three different Olympics in three different decades. My last major medal was the World Short Course bronze medal in 1991. I was a Commonwealth record holder for 12 years, and still hold the British record for the 400 I.M. after 20 years. I was fortunate enough to be voted Sports Woman of the Year twice and altogether I broke or re-broke over 200 British swimming records in my career. I now work as a TV presenter on sports programmes amongst other media and PR work.

My father was my coach and mentor. He gave up his job to coach and ferry me to training every day and was always my 100 per cent support system along with my mum. He always said, 'If you are going to do something then do it to the best of your ability and you'll never be disappointed.' I'm a great believer that we all have something we're great at – the secret is finding it!

MY ADVICE: *Anything worth having is worth working for. Most of my sporting friends weren't successful first time so don't give up too easily. I tried many times!*

Jonathan Edwards
Athlete

I am a triple-jump athlete. I made my first appearance for Great Britain at the 1988 Olympic Games. Since then I have won two world titles (1995 and 2001), a European title (1998), an Olympic title (2000) and a Commonwealth title (2002). I also hold the triple jump world record.

I would have to say that the most influential and inspiring factor in my life has been my faith. So, if I had to crystallise that to a person, it would be Jesus. And, of course, my faith involves being part of a community, and I would include that community as part of the reason I have achieved what I have. Jesus provides teaching for me on how to live, and his own life is an example to follow.

Ultimately, Jesus was willing to sacrifice his life to achieve God's purpose for the world, and that example of sacrifice has underpinned my own success as an athlete.

MY ADVICE:
Have faith in God and be prepared to make your own sacrifices.

Mark Harris
Professional Surfer

I enter professional surfing competitions and, by way of example, in 2002 my contest results were:

1st Headworx in the B.P.S.A (British Professional Surfing Association) Open and 2nd Fat Face B.P.S.A Night time, both in Newquay in May; 3rd Headworx in the Jersey B.P.S.A. Open in September; 2nd Surfing Life South Coast B.P.S.A. Open in Plymouth in October; and 1st Headworx North East B.P.S.A. Open in Scarborough followed by 2nd Headworx North Devon B.P.S.A. Open in Croyde both in November. In 2002 I was awarded B.P.S.A. Pro Tour Champion. I am sponsored by Quiksilver, Reef Shoes and Electric Sun Glasses who are a huge support which enables me to surf professionally.

There are many people who inspire me in the surfing world for different reasons. Firstly, as a grommet growing up and surfing in Newquay, I've had lots of great surfers to look up to, like former European champions Grishka Roberts and Spencer Hargraves, and the current European Number 1, Russell Winter. They are all from Newquay, grew up surfing my local waves, and have been very successful on the pro tour, putting British surfing on the map and inspiring me.

Surfing is a very stylish sport in the way you express yourself on the waves – every surfer having their own style. I love watching all surfing and my favourite surfer is Joel Parkinson. He has an amazing style and I always get amped for a surf after watching him on a surf video. My dad also inspires me because I love watching him surf and seeing how keen he is at 55. He went surfing today in a wind chill of −5, got loads of waves and was fully stoked, classic!

MY ADVICE: *Surf however you want to – if it feels good do it. Get wet as much as possible because Britain gets waves as good as anywhere in the world on their day!*

Gary Lewin
Sports Physiotherapist, Arsenal Football Club and England Football team

I have been the Arsenal first team physiotherapist for 16 years and the England physiotherapist for the past six years.

When I left school I joined Arsenal as an apprentice goalkeeper, but, at the age of 18, I was released by the club as I was not going to make it as a professional footballer. Like most youngsters, it was my dream to play for the team I supported as a boy, so this was a very difficult time which left me at a crossroads. Should I drop down to the lower leagues and continue playing or should I study to gain professional qualifications? It was at this time that I received invaluable advice and guidance from two people in particular.

Firstly, the Arsenal and England physiotherapist at the time was Fred Street, who not only actively encouraged me to take up physiotherapy, he arranged for me to visit Guy's Hospital School of Physiotherapy. It was after this visit that I decided to follow this path.

The second person that was instrumental in my progress was Alf Fields, an ex-professional footballer who looked after the Arsenal youth team players at the time. Alf encouraged me to believe in myself and never lose sight of my goal. He said if I remained disciplined I would succeed. It was his undivided support, counselling and general advice that kept me focused on becoming a physiotherapist instead of trying to become a professional footballer in the lower leagues.

I left my playing days with Arsenal behind in 1982 and moved on to Barnet FC on a part-time basis. I wanted to keep my options open and combine some kind of playing career with gaining a professional qualification. Fortunately, I had nine 'O' Levels which enabled me to study for two 'A' Levels in human biology and pure and applied maths. I returned to my old school and successfully took the two 'A' Levels in one year. I then applied and was accepted to train at Guy's Hospital, London. Whilst studying at Guy's between 1983 and 1986, I stopped playing football but concurrently worked with the Arsenal medical staff who were responsible for the reserve and youth team enabling me to gain invaluable experience in sports medicine.

Immediately after completing my qualifications in 1986, I was taken on at Guy's Hospital but I gave up my post there in September of that year when I was offered the position as the first team physiotherapist at Arsenal.

It was the constructive and reassuring advice of Fred Street and Alf Fields that gave me the determination and confidence, not only to gain professional qualifications but to achieve my lifelong ambition of working in professional football. I will be forever indebted to them both.

MY ADVICE: *During your life there will be times of failure but never lose your self-belief, your self-discipline and your determination to succeed.*

Stephen McClaren
Manager, Middlesbrough Football Club

After a playing career which included Hull City, Derby County, Bristol City and Oxford United, I started coaching the youth and reserve teams at Oxford. Four years later I became Assistant Manager at Derby County, then moving to Manchester United as Assistant Manager after three-and-a-half years. Whilst at Manchester United I became involved in the England set-up as Coach. I continued working with England even when I became the Middlesbrough Manager at the beginning of the 2001–2002 season.

Bill Bewick is a sports psychologist who I met at various coaching courses. He was one of our speakers. He started doing work for me at Derby, then Manchester, and is now my Assistant Manager at Middlesbrough. He taught me about the mental side of the athlete and teamwork. He has worked closely with me to develop my coaching and managing. He became my mentor, and someone I could share my ideas with, offering me advice and using the experience he has gained to guide me through my career.

The best advice Bill gave me was to be different, to develop my own style of coaching and managing, and not to copy other people.

MY ADVICE: *Attain all the qualifications necessary to work at this level. Develop your own style. Seek out an older respected person who can pass on* *their experience to you. Learn from mistakes and don't be afraid to make them! Work damned hard.*

Michael Owen
Professional Footballer, Liverpool Football Club and England football team

At seven years old, I joined Mold Alexander, and at eight I was picked by Deeside Primary School. I moved up to Harworden High and was approached by a number of clubs, but chose Liverpool. At 14, I went to the FA School of Excellence where I began to realise my dream.

My boyhood hero was Gary Lineker, but my dad, Terry, who was a former professional footballer with Everton, Bradford City, Chester and Cambridge, was undoubtedly my inspiration. As soon as I could walk he had me kicking a ball, but he never forced it upon me. He helped me develop my own opinions and stressed I should enjoy the game first and foremost. As an ex-professional he could always offer plenty of advice, but there was one lesson he drummed in: follow up the ball in the goal. It is remarkable how many goals I have poached because of this advice.

MY ADVICE: *Always concentrate on your game and seek to improve as you can always learn. Work hard and don't get carried away with any success you may have, and you must take it one step at a time. You cannot afford to look too far into the future as you never know what may be around the corner.*

Gareth Southgate
Professional Footballer, Middlesbrough Football Club and England football team

I have played for Crystal Palace, Middlesbrough and Aston Villa. I have over 50 caps playing for the England football squad.

Alan Smith was my first coach at Crystal Palace, when I left school. He went on to be the Manager and basically was in charge of me from when I was 16 until I turned 24. When you leave school I don't think your parents can help you quite as much, particularly in professional football. You are quite reliant on working with quality people. Alan helped me as a player but more importantly continued my development as a person. He believed in my ability but could be critical at the right times. He showed me the rewards that could be achieved from success, but was quick to bring me down to earth if I ever got carried away. Without Alan's help, support and advice, I might never have gone on to have a career in professional football.

MY ADVICE: *Football is a tough profession. Don't ever think you can stop learning or improving. Look after your body as it is the tools of your trade, and listen to advice from people you respect.*

Tony Stephens
Sports Agent, SFX Sports Group (Europe)

From 1982, I was the Commercial Manager at Aston Villa Football Club and then became Marketing Director of Wembley Stadium four years later. I was appointed Marketing Director of the SFX Sports Group in 1988. SFX is the world's largest sports management and live entertainment organisation, and my personal clients include David Beckham, Alan Shearer and Michael Owen. We also represent stars like Michael Jordan and Andre Agassi.

In life you become an amalgam of all the people who have impressed you. Talk or write to successful people – you will be surprised how much help they will give you. Everyone started somewhere.

MY ADVICE: *Begin by pretending to be the person you are trying to be – and then gradually you become that person. Keep stretching yourself: you never go back to the same shape. Remember, you are in life what people perceive you to be.*

Never accept 'no' for an answer. Don't think about problems, think about possible solutions. Don't worry about losing the occasional battle, as long as you win the wars!

Try to work with people you like, on projects which stimulate you and for people who pay their bills on time.

arts and entertainment

Richard Eyre
Writer and former Director, Royal National Theatre

I grew up in the west of England, in Dorset, in a landscape that to today's eyes would seem like a theme park: little churches, sandstone villages, valleys, hills, downland and the burial mounds, earthworks and standing stones of Celtic Britain. Our milk was delivered from a churn on a cart, I could see our butter being made or our bread being baked and, if I'd wanted to, I could have seen our meat being slaughtered. I could watch the blacksmith making horseshoes and the thatcher laying straw on cottage roofs.

What I couldn't do was watch much drama: the nearest cinema was eight miles away, the nearest theatre where I could see a play was at least ten times as far, and until I was ten we didn't have a TV set. If you add to this the fact that my parents had little or no interest in the arts it's a marvel that I became an actor, then a director and ended up running Britain's Royal National Theatre. None of these things happened on my own initiative. Like most people in the arts, I've depended on the kindness of patrons – the people who take an interest in you, who form your taste, who change your way of looking at the world, who sometimes save you from yourself.

As a child I wanted to be an actor. I suppose I wanted the gift of fluency and love. The search for approval is the force that sustains all actors and the lack of it – insecurity – is the actor's fuel. I certainly wasn't lacking that. What I lacked – as I eventually learned – was a talent that was more than a facility for mimicry, more than a readiness to be the comic turn at parties, more than a knack for dazzling the class when reading aloud, and more than a dizzying simulation of self-confidence. No amount of effort or education could compensate me for my lack of talent. I've learnt that actors are born, not made.

Like many aspiring actors I was shy, I was reserved, and I was more comfortable speaking in any voice but my own. Because we're so obsessed by class, we English get a lot of practice at this – it's often more comfortable or more liberating to pretend to be what you're not. I acquired a skill as a mimic, partly as a passport out of being middle class, partly as a weapon: I was able to imitate my friends and my teachers.

There was one teacher I never had the desire to mock, rather the opposite. He was an English teacher, an ex-Commando Major who had lost his leg in the D-Day landings. He used his stick to gain our attention, banging it on his tin leg or hurling it like a lance at recalcitrant pupils. He had a voice like an English Spencer Tracy and he loved reading aloud. One reading convinced me of the power of performance and of descriptive writing: Hemingway's *The Old Man and the Sea*. I unhesitatingly identified the Old Man with the Major, and when he finished the story there was a silence in the classroom that could have been carved into a monument. He took an interest in me, thought that I had a talent for acting, and wrote a play for me: *The Man Who Won the Pools*. I was that man. We performed it after the school prize-giving, to applause that intoxicated me and corrupted me irrevocably.

After leaving school, I became a barman and wine waiter in a restaurant in Somerset, and I continued to work there intermittently during my university years. Working in a restaurant was a rehearsal for working in the theatre, and I was attracted to it for many of the same reasons: there was a satisfaction in being able to recognise success as it occurred – the satisfied customer – and I found the hours attractive. I liked working during other people's leisure time and having time off when everyone else was working. It gave me a sense of living by different rules, an illusion, of course, but a fantasy that sustains many actors and directors.

I became a professional actor much as I might have become a soldier in the nineteenth century; I didn't seem to be fitted for anything else. Anyone can become an actor: all you have to do is to find someone to conspire in your delusion by offering you work and obtain an Equity card. In my day you simply applied for one and paid a subscription; nowadays there's a little more to it: you have to serve a mandatory twenty weeks' apprenticeship. The catch, of course, is that to get the work you need the card, and to get the card you need the work. I know an actress who got her card as the stooge in a knife-throwing act. It's not the worst apprenticeship; an actor always needs to be equipped to take anything that's thrown at them. I had no such training, and I embarked on my life as an actor armed only with my availability, my optimism and my defiant description of myself as a professional.

I gave up acting when I was working in the Christmas show at the Phoenix Theatre in Leicester. The show was *The Boy Friend*, about which I was as impartial as a hawk with a dead mouse. I hated it. I wasn't alone; like prisoners of war counting flies, the chorus, or at least the male half, developed their own survival techniques. We sat motionless in our dressing room before the show, our feet on the table, staring inscrutably at ourselves and our colleagues out of the corners of our eyes. The challenge was to see who could be the last to get changed, made-up (regular Riviera tan, Leichner 5 and 9), and get onstage for the first bar of the opening number. It was often the first note of the (shortish) overture that signalled an explosion of activity, with a degree of manic energy and commitment that disappeared as soon as we arrived onstage in our white shirts, trousers and deck shoes and told the audience that it was 'Nicer, much nicer in Nice'. Given our views on Leicester we could have sung that it was nicer in Anchorage, Alaska, with as much conviction.

I didn't have the will to continue as an actor. It was more than a lack of talent; I felt as if I'd been cushioned by a combination of exhibitionism and vanity, fuelled by sufficient confidence for the audience to supply the missing part and put it down to inexperience. And there had been enough co-conspirators in my fiction to encourage me to think I could earn a living out of acting. Confidence is nine-tenths of the business of acting, and when my cushion of confidence deflated I was left with nothing but despair.

To salvage some self-esteem I persuaded some of my fellow actors to be in a production of Ann Jellicoe's play, *The Knack*, which we rehearsed on the days that we didn't have a matinée and played for one performance on a Sunday night. After the performance the director of the theatre, Clive Perry, who hid his feelings behind a closely preserved cladding of diffidence, clinked his coins together and said this to me: 'Um . . . on that . . . um.' Pause. 'On that, if you want to be a director, you can become one. I'm not sure you'll ever be an actor. But you must choose.' And I did.

He asked me to do a production of the same play for a four-week run a few months later. I don't suppose doing what I do for a living will ever be as exciting, and I don't think I've ever felt quite so intensely the absurd privilege of getting paid for what you enjoy doing. I knew nothing about the process; all was intuitive. Ignorance (or innocence) seemed a glorious asset. It couldn't last. Like a child's acting, it may be successful in short bursts, but to sustain it, to repeat it – to become a professional – takes application and technique. I tried to acquire technique but rehearsals are a private province; no one likes to be observed, so it's hard to see enough to imitate, even if you have a model to follow.

My model at the time was (and still is) the director, Peter Brook. I wrote to him (how I found his address I don't know) and he replied, said he didn't know how he could help me, but invited me to come and talk with him. We met; he talked; I listened. He spoke with great clarity, with unforced charm and without any sense of talking down to me, although I was thoroughly and obviously ignorant and awestruck. Like all exceptionally intelligent people, he offered me the gift of his intelligence and required me to give my best in return. What impressed me then (and now) was not so much his expertise as a teacher as his doggedness as a pupil: he kept on asking questions. It's this capacity above all that persuaded me to emulate him – it's at the heart of what makes a director. I asked if I might be his assistant. 'Why?' he said. 'You're a great teacher,' I said.

'You can only learn from yourself,' he said, 'from doing it yourself.'

But you need someone to give you the opportunity to do it: you need a patron. I've often been asked how I became a professional director, to which I mumble nepotism, luck, bribery, or even hard work, but the truth is this: I had a patron. His name was Clive Perry and without his faith in me I would never have become a director.

* * *

Waheed Alli (Lord Alli)
Television Producer and Labour Peer

I left school when I was 16 with a handful of 'O' levels, and then found my first job at the Job Centre working for a group of financial organisations. I subsequently went on to work in the City of London and in 1992, I set up a production company, Planet 24, with Charlie Parsons and Bob Geldof. In 1999 the company was sold to Carlton and I took over as Managing Director of Carlton Television. I am now a television producer and also a member of the House of Lords working with the Labour Party.

The person who has inspired me through my adult life is Charlie Parsons. As my friend and colleague at Planet 24, Charlie had confidence in me and my abilities. He challenged me to think before I acted and most of all supported me in all that I did, and continues to do so. I first met Charlie when I was 17. He is a creative genius and I have learnt how powerful the imagination can be. Learning from him has given me confidence in my own creativity.

MY ADVICE: *Find a mentor – even someone your own age – who you can bounce ideas off. Trust your own judgement and be confident in your own creativity.*

Dr Andrea Ashworth
Writer and 2002–3 Hodder Fellow in Creative Writing at Princeton University

After studying and then teaching English Literature at Oxford University I wrote *Once in a House on Fire* – a memoir of my childhood, troubled by violence and poverty, in Manchester. (The book has been turned into a stage-play and is now being made into a feature film.) Through good fortune, the great work of my agent and publishers, and above all, the generous response of readers, I was able to contemplate a career devoted to writing. I am currently the Hodder Fellow in Creative Writing at Princeton University, USA, and I am finishing my second book, which will be my first novel. I also write short stories, essays and pieces of journalism. And I like to be involved, where I usefully can, with projects dedicated to helping children and young people in distress to improve their lives.

Among the many generous souls who've inspired and supported me, two fairy godmothers shine out especially in my progress towards happiness and fulfilment as a person and as a writer.

The brilliant and beautiful Professor Julia Briggs first rescued me when I was 17, helping me to escape my threatening, chaotic childhood in Manchester by offering me a place to study English Literature at Oxford University. She never allowed me to feel ashamed about everything I didn't know, instead celebrating my strengths as a reader, a thinker and writer–someone engaging honestly and enthusiastically (if at times bewilderedly!) with words and ideas. She encouraged me to dream and to live beyond the darkness of my past, seeing me for what I was and might be, not in the stark, sad terms of my background. She has always shown me that it is not only okay but that it can be *positively good* to create and re-create myself, over and over, bringing the past and the future together in my own way.

Another cherished friend and guide in my life is Michelle Kass, who became my literary agent long before I had finished my first book. She has been with me from my first published sentence and casts a crucial glow over everything I write and hope to write. Michelle invested her faith and time and energy in me and my writing, and has – as muse, editor, agent – blessed me with her genius for making beautiful things happen. Her ingenuity and love (and humour!) help me fluff my way through those clouds of doubt and confusion that tend to surround a writer, and her own love of stories, her understanding of literature's magic and her sparkly way with words are more inspiring than I can say.

MY ADVICE: *Michelle and Julia, like my mother and sisters and close friends, have helped me to see that, whatever your beginnings, and whatever the fears and confusions you may carry with you as you grow, it is possible to build your own world, to make a good, bright life and to be — to enjoy being — yourself.*

Peter Bazalgette
Chairman, Endemol UK

My job is to lead one of the UK's largest television production companies. We invent shows such as *Changing Rooms* and *Ground Force* and sell them around the world. We also import international hits such as the controversial *Big Brother* for British viewers. How did I get to this position? Let's gloss over the gross flattery of my superiors and the endless rounds bought in the pub. The terrible truth is that I served my time as a researcher and assistant producer under great practitioners such as Esther Rantzen.

I was inclined to nominate an English teacher, Brian Worthington, who encouraged me to start public speaking at the age of 12 and to enjoy entertaining people. But in the end I have chosen Will Wyatt as my mentor, a departmental boss at the BBC in the early eighties. He persuaded me I was a lousy reporter/presenter and that I should concentrate on producing. In particular he asked me to make the *Food & Drink* programme for BBC2. This not only provided me with a number of great dining experiences but also became a hit for over twenty years. Most importantly of all it provided the turnover for my first production company, Bazal, set up in 1987.

With the impetus to start a company, I've remained an independent producer ever since. And it made me work out how to both inform and educate people in a popular, accessible way. Most of all, it made me understand how important formats are to television. And that, despite what they say, there is nothing ignoble about entertaining people.

MY ADVICE: *Be media-savvy — watch TV, listen to radio, have opinions about it. Make your enthusiasm apparent by having worked on your student newspaper, community radio or local television. Get yourself work* *experience with relevant companies. Keep banging on doors and seeing folk – never give up!*

Peter Bennett-Jones
Chairman, Tiger Aspect Group, PBJ Management and Comic Relief

I was educated at Winchester School and Cambridge University where I read law. I was president of the University's two principal dramatic societies and toured with the Footlights. For the next five years, from 1977–1982, I worked extensively in theatre, producing and managing shows in North America, the Far East and the UK. Then from 1982–86 I was Managing Director of Talkback Productions and a Director of theatrical producers Pola Jones Associates. I founded Corporate Communications Consultants in 1986 and in 1988 formed Tiger Television with Rowan Atkinson. I became Group Chairman following Tiger's merger with Aspect Film & Television in 1993.

Tiger Aspect works with leading UK on- and off-screen creative talent and produces a range of award-winning comedy, drama, travel, arts, animation, factual and entertainment programming. Recent titles include *Fat Friends, Teachers, Lenny Henry in Pieces* and *Double Take*. At Tiger Aspect my personal credits include *Mr Bean, Harry Enfield and Chums, The Vicar of Dibley*, and via Tiger Aspects Pictures formed in 1999, we have made the films *Kevin & Perry Go Large, The Martins* and *Billy Elliot*. I am the lead producer of *Our House*, the West End musical by Tim Firth featuring the music of Madness.

As Chairman of PBJ Management, we represent the cream of UK comedy talent including Rowan Atkinson, Lenny Henry, Eddie Izzard, Harry Enfield, Chris Morris, The League of Gentlemen and many others. I am the Chair of Trustees of the charity Comic Relief and its new offspring Sport Relief, and am also the Director of the Oxford Playhouse.

I did attend a school renowned for grooming lawyers, doctors, civil servants, politicians and other 'proper' jobs. That I took a different path, working in the tinselly world of theatre, film and television, was down to the influence of the Art Master, the appropriately named Mr Drew.

I couldn't draw for toffee – I couldn't even draw toffee – and still can't. What Mr Drew actually taught me was a love of the creative process and what it is capable of producing. He instilled in me an appreciation of the value and beauty of art in its different forms. He also gave me the confidence to defy convention by encouraging the pursuit of what one truly wanted to do rather than what was expected of one; if you could make a career out of pursuing your hobby as a job, to go for it.

I went for it and precarious although my working life has been at times, it has never been boring. It has allowed me to work with an array of creative people and to share the pleasure of being associated with engaging new work on screen and stage. I have never regretted not going for one of those proper jobs.

MY ADVICE: *I would advise people setting out on the path of their working life to pursue what you are passionate about, which is not necessarily what is expected of you. Go for it.*

Melvyn Bragg (Lord Bragg of Wigton)
Labour Peer, Editor and Presenter of the *South Bank Show*

I have been very lucky in my life. Several people, most of all my parents, supported me enormously. I believe that inspiration for your future always comes out of yourself. It does, almost certainly, combine glimpses of a possible future from what you have heard in conversation, what you have read in books, comics, newspapers, what you have dreamed of and also what you have been taught.

But if I had to narrow this down to one figure apart from my parents, it would be Mr James, my History Master at my grammar school. His father had been a missionary in Madagascar and Mr James brought a missionary zeal to the raw working class grammar school boys he found himself teaching in the far north of England.

It was he who interested me in history and taught me well enough to apply for and get a scholarship to Oxford. He was a good teacher.

MY ADVICE: *Good teachers are the foundation of a good society. But you must also look inside yourself for inspiration and draw on all you read, dream and learn.*

Rob Brydon
Writer and Comedian

In the true tradition of overnight successes I have been working in the comedy industry for years. I studied at the Welsh College of Music and Drama in Cardiff, graduating in 1986. I worked first as a presenter for *Radio Wales*, and then working on *BSkyB* hosting a movie show. In 1993, I moved to London to further my comedy and acting career and became one of the most sought-after voice artists for commercials. Who can forget my legendary work for Somerfields and the ground-breaking Sudafed campaign?

I co-wrote *Marion and Geoff* for BBC2 with the producer Hugo Blick. This charts the life and lost love of Keith the cab driver played by myself and won the *South Bank Show* Best Drama Award. I was also voted Best Newcomer at the British Comedy Awards and Best Newcomer to the Network at the Royal Television Society in 2000, and Best Actor at the British Comedy Awards in 2001.

Alongside *Marion and Geoff,* I am also acting in television drama and continue to write and act in my own comedy with a live show tour in 2002. I have appeared in various films, among them Sean Connery's *First Knight,* and as the brutalised traffic warden in *Lock, Stock and Two Smoking Barrels.*

Roger Burnel was my drama tutor at Porthcawl Comprehensive in South Wales. Each year I played the lead in the school musical under Roger's direction. It was under his tuition that I passed my 'O' Level examination. He was an inspiration to me and many other people who have gone on to find careers in the theatre, film and TV business.

He treated the students in such a way that filled them with confidence, relating in a way that was adult whilst not forgetting the inexperience and limited skills of the individuals.

He still remains a friend and inspiration to me now.

Antonia Byatt
Director, The Women's Library

I'm Director of The Women's Library, Britain's biggest collection of women's history, part museum, part library, and part events venue. I'd worked in arts programming at the Royal Festival Hall previous to this and the Arts Council before that, so my skills are to do with opening up access to cultural life and hopefully enriching people's lives.

People who work in the cultural sector need to be pretty dedicated – odd hours and small resources. So I've needed to be very determined about making things happen. Josephine Butler has always inspired me. A middle class Victorian lady, she campaigned against the Contagious Diseases Acts in the mid-nineteenth century. She stood up for prostitutes' human rights and women's equality. It took a lot of guts to get up on a soap box and talk about sex in those days, and there wasn't TV to help, so she tirelessly travelled up and down the country. She was a mother too! I feel I owe it to her to let more people know about the Library and what she, and other women, did to make things better for us.

Enid Chanelle
President, The Louis I Michaels Theatre Group (Theatre Royal Haymarket and Strand Theatre in London)

At the start of my career, I applied for a job as a window dresser in a fashion store in Bournemouth, where the owner was Louis Michael. I was lucky that from the outset he trusted my flair and imagination and gave me the freedom to work the way I wanted.

Eventually, we brought our different talents to the table whereby he took care of finances and administration and I was allowed to carry out my artistic vision.

He told me that it was vital in business life to have a dream, his dream being to create a fashion empire which he entrusted to me to build up for him.

His second dream was to own theatres in London and around the country, above all the Theatre Royal Haymarket and we embarked on this venture together.

My recipe for success was energy, enthusiasm, drive and focus and he supported me all the way to put this into practice. He brought out the best in me by encouraging me to realise my goals.

MY ADVICE: *Have a goal and go for it. Create a team spirit and give credit to all who contribute to success. Inspire and motivate people around you and make them feel not that they work for you but that they work with you. Enthusiasm is infectious, use it to sell your ideas. Honesty and integrity are paramount in business.*

Mavis Cheek
Author

I grew up in the fifties. My mother was a single parent and worked in a factory. We lived close to the bone. I failed my eleven plus exam twice (!) and went to a secondary modern, staying in the 'B' stream. I was quite unconcerned about being considered half-brained, coasted through school, and left at 16. After 12 happy years of working, I decided to get an education. Hillcroft College for Women, an inspirational institution if ever there was one, offered women without paper qualifications the opportunity of a high-flying, fully rounded education. There, in two years, with fine tutors and a powerhouse Principal, Janet Cockerill, I found the other half of my brain. Alas, Hillcroft now runs mostly short courses teaching skills, rather than the mixture of cultivation and aspiration I received. Such, as they say, is life.

After I graduated from Hillcroft with a distinction in arts, I began my writing career in earnest. Journalism and travel writing at first, then short stories, and eventually, in 1988, my novel *Pause Between Acts* was published and won the *She*/John Menzies First Novel Prize. My latest, and tenth book, *The Sex Life of my Aunt*, was published in 2002.

MY ADVICE: *Don't ever let anyone tell you you can't achieve your good ambitions (and look beyond a WAP phone).*

Marika Cobbold
Author

I left my native Sweden for England at the age of 19, having married an Englishman. In my late twenties I decided that I wanted to write. I had two young children, no degree, no previous experience of writing apart from school, and English was my second language. But I was a passionate reader and the idea of writing my own books was my dream. I was introduced to Elizabeth Buchan, now a bestselling novelist, who, in spite of having two children of her own and a full time job in publishing, had embarked on writing a novel. I gave her all my reasons for *not* being able to fulfil my dream: lack of time being the biggest. 'Steal time,' she said. 'Set yourself a realistic target, however modest, then stick to it. One page a day doesn't seem much, but you watch them stack up. Within a year you would have a full-length novel.'

Five years of writing later I showed Elizabeth the manuscript of what would become my first published novel – *Guppies For Tea* – together with a fistful of rejection slips and a mass of depressing statistics on the chances of getting published. Elizabeth advised me to send the novel to a competition for new writers. I argued that my novel did not fulfil the subject criterion for the competition.

'Think laterally. If the obvious route has not worked,' Elizabeth said, 'go sideways. If you've got something to offer, someone, somewhere, will recognise it.' She was right; my novel won the competition and the judges recommended it to a publisher who decided to take it on. It was published, successfully, a year later.

MY ADVICE: *My advice to a young person wishing to be a writer is – be a reader. Write something every day. Don't wait for inspiration to come to you, go find it! And remember: at the end of your life it's not what you've done that you're likely to regret but what you have NOT done.*

Jilly Cooper
Author and Journalist

Towards the end of the 1960s, I was terribly depressed about my career, having been sacked from 22 jobs for being dreamy, inefficient and generally hopeless. At a dinner party in a flat off Regent Street in London, however, I sat next to the marvellously genial, rubicund editor of the *Sunday Times* colour magazine, Godfrey Smith. I proceeded to regale him with tales about the problems of being a young working wife: making love all night, leaving for work at eight, and not getting home until seven in the evening because of London traffic and then having to clean the flat, iron my husband's shirts, cook dinner before falling into bed and making love all night again. This continued day after chaotic day, until after six months one died of exhaustion! I was clearly as hopeless at running my home life as I was in an office. Godfrey roared with laughter – he had the most wonderful, rumbling, earth-shattering laugh – and said, 'Write about this, 1,500 words, and I might use it in the magazine.'

When he subsequently invited me to lunch to meet Mark Boxer, the editor of the *Sunday Times Look* pages, I rolled up with my piece. Godfrey read it at once, punctuating my rather shy conversation with Mark with great bellows of laughter. He then bought the piece on the spot offering me £100, which in those days was enough for us to live on for about six months!

Entitled *A Young Wife's Tale*, it appeared in the colour magazine with a divinely flattering photograph of me and Felix, the baby my husband Leo and I had just adopted. The following week I was offered nine jobs, culminating in the offer of a column in the *Sunday Times*, which I joyfully accepted. This continued for 13½ wonderful years. Godfrey, who was entirely responsible for this amazing break, has been a friend and adviser ever since and is our daughter Emily's godfather.

I also regard him as the perfect role model. He writes like an angel, apparently effortlessly and carrying his massive erudition so lightly. I, however, know how much trouble he takes with every word. He is also incredibly generous in praising other writers, which is a rare quality in the literary and journalistic world, and has been responsible for bringing on so many new talents.

MY ADVICE: *Always say thank you to anyone who helps you in life – people who have been kind enough to interview you, or give you a leg up, or give you an opportunity to work, or to meet interesting people. It takes five minutes to drop a line to them saying thank you. I always hugely appreciate it when people bother to do this to me, and remember them. Put more crudely and cynically: always be nice to everyone on the way up because you never know if you're going to meet them on the way down. And Charles Clore's wonderful motto: 'The harder I work, the luckier I get.' – I believe in that too.*

Jon Culshaw
Impressionist, *Dead Ringers*

I am an impressionist on BBC2 and Radio 4's *Dead Ringers*, ITV1's *2DTV* and my own show *Alter Ego*. I have previously worked on *Spitting Image* and appeared on a Royal Variety Performance, *Parkinson* and *They Think It's All Over*. I once phoned 10 Downing Street in the voice of William Hague and was put straight through to the Prime Minister.

After leaving sixth form college I became a presenter on local radio before moving into voice artist work, and then relocating from Lancashire to London to work on *Spitting Image*.

Eric Seal, the Vice Principal of St John Rigby College in Lancashire, was very encouraging to me at a crucial moment. As a teenager I was at an awkward crossroads, not sure of what to do next. Other teachers told me things like 'An impressionist? You're living in cuckooland, laddie.' But Eric went against conventional teacher advice and told me not to worry about my lack of interest in academic subjects. He said the key thing for me was that I had 'great talent and a hell of a lot to give'. His advice to me as a student was 'Go after your goal with absolute confidence and determination – and make it.' So I thought, 'Right then, I will.' From that point on I knew I was on the right track and with dedication and resilience I was going to do all right. I've always been grateful to him for that piece of encouragement.

MY ADVICE: *Do what you love and what you know you are best at. Enjoy it and do it with a vengeance.*

Kate Fawkes
Creative Consultant and Writer

I started out as an actress, then moved into film and television production, including working for the Jim Henson Company as Head of Development, on *Storyteller: The Greek Myths* and Emmy-winning *Living with Dinosaurs*. I joined HIT Entertainment in 1989 and ended up running the production division, where I was the executive producer on many award-winning animated series, such as *Bob The Builder*, *Angelina Ballerina*, *Kipper*, *Brambly Hedge* and *Percy the Park Keeper.* As a single parent, the rigours of such a high-energy job became too onerous so I left the company in 2001 and am now happily working from home on a small number of handpicked projects.

My great friend and mentor, producer/writer Moira Williams, gave me inspiration at a pivotal time in my life. Having bumbled through school, drama school and a stint on the stage, I moved to working behind the scenes as a producer's assistant, first in film, then in television. I loved reading scripts and was full of ideas, but at first had no confidence in myself to speak up and be counted. Until I met Moira Williams. She and I were working for a not-very-happy production company, she as a development guru, me as a frustrated P.A. Comrades in adversity initially, our relationship has developed over 15 years into a long lasting friendship. Her fabulous sense of humour, inventiveness and dedication to her work has proved a wonderful font of inspiration on a personal and professional level.

Moira was the first person to believe in my ability to spot a strong story. She encouraged me to put my ideas on paper and to get involved with the whole production process. On her advice I went off and became a full time script reader for two years before I got a job in development at the brilliant Jim Henson Company. When I went on to HIT Entertainment I had the company's backing to put my instincts and skills to good use. Spotting *Bob the Builder* when he was just a three-page proposal was testament to that gut reaction.

MY ADVICE: *If you have a great passion for storytelling, if an idea can make you as breathlessly excited as falling in love (well, nearly) then that's just the start. You need energy, dedication and a very strong sense of your own worth creatively. Be receptive to others' ideas and learn to listen to your gut reaction, as that is a better guide than anything else.*

Mike Gayle
Novelist

I started off writing for my university magazine about music which led me to start a music fanzine with my best friend Jackie Behan. This led me into the world of journalism. Following a year-long stint on a listings magazine I moved to London and did a post-graduate diploma in magazine journalism. On graduating I was offered the opportunity to launch a magazine based on my own idea. It didn't happen in the end but helped me get my freelance career off the ground. A year later, having become an agony uncle for the teen magazine *Bliss,* I joined *J17* as features editor. While there I had the idea for my first novel, *My Legendary Girlfriend.* I went freelance again and wrote my novel, in my spare time, and a year later the manuscript was complete. I sent it to an agent and in October 1997 it was bought by Hodder and Stoughton. Since then I have written three other books: *Mr Commitment, Turning Thirty* and *Dinner For Two* which have all been *Sunday Times* top ten bestsellers. The books have now been translated into seventeen different languages. I am currently working on my new novel *His 'n' Hers.*

The person who inspired me most during my writing career has to be Jackie Behan. I've known her since I was seventeen when we both attended the same sixth form in Birmingham and we ended up going to the same university. The way that Jackie inspired me on the surface appears quite simple and yet it had tremendous results. Put simply, she told me I was good enough and it worked wonders. Without her support I strongly doubt whether I would ever have shown anyone my budding journalism but because of her I got my first article in print for a listings magazine in Manchester. Seeing my name there in black and white for the very first time was the beginning of everything I've achieved so far. But it was a first step that I would never have taken without her.

MY ADVICE: *For anyone who wants to be a writer you have to believe that you can do it; then turn that belief into action; then show it to the world. And if you fail pick yourself up, dust yourself off and then do it all over again.*

Bonnie Greer
Playwright, Novelist, Critic and Broadcaster

I have had one novel published, many short stories, and another novel will be published in 2004. I have won an award for my playwriting and have had many plays produced. I have my own column in the *Mail on Sunday* every week and I am an arts critic on BBC2's *Newsnight.*

My father, Ben, who is dead now, did his best, along with my mother, to make sure that I had the best education he could afford. He wanted me, as a black woman, to have more options in life. It was not easy for him because I had six other brothers and sisters. Our mother did not work. Dad worked in a factory making tin cans six nights a week. He had very little education himself, but he loved books and conversation. There was a great deal of reading and talking in our home.

I was the first person in my family to attend university. I had to pay for it myself. Once I had no money and my professor, his name was Ben, too, paid my fees out of his own pocket until I could earn more money. They both would have been brought up to expect a woman to stay at home, yet through their help and belief in me, my father and my professor gave me the courage to believe in myself, to even have the courage to move to a foreign country.

MY ADVICE: *Get all the education you can. Let no one prevent you from learning, most of all yourself. Have a goal, but leave room in your life for the unexpected to happen. Everything good that has happened to me has always come out of the blue. Remember: neither your colour nor your gender need stop you.*

Alan Grieve
Chairman, The Jerwood Foundation

I am Chairman of The Jerwood Foundation, an international foundation dedicated to imaginative and responsible funding in a wide diversity of fields which include the arts, education, design and other areas of human endeavour and excellence. Our grants have funded the new RADA theatre, the Jerwood theatres at the Royal Court, the Jerwood Medical Education Centre at the Royal College of Physicians, the Jerwood Gallery at the Natural History Museum and many others. I am also Chairman of the Jerwood Charitable Foundation, a UK charity supported by the Foundation to sponsor the visual and performing arts, education in the widest sense, conservation, work in prisons, medicine and science. I qualified and worked as a solicitor for many years, including acting for John Jerwood, before turning my attention full time to the running of the Foundation upon his death in 1991. I continue now to develop and expand the widest range of support in our chosen fields.

It must have been in the late 1960s when John Jerwood telephoned me from Tokyo where he conducted his international pearl business. He told me he had suffered serious losses of pearls being cultured on Escape River on the North West Australian coast within the Barrier Reef. The only speedy access was by a two-seater biplane flying south out of Papua New Guinea, and I would then need to prepare an insurance claim against Lloyds of London. The questions were clear – Would he recover all or most of his losses? Could and would I do it? When could I leave London as the evidence of storm damage would be difficult to get and might be lost?

Via Tokyo, Singapore and New Guinea I arrived in monsoon weather flying in at 500 feet over shark-infested waters. The so-called air strip was marked by eight-foot ant hills, and only one bushman spoke Australian English; the rest were Japanese pearl farmers and divers. I killed hundreds of large cockroaches each night in my hut on stilts, lived on raw fish, never walked on the beaches because of the snakes, never contacted the outside world in three weeks via the once-a-day radio link; but I gathered all the evidence I needed ahead of anything Lloyds had even dreamt could be done. They settled handsomely!

I knew very little about cultured pearls and spoke no Japanese. The Barrier Reef was fairly unknown territory then and not an adventure holiday.

MY ADVICE: *It seemed to me then, and it still does, that if you want to do something you don't know about, then learn on the hoof, and with one-third knowledge, one-third timing and one-third luck you'll succeed.*

Tony Hall
Executive Director, Royal Opera House

Everybody needs a mentor: someone who knows you, knows what you are doing, has probably been there themselves, and is older than you, so you get perspective, but not so old they have forgotten what it is really like.

I am lucky as I have had a number of people at different times in my life who fulfilled that role. But one person who has been my mentor most consistently was my former editor of BBC2's

Newsnight, whom I met when I joined the programme more years ago than I care to remember. He was, and is, a great television journalist, a great television producer and a great creative head.

We met when we first realised we lived in the same street in Twickenham. I went on to work for him for many years, through the great reforms of news in the late 1980s. We launched new programmes, we went through great crises and great triumphs too. It was exhilarating stuff.

He never failed to give you feedback on how you were doing – the bad news as well as the good. He also made it clear how he felt about what was going on – in a very honest way. He cared for the people he was working with, and I know a number of people who owe an enormous amount to him, including me.

I made a big change in my career at the age of 50. I left a job as Chief Executive of BBC News where I had been for over a decade – and a job I loved. I came to the Royal Opera House as Executive Director – a place I had loved going to for years. One person's advice was invaluable: and you have guessed it. What was even better was that the pros and cons were delivered over an extremely good bottle of wine. Everybody needs a person like that and I am sure if you think about it, you have got one too.

Nigel Havers
Actor

As the son of a former Chancellor and Attorney General, I broke with family tradition in deciding to embark upon a theatrical career. I trained at the Arts Educational Trust in London and my early stage work included Richard II and Edward II for Prospect Theatre Productions. I have acted with the Royal National Theatre, on tours, and in the West End. Most recently I played Serge in the London stage show and touring productions of *Art* and in the *Play What I Wrote* at the Wyndhams Theatre. I have also achieved success in British television in drama and comedy, recently completing *Murder in Mind* and a second series of *Manchild* for the BBC. My film credits include *Chariots of Fire, A Passage to India, Empire of the Sun* and *The Whistle Blower.*

In my early years definitely the most inspirational character was the headmaster of my prep school. Charles Blackburn was a former member of the Cambridge Footlights, and was passionate about acting and the arts. Actors and writers such as Angus Wilson were amongst his closest friends and all boys were encouraged to perform in his plays, which now that I look back on them, were astonishingly professional. Charles treated us as adults, which is not to say he didn't maintain a firm hand, indeed we all had the utmost respect for him, but he never talked down to us. Our opinions were listened to and valued and he had the admirable knack of assessing each individual's ability and then leading them in the direction they were best suited to. Above all he instilled a confidence and a belief in oneself that anything is possible.

MY ADVICE: *As my mentor, Charles Blackburn, used to say, 'Don't think dear, you haven't got anything to think with!'*

Tony Hawks
Comedian and Author

I work as a broadcaster, writer and performer. I was a team captain alongside Jo Brand in the BBC2 series *The Brain Drain*, I have made numerous appearances as a guest on *Have I Got News For You* and *They Think It's All Over*. I am a regular on BBC Radio 4's *Just A Minute*, *The Newsquiz* and *I'm Sorry I Haven't A Clue*.

I have written three bestselling books, all based on wacky bets: *Round Ireland With A Fridge*, *Playing the Moldovans At Tennis* and *One Hit Wonderland*. I have recently completed a sell-out tour of the UK with *One Hit Wonderland*, the show about my latest book.

I was inspired by my history teacher, Mr David Akers. He was clearly a frustrated performer and he would bring his guitar to certain lessons and sing songs which he had written about episodes in history. I was moved by his song about the First World War and I still remember a catchy little tune about Bismarck. From watching this man, and seeing the joy which these songs brought him, I knew that it was important to follow your heart and to try hard to make a career out of what you enjoy. I have been lucky enough to do this.

Mr Akers did me another favour recently when I was able to talk about him for one minute uninterrupted on *Just A Minute* for BBC Radio 4 – the subject was 'my favourite teacher'.

MY ADVICE: *I would advise aspiring performers to check their motive. Do you want to do this because you want fame or recognition, or because you love it? If it is the former then I would say you will almost certainly be bound for some form of disappointment. Also remember that it is a business which cannot cater for everyone's talents. You may have to earn money in another way and do your performing for fun. This will not mean that you have failed. And, hey, don't take it all too seriously. It's only life after all.*

Penny Johnson
Director, The Government Art Collection

As Director of the Government Art Collection since 1997, I lead a team of 13 people curating a British art collection for display in British government buildings in the UK and around the world. Previously I was the Curator at the Towner Art Gallery and Museum in Eastbourne, and the Assistant Keeper of Fine Art at the Stoke-on-Trent City Museum and Art Gallery (now the Potteries Museum). I have a degree in fine arts from the University of East Anglia, and a post-graduate diploma in Art Gallery and Museum Studies from the University of Manchester, and was later awarded the Museums Association Diploma.

Miss MacQuaide was the person who first inspired me in my career. As my teacher when I was ten, she reinforced my interest in art by devoting lesson time not only to making art, but also looking at art, and in particular impressionism and post-impressionism. I liked her enormously and she was important to me for fostering a strong interest in art, which led me to study art history. She developed my love of colour, encouraging me to present a talk to the rest of the class about complementary colours. I explained the way I thought this worked with rectangular sheets of colour with the three primary and secondary colours painted and mixed by me in advance. She also took us to the Tate Gallery to look at the paintings she had shown us and where we bought postcards for our special Tate Gallery postcard album. At my next school I had practical art lessons but had to wait until the sixth form for further art history.

The next major encouragement in my career was seeing and hearing Marjorie Allthorpe-Guyton give a talk about working at the Norwich Castle Museum while I was studying art history at the University of East Anglia. Here was a striking young woman, only a few years older than me, doing exactly what I imagined I wanted to do. She had studied at the same university and was a hugely influential role model for me. She is now the Director of Visual Arts at the Arts Council of England. There are many people since whom I have admired and still admire and from whom I have learnt, but Miss MacQuaide and Marjorie Allthorpe-Guyton are the most vivid for me.

MY ADVICE: *The key to success is to find out what you want to do and what you care about and then be very focused and persevere, taking every opportunity to achieve your chosen career.*

Clive Jones
Chief Executive, Carlton Television
and Joint Managing Director, ITV Network

I started out in journalism as a graduate trainee journalist on the *Yorkshire Post*, and then worked my way through various jobs on the *Morning Telegraph*, Sheffield. I first worked as a news editor at Yorkshire Television, and in my 25-year television career, I've worked for a long spell as an award-winning news and documentary programme maker. At Carlton Television, I am proud of my role in creating the Cultural Diversity Network that ensures equality, and fair representation is a key part of the strategy and objectives of every broadcaster in the UK. I am also a member of the committees advising the British Government on the development of the national curriculum in British schools and to chart future education and training needs for the old and new media in the UK.

Kate Lawrence was my history teacher for 'O' (now 'GCSE') and 'A' Levels in Newbridge Grammar School in South Wales. She showed me that study was fun, school was a great place to be and working hard was something I wanted to do for myself not just for her or my parents. I've never forgotten her.

MY ADVICE: *Trust your teachers.*

Dafydd Jones
Photographer

I left school at 16. I had not got on very well with my headmaster at Oxford Grammar School where I was considered rebellious and difficult. I bummed around for a couple of years then, at 18, brought a portfolio of my paintings to Oxford polytechnic where I met Len McComb who ran the art foundation course there. He immediately said that on the strength of my portfolio he would take me whether I had any GCSEs or not. He was the first person to show confidence in my potential. He taught drawing and how to look at things, how to look at the shapes and the negative space, not just the subject. There was absolute silence when he spoke to a class of 35 students: we all felt he really understood each one of us. I remember him as autocratic and old fashioned but a very dedicated artist and a very good teacher. Yet, by the age of 50, he had received little recognition until Carel Weight introduced him to Ron Kitaj who was curating a show at the Hayward called the Language of Drawing in which Len was given pride of place. This made his name and for a while he went on to become head of the Royal Academy of Arts.

I admired and respected his dedication to his art and also his teaching. Without his interest in me, and his encouragement, I might have gone onto a graphics course as an easy option. It was he who said I had an unusual talent, was an eccentric, and steered me onto the fine art course which eventually led me into the sort of photographic work I do today.

MY ADVICE: *My advice to other young people would be to follow Len's example of dedication to his art. Photography as a profession is wide open to newcomers because you really are only as good as your last picture.*

Mary Loudon
Author

I am an author, and I write books of non-fiction short stories. I do this by tape-recording many long conversations with people, and then cutting and editing those conversations (usually by around 90 per cent) so that the main strand of a story is teased out, but is still in the subject's own words. I write this way because I am fascinated by the way other people live, think, and deal with their lives, and I find it more interesting than making up my own stories and writing novels. My books are: *Unveiled, Nuns Talking; Revelations, The Clergy Questioned;* and *Secrets & Lives, Middle England Revealed.* I have contributed to three anthologies, won four prizes for my writing, and been a judge for the Whitbread Book Awards. My work means that I also appear on television and radio, and give public talks, all of which I enjoy very much.

I had a wonderful junior school headmistress called Miss Pope. She was hearty, kind and intelligent. She loved children, and she had the gift of being able to extract the best from absolutely everyone. I always loved writing; she always encouraged it. But more than that, she taught me some valuable lessons about resilience. When I left her school, and went to secondary school, I was badly bullied. I was sworn at, called names, beaten up and teased for months and months. I was desperately unhappy, and I used to talk to her about it. 'Never stop being yourself, Mary dear,' she said. 'There's nothing wrong with you. You do what you need to do, and ignore the rest.' It sounds easy to say, and it was by no means easy to execute, but I did what she suggested, and gradually it worked.

MY ADVICE: *Don't let anyone stop you from being who you are. Take courage from those who support you, and do what YOU need to do. Don't ever let anyone tell you that you're worthless. As I got older, I realised I had lots of friends, and that bullies are everywhere in life (in adult life, too), but can be ignored, or even told where to go! These days, I don't let anyone push me around, and I'm careful not to do the same to others. In order to succeed in your life, whatever you do, and whoever you are, stay kind, reasonable, polite, and determined. Always work hard; always remember that everyone has good and bad times, and when your own times are hard, seek support from someone nice. And ALWAYS thank people for their help (however minimal).*

Joanna Lumley
Actress

My career has included being a photographic model; a Bond Girl; an Avenger; a writer and Jack of all Trades. I have said 'Yes' to many opportunities allowing me also to be, from time to time, a presenter, a traveller, a reader, a helper and a performer of stage, screen, TV and radio. You name it, I have had a go.

Mrs Curran was my elocution and drama teacher at St Mary's School, St Leonards on Sea. She said I moved well and was a natural actor. It gave me confidence and belief in my ability. She wasn't just being kind. It made me feel stronger.

MY ADVICE: *Never give up. Never give in. Never be late. Volunteer for everything. Be polite. Smile. Learn from everything. Remember tomorrow.*

John MacAuslan
Director of Administration, the National Gallery

My wife's grandfather told me to make a complete career change at least three times in my life. I am not quite there yet. I worked in the Treasury on public services and economic policy from 1976–82 and again from 1985 until 1994. I developed high technology materials for Raychem UK in the mid-1980s and I'm now the Director of Administration at the National Gallery in London.

I have been so privileged – I mean in the things that really count, rather than in money terms. I've been inspired by family, friends, teachers, work colleagues – so many that I could not single out just one. Some of them would be very surprised to know I learnt so much from them. Trying to understand people from very different centuries and places has always been an inspiration. How did this make a difference? I learnt that thinking and listening are enjoyable, that hard work can be fun, and lots of different things are fascinating once you get into them: the deeper the better. I became optimistic.

MY ADVICE: *Work, like the rest of life, is too deep and rich to be summed up in slogans. But if I have to: do your best to show courage, truthfulness, wisdom, goodwill, fairness and humour – and then all you'll need is a bit of luck.*

Sir Cameron Mackintosh
Theatrical Producer

I have now produced hundreds of successful musical productions around the world. Current productions include *Les Miserables, The*

Phantom of the Opera, Miss Saigon and the recently acclaimed productions of *The Witches of Eastwick* and *My Fair Lady* as well as the Royal National Theatre's production of *Oklahoma!* in New York. I also own seven West End theatres in London – the Prince Edward, Prince of Wales, Gielgud, Queens, Wyndhams, Albery and the Strand. In 1985 my company received The Queen's Award for Export Achievement.

I have been fortunate to have the inspirational figure of the musical composer Julian Slade in my life. At the age of eight, I was taken to see his show *Salad Days* about a magic piano that makes everybody start dancing. Julian himself was playing the piano in the orchestra and at the end of the performance I was so captivated that I rushed down to the orchestra pit to meet him. He took me on stage and explained to me how everything worked. At that moment I decided that when I grew up I wanted to be the person who put shows together – the producer. By treating me seriously Julian ignited my imagination and I will always be grateful for his friendship and faith in me.

I remember once, following the closure of one of his less successful shows, Julian wrote to me, 'I refuse to be beaten.' Doing what you believe in is a vital ingredient if you want to succeed in life.

MY ADVICE: *In the theatre no one really knows what is going to succeed and, whatever anybody thinks, it is almost impossible to guess what the public wants to see next. All you can do is trust your own taste and do it as well as you can and, with a little bit of luck, the public will like it as well.*

Davina McCall
Television Presenter

My road into the world of presenting has been a colourful and varied one. I sang with a band until I was 19 before going solo. Dissatisfied with my near misses in the record industry, and despite the help of Eric Clapton producing my demo, I gave up singing and took a job as a booker at the model agency Model's One on the men's desk. I ran a restaurant for two years and also worked as a singing waitress in Paris. The last few years have been huge for me. I have fronted three series of *Don't Try This at Home* for ITV involving a death-defying bungee jump; presented the cult dating show *Street Mate* for Channel 4, hosted the *Brit Awards 2000* for ITV and the *British Fashion Awards 2000* for BBC2. I have also hosted three series of the biggest reality game show *Big Brother* for Channel 4, and ITV's big money game show, *The Vault*. Recently I have presented *Popstars – The Rivals* for ITV1. During 2000 and 2001 I also took part in Comic Relief's fundraising programme screened on BBC1 visiting Kenya and Uganda to provide updates on the charity's work in East Africa.

I never really thought TV presenting was a 'proper job' so the idea of becoming a presenter didn't cross my mind until I saw MTV for the first time. Everyone on the channel looked like they were having a blast but there was one man that shone – Ray Cokes. He was BRILLIANT. He was hilariously funny and totally unscripted. He was utterly inspiring and watching him made me want to get into television, in particular on MTV. So I made a show reel and sent it out to a couple of people. There was someone that saw my screen test who believed I had potential. He didn't have the power to hire me, but decided to help me. He was a researcher and I was a nobody but for some reason he wanted to help me and I was very grateful. Every couple of weeks he would send me information on companies that were looking for presenters, who I should speak to, etc. He also gave me sound advice regarding my show reels.

His kindness came at a time in my life when I really needed a helping hand. I had just got clean (from alcohol addiction), and was back living with my mum and dad, and had a car but couldn't afford to put petrol in it. His biggest gift was that he believed in me. That gave me the courage to keep plodding away. Three years on I got a job at MTV with Ray Cokes! And my friend, the researcher, sent me a big bunch of lilies. His name was Duncan Gray. Now he's a big wig at Granada and I work for him! How great is that?

MY ADVICE: *Have the courage to keep plodding away, finding out all you have to do to get what you want in your career.*

Gil McNeil
Author, Consultant to Brunswick Arts and Publishing Director of PiggyBankKids Projects

After working in a variety of junior jobs in the film business and in an art gallery I moved into book publishing, working first as a literary agent, then at Virago Press. I worked as Rights Director at Virago and was appointed to the Board there. I'd always wanted to write, and eventually left to launch my freelance career by taking on consulting work. I also began work on my first novel, *The Only Boy for Me,* which was published in 2001, and my second novel, *Stand By Your Man,* which is published in late 2003.

I've always managed to find people who inspired me wherever I've worked: usually because they had a real passion for what they were doing, sometimes just because they were especially generous in the way they passed on their skills, and occasionally I've learned from people whose example showed me how NOT to do things! I was very lucky to have some wonderful teachers when I was at school, and my mum and dad have both been the kind of parents that everybody needs: always there for you when you need them, ready with advice and support. And working with Sarah Brown over the last few years and setting up PiggyBankKids with her has been an inspiration. Her integrity and kindness has persuaded many people to help with the charity, and driven the creation of a new initiative that will make such a difference to supporting opportunities for children and young people.

Alongside my writing and my role at PiggyBankKids, I work one day a week at Brunswick Arts, providing a consulting role to the development of the arts PR business. Alan Parker is the head of the Brunswick group of companies, a corporate PR business with offices all over the world, and he combines passion and enthusiasm in a really infectious way: you just can't help being carried forward by his energy and enthusiasm. Alongside his position as head of the extraordinarily successful PR business he founded and his day-to-day work advising the UK's corporate leaders, he shows a passionate interest in his staff, his family and in the arts. He also provides a home to two charities, PiggyBankKids and Pilotlight within the

London office. He firmly believes that work should be fun and if it's not fun then you should be doing it differently. He works incredibly hard, but he always seems to be enjoying it, which seems to me to be the secret of real success.

MY ADVICE: *Work hard, and don't be afraid of change. You don't have to have a plan for the next 20 years already fixed when you get your first job. As long as you can pay the bills you can always try something different. Aim for the best you can be, not the easiest. And make sure you enjoy it.*

Andrew Motion
Poet Laureate

I can still see the classroom: filling the ground floor of an awkward, half-timbered barn of a building. I can still see the book open in front of me: the right-hand page printed with Thomas Hardy's short lyric 'I look into my glass'. And I can still see my new English teacher: a florid-faced, softly-spoken shy man named Peter Way. Until that day, I'd had no more than a mild and easily-unsettled interest in poetry; after that day, nothing was the same. Without any ostentation, but with a compelling devotion, Peter Way made me feel that poetry was a central part of existence, not merely a fanciful addition to it – and everything he said was either dramatised or reinforced by Hardy's poem. It's a clichéd phrase, but it's true – he changed my life.

John O'Farrell
Writer

I got into comedy writing via Radio 4. I kept handing in comedy sketches for specific shows until I was commissioned for a few minutes every week. From there I went on to write for productions such as *Spitting Image*, *Have I Got News For You* and *Chicken Run*. Now apart from a weekly column in the *Guardian* I concentrate on writing books. Publications to date are *Things Can Only Get Better*, a memoir and *The Best A Man Can Get* and *This Is Your Life*, both novels.

All sorts of people inspired me, but two particular teachers stick in my memory. First there was Richard Butler who taught me when I was nine. Every week we would do 'drama' and my friends and I would put on a comedy sketch and Mr Butler was kind enough to pretend to laugh at my jokes. Then at secondary school a teacher called Barrie Williams introduced us to satirical works such as *Gulliver's Travels* and *Animal Farm*. His enthusiasm for comedy shone through and he encouraged me and a friend to write humorous pieces for the school magazine. There were of course lots of other people who helped me along the way. When Gwyneth Paltrow won her Oscar she thanked everybody she had ever met in her whole life. I would like to go one better but there just isn't room here to write all their names down.

It was a revelation to discover that grown ups found the same things funny that I did. The fact that both those teachers were positive about my sense of humour in my school reports made me wonder if it was something I might do more with. There was also a teacher who said, 'O'Farrell, you can't spend the rest of your life making jokes', which immediately made me think, 'Now there's an idea!'

MY ADVICE: *In writing, as in anything else, you get better from just doing it. Whether you are writing for a school magazine, short stories for competitions or a play to put on at some local theatre, just get something down on paper. It may not be great stuff to begin with, but at least you'll have something you can improve. With experience, perseverance and a willingness to accept constructive criticism, eventually you'll discover you have the ability to produce work that you can read back with pride and confidence. Hang on, can I write this all out again?*

Charlie Parsons
Television Producer

I am now the Managing Director of Castaway Television Productions, and the Creator and Executive Producer of *Survivor* (global TV programme and brand). I was previously the co-founder and Creative Head of Planet 24 UK which I set up with Waheed Alli and Bob Geldof. We created *The Big Breakfast* after a 1992 Royal Television Society seminar reached the conclusion that it was impossible to come up with a new successful idea for breakfast television and other programmes.

I originally started out as a journalist on the *Ealing Gazette*, and then became a programme researcher on London Weekend Television working on several programmes before becoming Series Editor of *Network* 7, and then Creator/Executive Producer of *The Word*, the groundbreaking youth entertainment series (1990-95) and the first programme on British TV to capture an audience valuable to advertisers late at night.

Not one person inspired me, but many. At school, my English teacher, Jonathan Smith believed in ideas. In television, my first boss was Greg Dyke – he believed anything was possible. Also Jane Hewland, a genius TV producer, challenged the conventional orthodoxy about how things could be done. And best, and finally, my partner Waheed Alli gave me confidence.

The combination of these great people meant huge confidence, the knowledge that you have to make mistakes to succeed, that you must be bold and challenge and question – and ultimately believe in yourself.

MY ADVICE: *Don't believe a word I say – just get out there and do what you want!*

Ian Rankin OBE
Novelist

I started writing stories at the age of five, but waited a further twenty-one years before my first book was published. I am the author of the *Inspector Rebus* series of novels, and also often appear as a critic on TV and radio.

Probably the biggest influence on my early career was one of my English teachers in high school. His name was 'Mr Gillespie' (I later learned that his first name was Ron). He was young, hadn't long been out of university, sported long hair, spoke with a working-class Glasgow accent, and was passionate about his subject. He connected to us 15 and 16 year olds straight away, bringing records to school for us to listen to. We'd then have to write essays about the lyrics of such great songwriters as Paul Simon, Bob Dylan and Neil Diamond. We also had to write short stories, and Mr Gillespie was very enthusiastic about my writing, sometimes reading bits of my stories out to the class. Later on, when I was in my final year, he taught a class on TS Eliot, and made that difficult poet seem easy and relevant. Mr Gillespie had studied Greek and philosophy, showing me that it wasn't just 'posh' people who could be clever. He also made me think my own creative writing was a worthwhile enterprise.

MY ADVICE: *These days, I am often approached by people, young and old, who want to be writers. I tell them they need to believe in the merits of their work. They need patience, because they will have to face criticism and rejection along the way. They'll also need luck. But no matter how much luck they get, they'll never have Mr Gillespie.*

Irving Rappaport
Mediator, Producer, Ventriloquist

Currently, I divide my time as a mediator, a consultant in electronic democracy, a film producer and a ventriloquist. I actually started out by studying medicine when I left school and worked as an oral and dental surgeon for seven years. I then changed direction to become the manager of a punk rock band and an independent film producer, was the co-founder of Palace Pictures in the early 1980s and moved on to be Managing Director of Virgin Film and Video distribution before returning again to film production. By 1992, I was ready for another change, got a degree in Ecology, supervised an expedition to the West African Sahel and then became the Land Resources Manager of the Lea Valley Park in the UK.

In 1995, I became fascinated in finding out whether the internet could allow ordinary people to help politicians make better decisions about the things that affect our lives, and founded UK Citizens' Online Democracy to experiment with and promote 'electronic democracy'. I am still working as an electronic democracy consultant to the Hansard Society. Alongside this, I have maintained my interest in the entertainment world, most recently with a production of Neil Simon's '*The Seven Year Itch*' starring Daryl Hannah in the West End of London. Between 1997–99 I qualified in counselling, hypnotherapy and mediation and now work as a commercial and community mediator. I have also just started learning to be a ventriloquist and recently appeared at the National Theatre.

Many people have inspired or guided me. Here are some of them: my two daughters and grand-daughter for constantly reminding me that life is meant to be enjoyed and that we are all designed to grow and evolve; my witty and wise brother David Rappaport who was small and beautiful and taught me that less is often more; Mrs. Wellington, my primary school teacher, for telling me the story of the boy and the butterfly which made me realise that you have to work hard exercising your wings before you can fly; Ken Dodd, comedian, for staying young at heart and proving that laughter is the best medicine; Gerry Webb, space expert, for giving an amazing lecture under the railway arches on Walthamstow marshes which opened my eyes to life on and beyond this planet; Mr Dixon, my English teacher, for encouraging me to write and for appreciating my efforts; Dag Hammarskjöld, Secretary General of the United Nations (when I was a kid), for providing a fine example of how to make peace by honouring the different cultures and peoples of the world; John Allen, inventor of Biosphere Two (the world's first self-sustaining, sealed, miniature world in which eight people lived for two years), for superbly demonstrating the difficult trick of building and running a team according to the maxim 'beauty is the supreme attractive force'; Mr Questle, my religious teacher, for challenging my mind – and awarding cash prizes for clever answers!; Ken Campbell, actor/writer/director, for hilarious stories, sensational theatre and introducing me to the benefits of 'supposing' rather than believing and the notion that 'it's only true if it makes you laugh'; John Dowie, for his big heart, enchanting poems and allowing me to perform his one man show *'I was Jesus's Dad'*; Richard Bandler, for teaching me how your attitude to life governs what you get out of it and for showing me how to be 'the best you can possibly be' – I've still got a lot to learn!; Oberto Airaudi, for dreaming up the magical, fabulous, underground 'Temple of Mankind' and the talented, hard-working people who built and adorned it; my close friends for always being there.

MY ADVICE: *Live life to the full! Be passionate, totally dedicated and focused. Take complete responsibility for your own life and never resort to blaming others when things seem to go wrong. Always remember that God is working through you and that He/She presents you with obstacles and challenges so that you can grow – all you have to do is pay close attention and be prepared to change. Every human creation or activity starts out as just an idea and your unconscious mind is much more powerful than you realise, so always follow your dreams and never be discouraged by your fears. 'Love your neighbour as yourself' by recognising the good in people rather than judging the bad – the negative traits you see in others are merely a reflection of your own. Happiness is a figment of your imagination – so let your imagination run riot! Train yourself to listen and observe very carefully – you'll win friends and learn a lot. And finally, don't believe a word I've told you – just 'suppose' it and then try it out for yourself.*

Richard Rogers (Lord Rogers of Riverside)
Architect and Chairman, Richard Rogers Partnership

I studied at the Architectural Association, and then as a Fulbright, Edward Stone and Yale Scholar at Yale University in the United States. I now run my own architectural practices in London, Tokyo and Spain. As an architect, I have chaired the UK Government's Urban Taskforce from 1997–99. In addition, I am also the London Mayor's Chief Adviser on Architecture and Urbanism, and an Adviser to the Barcelona Mayor's Urban Strategies Council. My other voluntary commitments include Chairman of the National Tenants Resource Centre, Trustee of Médicins du Monde's UK Board, and Patron of the Society of Black Architects. I have been fortunate to receive many architectural awards and honours from around the world.

When I was 12 my parents decided that it was time to take a different approach to my education. I'd spent seven extremely unhappy years at a small traditional uptight English private school, totally unable to cope with both the educational system and the social expectations that went with it and as a result of this I had few friends. My aim in life at that time was to move from the bottom of the class to the second bottom of the class. In desperation my parents sent me to a school for children with special needs. It was a small school and there were about 20 children with a very high proportion of teachers (about four to five). Here I met an exceptional teacher who spent the year giving me confidence about my own ability – a confidence I had totally lost. He talked to me, he gave me books to read and even helped me with sports. By the end of the year I was not only able to take my common entrance exams but suddenly became good at sport. Later it was acknowledged that I was dyslexic but in those days the condition was not recognised.

MY ADVICE: *There were at least two positive outcomes from this period. Firstly I never believed it when people said something was not possible. I learned that if you really wanted to do something it was nearly always possible. Secondly, I learned to work extremely hard on things that interested me and I never saw a difference between work and play. This enjoyment has become even greater as I have grown older.*

Sir Nicholas Serota
Director of Tate

I have been Director of Tate since 1988. During that period we have presented major exhibitions including those devoted to Cézanne, Whistler, Sargent and, most recently, Matisse and Picasso. We have also opened Tate St Ives and other regional ventures, and have developed new galleries in London, notably Tate Modern but also a renewed Tate Britain.

In the summer of 1966, while studying Economics at Cambridge, I came to realise that I was spending more and more time in museums and galleries and looking at contemporary art. The art history course at Cambridge takes a very small number of students but at that time was led by Michael Jaffe, an art historian with a special interest in Rubens and Raphael. I approached him to see whether I could change courses and after a searching interview he agreed. Michael's particular strength as an art historian was a belief that you should look first at the painting, sculpture or drawing and use your eyes to make an assessment, turning to the documents or the historical circumstances only as a support. In this he was unlike many historians who preferred to work from photographs or texts. This commitment to 'looking' was reinforced by my contact with David Sylvester, critic and friend of Henry Moore and those artists who emerged in America in the 1950s and 1960s, such as Willem de Kooning and Jasper Johns. I worked with David on the installation of several exhibitions and learned from him how critical it is in making exhibitions to place sculptures and paintings in relation to each other and in relation to the space which they occupy.

Both of my mentors taught me to rely on my own eye and on my own judgements. However, they also taught me to listen to the comments of others. Every judgement can be improved by taking account of other points of view.

MY ADVICE: *Keep your options open at school for as long as possible. You never know when new interests might develop, as they did for me in my last years at school and early years at university. Once you decide, try to make contact with people at the leading edge of your profession.*

Ralph Steadman
Artist and Writer

I grew up in Kent, and did military service with the Royal Air Force. My early career included a variety of odd jobs including trainee manager at F. W. Woolworth in Colwyn Bay, North Wales and apprentice aircraft engineer with De Havilland Aircraft Company in Cheshire. I then went to East Ham Technical College and the London College of Printing and Graphic Arts. Since then, I have written and illustrated a wide range of books for children and adults, and shown my work in many group and individual exhibitions. I have received a number of awards for illustration from around the world. I have also designed for the theatre, television (including the opening credits for *Harry Enfield's Guide to the Opera*) and commercials (the Oddbins and Sony adverts) and contributed to newspapers, magazines, CDs and my own website, www.ralphsteadman.com.

Leslie Richardson was my art teacher at the London College of Printing and Graphic Arts. He told me not to worry about art and being an artist, but to absorb ALL influences of life, good or bad. He encouraged me to let the mind do the digesting, sifting, rejecting or retaining. My job was to learn to look by drawing and drawing – and reading. Drawing forces you to look and reading encourages you to think.

MY ADVICE: *Bring back drawing if you want to be an artist, photographer or even a conceptualist. Drawing constantly helps to develop coordination between hand, eye and mind. Don't be fashionable. Listen to your instinct. Follow your heart. If you want to write or become a ballet dancer – do so!*

Don't be pigeon-holed, but keep pigeons by all means. Be objective, ie, don't court popularity – applause is the echo of a platitude. Laugh a lot – even if it hurts!

Penny Vincenzi
Novelist

A posh secretarial course led me to being junior secretary on *Vogue*. Then, via a series of steps, I went to the *Daily Mirror*, where I worked for Marje Proops and then Felicity Green, at that time assistant editor and woman's editor of the paper. I started writing, moved on to being first fashion editor of *Nova*, wasn't very good at that, got fired, turned to beauty writing and finally to features, and wrote, in particular, profiles, which is what I'd always wanted to do. By this time there were two children (later four), so I went freelance and worked for every publication you can think of, from *The Sunday Times* to the *Sun* and from *Tatler* to *Woman's Own*. Finally, I became Deputy Editor of *Options* magazine, when I was approached to write my first novel. This book, *Old Sins,* was published in 1989 and since then I have written ten more.

What inspired me? Those two ladies on the *Daily Mirror*. Marje spotted my ambition and encouraged me, let me do research for her (I was actually her secretary) and help with ideas and so on. She also saw me through my first pregnancy and became a second mother to me. Felicity gave me my first writing job and trained me professionally; I always say she brought me up. They were both dynamic, inspiring and immensely generous, professionally as well as personally.

It made a difference. They both taught me to be painstaking, to work when I was exhausted, to check everything, and never to give up and say I can't do that. I found I could! The best advice was from Felicity, who told me to take nothing for granted and never to take no for an answer. I think it gave me more confidence: although not at the time, I was very often terrified in those early days!

MY ADVICE: *Go for it. Take a job, however humble, in the right area. Work for nothing if you can afford it, even part-time on hospital radio, if radio is your ambition, for example. Just get some experience under your belt. Don't mind what you're asked to do. Remember the most brilliant graduate is not necessarily of any use in an over-stressed, over-worked office until he or she knows how it actually works. Willingness to muck in and slave is almost always remembered. If it isn't, remind them, politely. And look for a mentor, someone to hitch your star to, someone sympathetic to your ambitions, someone who will champion you.*

Marina Warner
Author

My writing spans fiction, criticism, and history including novels and short stories as well as studies of female myths and symbols. My most recent books are *The Leto Bundle, Fantastic Metamorphoses, Other Worlds (2001)* and *Murderers I Have Known,* published in 2002.

I grew up in a transitional period for women, and I was tugged between the conventional destiny of Catholic girls of 'good family' and my own sense of a larger horizon. When I was 17 I met a student who was six years older than me who also came from a background (Chinese, as it so happened) that had highly traditional and authoritarian views of what a daughter should do, and she helped me see that it was possible to remain on good terms with parents and at the same time attempt to make another life, to create another destiny. Irène Pih (now Andreae), who became my friend and the chief influence on my life, was studying Chinese history for a PhD at the Sorbonne in Paris, and she fortified my resolve to be a writer. At the same time she was – is – also extremely interested in emotional and sexual independence (this is very different from Chinese or Catholic ideas!) and so she helped fashion the feminism of my youth. It has changed in character over the years, but the spirit remains.

Women have helped me all along the way: the generation after the war, moving inch by inch into positions of greater influence than before, have been my commissioning editors, publishers, agents, sponsors, hosts, all over the world. Women like Pat Kavanagh, Carmen Callil, Liz Forgan, Wendy Doniger, Elisabeth Sifton, Alison Samuel showed interest in me and gave me support at crucial times.

MY ADVICE: *It is very hard to believe in your own work's worth; others really do have to do this for you and inspire the courage to continue.*

Alan Yentob
BBC Director of Drama, Entertainment, CBBC

I was appointed Director of Drama, Entertainment and CBBC in 2000, putting me at the creative helm of the BBC and with overall responsibility for BBC drama, entertainment and all aspects of the BBC's children's output. In addition I oversee BBC Talent and BBC Films.

I joined as a general trainee in 1968 taking my first job in the World Service. From 1973–75 I was a producer/director with Omnibus, where my films included *Cracked Actor* with David Bowie. In 1978 I created the arts series *Arena*, and was Editor until 1985 when I became Head of Music and Arts. I was appointed Controller of BBC 2, before becoming Controller at BBC 1 in 1993, and then Director of Television in 1997 for three years. My outside responsibilities include sitting on the South Bank Board and Chairmanship of the ICA. I am also a Trustee of the charity Kids Company.

The person who most inspired and motivated me when I joined the BBC as a raw, young trainee is called Leslie Megahey. Leslie was a little older than me and had arrived at the BBC by much the same route two years earlier. It was his generosity in sharing his passion and know-how which gave me the confidence to try things out and take risks which might otherwise have seemed intimidating. We became close friends and colleagues in the Music & Arts department of the BBC. Leslie's enthusiasm and commitment were infectious. Together we immersed ourselves in the arts and in the craft of film-making. Leslie was endlessly curious and was a great believer in finding inventive ways to tell stories. It was this approach which enabled us to use the modest means at our disposal to great effect. We remain great friends to this day.

MY ADVICE: *Always seize the opportunity to learn new things.*

Don't be afraid to ask for advice and help from others.

Be patient but persistent.

Never allow cynicism to corrode your enthusiasm.

Have faith in yourself.

film business

Sir Alan Parker
Film Director and Chairman, Film Council

Having been asked to write this piece I had to think hard. I've been blessed with many helpful people who have shaped my life. There was my Uncle Jim who would hurry home from being a conductor on the No 19 bus route to help me do my homework and, when the Arsenal weren't playing, take me to the magical Astoria cinema. There was my boss in advertising, Colin Milward, who allowed me to experiment with a camera, learning to make TV commercials in the agency basement and who then 'sacked' me, forcing me to take up directing full time. There was my friend Fred Zinnemann, the great film director, who politely critiqued each new film of mine with the deft expertise of a Viennese abattoir butcher. But I've chosen to write about my old Boys' Brigade leader, Terry Currey.

Growing up in Islington, North London, in the fifties before the area's gradual gentrification, the Boys' Brigade wasn't just a marching band heard for miles around on the last Sunday of every month: it was our boys' club; the only one around. There were the Boy Scouts at St Mary's but curiously they were thought too posh and sissy for us working-class kids from the council flats.

Located in the dingy Victorian basement of the old Islington Chapel in Gaskin Street, the BB supplied all our needs every day, week in week out, as it dominated and defined our lives. For most of my time there it was organised and presided over by Terry Currey. Mr Currey, as we always called him, was officially the 'Captain' of the 17th London Company of the BB. Monday night was 'club' night (table tennis and snooker), Tuesdays, gymnastics, as we deftly dodged the iron pillars that supported the chapel upstairs. Wednesdays, swimming at the tuppenny bath at 'The Tib', the public baths off Essex Road; Thursdays, band practice or athletics in between football seasons (which seemed to stretch throughout the whole year – ignoring cricket, which wasn't big in Islington). Band night was eventually abandoned because we had the distinction of being the worst drum and bugle band in Britain. Fridays were 'drill night' where we spruced up in starched white haversack and polished belt and marched up and down with as much precision as a guardsman after a bucket of vodka. Saturday afternoon was football at which we excelled – no mean feat considering that most of us were exhausted, having already played a game in the morning for our schools. Our success on the football field was mainly due to our brilliant captain, Peter Shreves, who ended up, for a brief time, as the manager of Spurs. (A heretical thought to all of us who grew up so close to Highbury and Arsenal.) Sundays, a priority for Mr Currey, if not for us kids, was Bible Class. One hour every Sunday morning, and if you didn't turn up you couldn't enjoy the rest of the week's activities. That was the catch. Our spiritual diet was always followed by our ritual trip to Chapel Street Market and a visit to the sarsaparilla and apple fritters stalls.

Mr Currey organised everything with tireless patience and an enthusiasm that bordered on crazy, considering the bedlam we mostly engendered. Not that we appreciated this skinny, pallid-faced man with curly hair and big geeky glasses at the time. His 'day job' was a postman and we would giggle whenever we caught sight of him in his uniform, riding his bike along Upper Street with a huge canvas sack over his shoulder. He had a family of his own (his wife, Hilda, also an avid church person, oversaw the sister organisation, the Girls' Brigade – any contact with the members of which was strictly discouraged) but night after night, Mr Currey devoted his life to us scruffy, ungrateful hooligans. Whenever we turned up at 'all London' BB marching functions we were a shambles: always the worst turned-out, eliciting derisory groans from the other London companies with their shiny, magnificent bands flanked with sergeants and corporals, their arms sparkling with acres of metal proficiency badges. Bringing up the rear, we would shuffle along, our 'band' section more for show than musical pleasure. It was hard enough to keep in step let alone bash a drum at the same time. Our incompetence was lost on Mr Currey, however, as he proudly marched at our side, seemingly oblivious as to our awfulness. Curiously, he was an excellent musician himself, which must have been exasperating for him, although he never showed it. He played the church organ in the chapel upstairs and at the annual summer camp – the only holiday for a lot of the kids – and he would pump away at his piano accordion with gusto. We would all squawk along enthusiastically, 'She'll be coming 'round the mountain,' whilst sipping the weakest, most hideous cocoa ever brewed, sheltered from the rain under leaky, mildewy, ex-army tents probably captured from Rommel. We loved it.

I never could understand why this gentle man would give so much of his time to such grubby ingrates. It's easy to be cynical looking back – certainly he was driven along by his Christian faith but, in a way, he was a religious Canute, as the world washed by and the more secular times we were living in were changing so rapidly. The Boys' Brigade had been started in the slums of Glasgow by William Smith in 1883 and even by the late 1950s learning to play the bugle, whilst wearing a daft pillbox hat, was losing its charm as Elvis, Lonnie Donegan and 'Dance Night' at the Tottenham Royal gradually distracted us. But Mr Currey never lost faith. Indeed, he went on persevering for another forty years until he finally threw in the towel when the once populous 17th was down to a membership of just two boys – both of them, I think, his relatives. I wrote a letter to him at the time because I knew what a choker it would have been for him, having struggled for so long to keep the Company and his ideals afloat. With the benefit of hindsight and grey hair, I realise how much we actually admired him. Hardly any of us ended up religious, as he had probably hoped – as the kid who got to the grammar school, I was always the one who had to read the lesson from the Bible on Sundays, proficiency in reading not being the strong point of my more sporting fellow company members. The BB was a significant part of our lives. In a taxi last year, the cabbie looked in his rear view mirror and said to me, 'I know you. You're little Alan Parker.' Then followed a lengthy conversation about my movies, Arsenal, but mostly our BB days, with a fellow 17th boy (older than me – hence I hope, the expression of the diminutive).

So why was Mr Currey important to us – this bespectacled, lanky, not overly educated, pasty-faced postman who played the accordion, made bad cocoa, lost at table tennis and spoke to us of Jesus? We admired him because of his, maybe ingenuous, lack of guile. He gave his time to us because he genuinely believed that helping us bunch of scruffs was worthwhile. Trite as it might sound, Mr Currey was a genuinely 'good' man. He had an innate decency, modesty and genuine, selfless values that maybe were missing in our normal lives, and indeed were probably frowned upon on those cynical street corners. We never thought of him or treated him as a hero but, without us even knowing it, or him ever seeking it, he was an extraordinary example to us all.

I have lived a good many years since my BB days but have yet to meet a better man.

* * *

Tim Bevan
Film Producer, Working Title Films

I am now the producer or joint producer of over 50 feature films in the UK and the USA including *Four Weddings and A Funeral, Elizabeth, Notting Hill, Billy Elliot, Bridget Jones's Diary, Captain Corelli's Mandolin, The Guru, The Ali G Movie, About A Boy* and in 2003, *Johnny English, Love Actually, The Shape of Things,* and *Calcium Kid.* I first started my own music video production company when I was 21, and then formed Working Title Films in 1983 and produced the film *My Beautiful Launderette* when I was 24.

What inspired me? Movies of the 1970s – how could I get to be part of this world? In the early 1980s I worked as a runner for Charlie Crichton, ex-Ealing Comedy Director. He was an inspirational character, unpretentious, still passionate at the age of

80. He taught me to unashamedly pursue the world of film.

MY ADVICE: *For every 100 shut doors there will be one that opens; believe in yourself and create your own opportunities. I did. Be tenacious. Take risks — get noticed.*

Nik Powell
Executive Film Producer, Scala Productions

Everyone knows Richard Branson's life story and his achievements and notoriety. I was fortunate to meet him when I was four years old and we grew up in the same village and became best friends. We launched a student magazine, a pro-choice campaign, Virgin Mailorder, Virgin Megastore and the Virgin Records company together. I am writing this while travelling on one of his aeroplanes! We separated as business partners in 1981, with the sale my 40 per cent shareholding, but remain firm friends.

What did Richard teach me? Fearlessness, courage, hard work, boldness. Never judge a book by its cover, but take care of your own 'cover' because everyone else *does* judge a book by its cover! Never overestimate other people's intelligence and power, however high and mighty they might seem. That one person CAN make a difference. That making a difference IS important, however small that difference is.

I have since worked in film production as executive producer for many successful films including *Company of Wolves, Letter to Brezhnev, Mona Lisa, Shag, Scandal, The Big Man, The Crying Game, Fever Pitch, Twentyfour:Seven, Divorcing Jack, Little Voice, Last Orders, Black and White*, and *Leo* (aka *Leopold Bloom*), and currently in production *The Night We Called It Day* to star Dennis Hopper as Frank Sinatra.

MY ADVICE: *Take all the advice I learned from Richard Branson.*

David Puttnam (Lord Puttnam)
Former Film Producer and Labour Peer

When aged 17, I left school and entered the world of work; one of my first jobs was as a very junior account executive at an advertising agency, Collet Dickenson Pearce. My boss there was a man called

Colin Millward – a very hard taskmaster. He taught me more than anyone I have ever met, and he did it in a most peculiar way.

I'd take an idea for an ad into his office for approval and he'd sit biting his nails for a while and then, in his strong Yorkshire accent, he'd say 'It's not very good, is it?' and I'd say, 'Isn't it?' and he'd say 'No, it's not very good at all.' And I'd ask, 'What don't you like?' – 'You work it out, lad. Take it away, do it again. See you tomorrow.'

This went on for a year or so, although, because I was terrified of him, it seemed like an eternity. I'd leave his office and go back and stare at whatever I'd produced. Then I'd talk it over with a few colleagues, and we'd sit and curse Colin. But 99 times out of 100 he was right, and we would eventually come up with a genuinely better idea. Awards and recognition began to flow in abundance – so our self-esteem was very well catered for!

Years later I said to Colin, 'You were a real tyrant to work for, you know. You seldom gave us much in the way of encouragement and you never steered us in any particular direction.'

'No, I did something much more important than that, lad. I taught you to be self-critical and to start thinking for yourself.' And he did. He taught me that competency, or your first idea, is a point of departure, seldom ever a point of arrival.

Alan Rickman
Actor and Director

My theatre work most recently includes *Private Lives,* by Noël Coward in London and New York, and my film work includes *Sense and Sensibility, Michael Collins, Dogma, Truly Madly Deeply* and the *Harry Potter* series and, as director, Sharman MacDonald's *The Winter Guest*.

The people I think of as truly inspiring are all teachers. Colin Turner from school days, Maria Fedro, June Kemp, Robert Palmer, Michael McCallion from RADA amongst some very gifted others. However, the qualities they all share are perhaps best summed up by singling out Hugh Cruttwell. He died recently and was Principal of the Royal Academy of Dramatic Art during my time as a student there . . .

Throughout his working life he was an uncompromising enthusiast for the seeking of truth in the theatre. Why bother otherwise? Don't put it on display, make a gift of yourself to the material and make a gift of your work to your fellow actors and the audience. It sounds simple but is frustratingly difficult to achieve. Like almost every worthwhile endeavour . . .

Sir Ridley Scott
Film Director

Films I have directed include *The Duellists, Alien, Blade Runner, Thelma and Louise, White Squall, Gladiator, Hannibal, Black Hawk Down* and most recently *Matchstick Men.*

The first really good advice I received, and on which I occasionally reflect as I believe it changed the course of my life, was from my art master at grammar school. He advised me not to continue my education into the sixth form, but instead to leave school and enrol at the local art school where he thought my real passion and talent could be realised. I did, and he was absolutely right – many thanks to Mr Cleland.

My four years at the West Hartlepool Art College focused and nurtured me creatively. Although the path ahead was uncertain, I quickly grasped the ethic of hard work and for the first time during my formative years realised a sense of personal achievement. With achievement, comes confidence and a greater sense of self-worth.

MY ADVICE: *As a film-maker I have been fortunate enough to find an occupation that is my passion and I start every day knowing I am doing what I love to do. I worked hard and took all the opportunities that were available to me. We are fortunate to live in a society that allows most of us the chance to explore and investigate all possible opportunities. The decision to take the advice of those around us is down to the individual and after that it is mostly hard work and dedication that brings the reward of success. You don't get to play soccer like David Beckham without thousands of hours of practice. Practice makes perfect, and perfection looks easy, but it isn't! Even natural talent requires hard work and most importantly the desire to succeed. Commitment, dedication, discipline and self-worth are the keys to success.*

At this stage in my life I still push out the boundaries and seek new challenges. It is important to make the best of every opportunity and strive to achieve the most from every task and obstacle we are set.

Keep striving and you will succeed!

music business

Brian Eno
Musician

I have been fortunate in having made the acquaintance of some brilliant and generous people. I have chosen to write about two of them.

When I was 17 my girlfriend Sarah (who I eventually married) took me to meet her mother, Joan Harvey. Joan was the first person I'd ever met who seemed to have thought her life out from scratch, who was ready to question any idea, including the ones she held most dearly. She lived in a caravan outside Cambridge – a caravan that was regularly visited by leading scientists and thinkers such as Francis Crick and Hermann Bondi.

What drew them there, and what drew me, was the clarity and originality of Joan's thinking. A committed philosophical anarchist, she also ran the Cambridge Humanists, booking some of the most adventurous thinkers to come and speak to them. She liked science, despised religion and was agnostic about the arts. She felt that artists tended to be slippery and self-serving, unable to articulate what they were doing, and generally sloppy thinkers.

Even though I was a young would-be artist, Joan liked me, and I liked hearing her thoughts. You could never guess what she might think about anything, and her ideas often seemed inconsistent at first hearing. However, beneath the surface of her thinking was a rigorously thought-out personal philosophy, and a genuine appetite to understand how other people think – to know on what basis people made their decisions.

Joan changed my life. I respected her singularity, her pleasure in questioning things, her excitement in the insecurity of not knowing the answer to something. She was someone with an appetite for uncertainty. One day she asked me what was probably the most important question that anyone ever asked me. She said 'Why does someone with a good brain like yours want to waste it by becoming an artist?'

This question shaped my life. I couldn't answer her, but ever since I've been trying. I felt that art did something good for the world, but had no idea what. Furthermore, I didn't know anyone who knew or was interested to find out. So Joan's question started me on a personal quest which lasts to this day – the desire to find out what art and culture does for us, why we want it and like it, and how it relates to other forms of human practice and knowledge.

The second person I will mention dates from about the same period of my life.

I met Peter Schmidt when he was teaching at Watford School of Art and I was studying at another art school. Peter was a painter. In 1938, when he was 8, his Jewish family had moved from Berlin to London. I'd heard about his experimental performances with Mark Boyle and The Soft Machine, and more particularly about his reputation as a special kind of teacher. As head of the entertainments committee at Winchester School of Art, where I was a 19-year-old student, I invited him to come to my college to do a performance there.

Peter was interesting – and slightly intimidating – because he was entirely free of any of the habits of tact that keep normal conversations ticking over. If he had nothing to say, he'd say nothing. But when he spoke it was quietly and calmly, even in a noisy room. I noticed that other people in turn became quieter and calmer to hear what he was saying – his behaviour was infectious. It was very much his philosophy that one should do, rather than preach, what one believed. I don't recall him ever telling anyone to be quiet – he simply was quiet himself.

His responses were often unusual and sometimes enigmatic, as though he thought out each question anew, almost from first principles. This made him a great teacher: if you asked him a question he wouldn't deliver a pre-formed answer, but would think aloud with you. He joined you in an adventure of discovery which could lead anywhere. He was the opposite of a snob, seeming to have no preordained cultural barriers – he engaged with music and art right across the cultural spectrum, and was intrigued by the sciences. I realised that even though I was 19 years younger and considered myself musically adventurous I was in fact much more limited than him in what I would listen to.

When I moved to London, where he also lived, I began to visit him regularly. We had intense conversations punctuated by long silences during which we'd listen to music or play Scrabble. Sometimes we went for long walks through South London or to the cinema. In the course of our meetings – which extended over about 10 years until his death in 1980 – we formulated a set of working principles based on our own practices as artists. We published these first in 1975 under the title 'Oblique Strategies', and they remain popular to this day.

Peter Schmidt was not a very successful artist in the commercial sense, but he was a good artist. Most importantly for me, he was really alive. His practice as an artist was a continuous celebratory probing of the world around him and his own perceptions of it. I realised that this was the kind of artist I wanted to be, and that success in these terms meant a great deal more to me than success in 'worldly' terms.

★ ★ ★

Jan-Willem Alkema
Drummer

During the 80s I mostly collected skeletons for my musical closet. I trekked around working men's clubs playing all the classics, played drums in a production of *Jesus Christ Superstar* at the Jersey Opera House, played in several no-hope pop bands, programmed Linn drums/over-dubbed percussion parts for dodgy albums including a reborn Christian soft rock artist (ouch!), went to Dubai with *Paddy goes to Holyhead* to play all the classics, embarrassed myself in blues/country bands, taught drums to wealthy children, gradually fell out of love with heavy metal and got funky.

With the bands *Compulsion* and more recently *China Drum,* I have recorded numerous albums, singles and EPs, made videos and toured extensively in Britain, Europe, the USA and Canada, and Japan, performing in all types of venue, from the tiniest toilet, to Arenas and festivals. Also, during this period there were plenty of radio, TV and in-store performances, ranging from a full band set-up, to playing guitar or hanging around drinking cups of coffee.

I currently own a Pearl DLX kit, an ABB handmade stainless steel kit and a Roland TD10 electronic kit. I also play guitar, write music and can sing if forced.

I wish to put forward the case for struggling entertainers. It is a well-known fact that most of us who want to entertain the masses will be seen by few.

My mentor, Bill Castle, was my drum teacher from age 12 to 15. He was a good teacher, able to convey the essence of what makes a good drummer, always adapting the lesson plan to suit my abilities and teenage mood swings. Far more importantly, he would invite me to watch him play. A real-life professional drummer at work, fantastic! He also made me audition for the National Youth Jazz Orchestra, and they were considering me for the position. But I did not have a burning passion for jazz: still, nice to be asked. I preferred *heavy metal*, for those under 25, think *nu-metal* without baseball caps and DJs.

Bill also illustrated the economic realities of a drummer's life. For a while he would be driving a newish Jaguar. A month or so later the Jag would be replaced by a rusty jalopy. This did not seem to bother him, and his infectious optimism was so stimulating. I knew what I was going to be, come what may.

I subsequently had what I still consider a very successful career as a drummer for about ten years, although I am by no stretch of the imagination a household name.

MY ADVICE: *To any young person wanting to follow a similar career I would say: learn your craft so that it becomes second nature. And show your passion by wearing your heart on your sleeve and be prepared to have it broken.*

Peter Cunnah
Songwriter, Producer and Performer

I first joined a band, The The Boy, when I was 15 in 1982. I formed D:Ream in 1991 and we had 12 top-40 hits between 1992 and 1995. I co-wrote the song *Things Can Only Get Better* which went to No. One for four weeks in 1994. Since 1996, I moved on to producing and writing for various acts.

Too many people inspired me over the course of my life to write about here. But one individual stands out as someone who guided me. I met Jamie Petrie in the Summer of 1989 when I first arrived in London. His spirit as a songwriter was so inclusive and encouraging that confidence and ability in my own songwriting emerged through our collaborations. We bonded as friends and seemed to share a chemistry. One of the results of this partnership was *Things Can Only Get Better*. We're still friends to this day and continue to explore what is now a mutual inspiration.

MY ADVICE: *You have to have a single-minded belief in yourself almost to the point of obsession, in order to survive the knocks and rejections you will receive along the way. Even to this day, after a No. One record, I still experience these setbacks. Tenacity and the 'hide of a rhino' are essential!*

Keith Harris
Chairman, Music Managers Forum

I was born in Newcastle-upon-Tyne and educated at Dundee University. I then worked as Promotions Manager for Motown Records UK from 1976–78, and then as Operations Manager for Stevie Wonder from 1978–82. In 1982 I set up my own music management company, Keith Harris Music Ltd, and I am the Managing Director. I am also the Chairman of African and Caribbean Music Circuit (Arts Council Organisation), Senior Fellow of the University of Westminster (School of Music, Film and Fashion) and Chairman of the Music Managers Forum.

The person who I have found to be most inspirational and who has been most influential on my career in the music industry is Stevie Wonder. We met in 1977, when I was working for Motown Records in the UK which is his record label. He was at that time arguably the world's number one recording artist, and I had been a big fan of his music for the previous ten years. The thing that inspired me most about him was the sheer positivity of his music and his personality. His 'nothing is impossible' approach to life made me realise that you should never give up hope of achieving your goals. He had overcome the odds of being blind from birth to follow his dream of reaching a worldwide audience with his music. By giving me the opportunity to go and work with him in America, he made real another seemingly impossible situation, that of a young British black person becoming personal manager to one of the world's biggest stars. It made me realise that you have to hold on to your dreams.

MY ADVICE: *Make sure that you have a genuine passion for this business before coming into it. If you think of it as just a means of becoming rich and famous you're likely to be disappointed.*

Gillian Porter
PR Manager, Hall or Nothing Music Promotions

Quick Biog: I left school at 16, went to local college for six months . . . first job was at Pinnacle Records (record distribution company – job: assistant to sales manager/general office duties); Roadrunner Records (rock label – job: v. small office /three people – so a bit of everything); Maggi Farran PR (independent PR firm – job: junior/regional PR working with mostly rock bands); Hall or Nothing PR (independent PR firm – wider roster/job: PR); EMI Records (job: Head of Alternative Press and Artist Development – the title was longer than the list of jobs I had to do . . . mainly press and a little A&R); Press Counsel PR (independent PR – job: PR); Hall or Nothing (er . . . back again). Also do a bit of DJ-ing on the side . . . disco and punk stuff.

The first day of my professional career got off to a rather underwhelming start. I had turned up at Pinnacle Records, a record distribution company based in the glamorous surroundings of St Mary Cray near Orpington, Kent (well, glamorous compared to the village in Central Scotland I had travelled down from) for two weeks' work experience and my introduction to the music industry.

This was my dream. I hadn't known until recently that you could actually work and earn a living in music even if you couldn't play a note or hold a tune. Unfortunately, nobody knew who I was or what I was doing there. I sat in reception feeling a bit silly, very nervous but with the attitude that I had nothing to lose and I did have a letter offering me the placement. Somebody in this huge building must know about me!

The person who came to my rescue didn't have a clue who I was or what 'holiday job' I was babbling on about, but seemed to take it in his stride and invited me into his office to explain the mysteries of this sprawling building with loads of people running around. This was George Kimpton, the General Manager of the company, and he seemed rather amused at this 17-year-old with silly punky hair. He listened to why I was there (I think the 'big' boss had agreed to me coming down and promptly, and not unreasonably, forgotten!) and then put me to work.

For the next two weeks I received an exhilarating crash-course education on all aspects of the job. I thought I had a rough idea of how things worked – I had bought and listened to lots of records, gone to gigs, wasted hours of my life hanging around in record shops, helped with a fanzine and putting on local gigs – but, of course, I knew nothing at all! George got me working in the warehouse packing records into boxes; I worked on the telephone taking orders from record shops; I was negotiating advertising rates with magazines; I went out with sales reps flogging records out of the back of their cars (hmm, looking back on it, maybe I wasn't supposed to mention that); I sat in on countless meetings – I was even invited in with the management of New Order to discuss the release of a new single – and asked my opinion on mixes. George breezed everywhere with me in tow, ignoring the quizzical glances as to what this wee Scottish girl was doing with him.

At the end of the fortnight George offered me the chance to stay, and madly enough I turned it down only to realise three days later what a mistake I was making. Thankfully the offer was still open and I moved to London about ten days later and I had my first job in 'the music business'! I stayed there for over a year where George continued to educate, encourage and enthuse me. He was quite a bit older than me, but he had such a love of music, and a wicked sense of humour, that he gave me untold confidence and knowledge. He always listened to me prattle on about whatever gigs I'd been to and my theories about good and bad record labels.

When I left the company I think he helped me get my next job. I've never quizzed him about that as I suppose I'd like to think I got it on my own merit, but I know he looked out for me.

I think the lasting impression George made on me was that it didn't matter that I didn't know anybody or had no experience. We worked in music and everybody's opinion was valid, even 17-year-old, snotty know-it-all-but-know-nothing-at-all kids like me. He treated me with the utmost respect and equality and I hope I have learnt that from him if nothing else. I certainly haven't learnt to love some of the old punk rubbish he used to play me continually.

MY ADVICE: *Get involved as much as you can on a local level . . . help out local bands. If you can write, try to help them out with a short biography, or press releases on gigs for the local papers/student press, fanzines etc. Start your own fanzine, it helps you to make contacts with bands, record labels, other fanzine writers etc. Listen to everything with an open mind and try and get out to hear as much live music as possible. Read the music press regularly so you know all about new bands/scenes/venues ... you need to be up to date with what's going on! Try and maintain as much enthusiasm as you possibly can, even if you are unimpressed occasionally. And have a good attitude — music should be fun and a pleasure.*

Tim Wheeler
Lead Singer and Songwriter, ASH

I have been with my band ASH since I was at school. Our big break came in 1994 when we were signed to Infectious Records and released the mini album *Trailer*. Tours followed with the likes of Elastica, although we needed permission from our headmaster at school before we could go out on the road! We had our first Top 20 hit in 1995 with *Girl From Mars* and, in 1996, we released our first full album, *1977*, which went straight to the top of the UK charts.

We had two Top 5 singles and the album went on to sell well over a million copies.

Our second album, *Nu-Clear Sounds*, was released in 1999 and charted at number seven in the UK. After that we took a well-needed break and I suffered from writer's block for a while before starting to write again. We set about recording our third album, *Free All Angels,* and felt that the public needed re-convincing – no easy task – and we needed to get back to our roots. Using the internet we re-established our fan-base, hitting small venues voted for by fans online. The touring and re-thinking paid off and, in 2001, after almost two years, our single *Shining Light* crashed into the Top 10. The album was released in May 2001 and beat Janet Jackson to the top slot in the charts. This put us back in our element and we had a summer full of touring: 44 European festivals, culminating in a triumphant headline set at Reading.

Free All Angels spawned five Top 20 singles and Hot Press awarded us gongs for Best Irish Album and Best Irish Single. *Q* magazine awarded us Single of the Year for '*Burn Baby Burn*'. I also won the Best Contemporary Song award at the British Academy of Composers and Songwriters' Ivor Novello awards for *Shining Light*.

Our latest album *Intergalactic Sonic 7s* reached number three in the UK album charts and we have recently signed a new record deal stateside where *Free All Angels* will soon be released.

Back at school, I had a great English teacher called David Parks. He taught me right through high school. He's a maverick kind of teacher, always doing things his own way. Pupils could identify with him; he wasn't too hung up on discipline. Also he's a novelist so he encouraged creativity, which is pretty rare in teachers these days. His literature classes were really inspiring for me: the dusty old school books came alive instead of putting you to sleep. When he heard my band ASH playing at a school concert, he gave me a stack of his records to listen to, and it was great stuff like the Rolling Stones, the Kinks, the Undertones and the Clash. I thought teachers were meant to be into Barry Manilow! I was really chuffed last year when he wrote me a letter saying he'd bought our latest album and he thought it was great. That meant more to me than a five-star review!

Roddy Woomble
Singer/Lyricist, Idlewild

I am lead singer and lyricist of Idlewild. Since our first mini-album, *Captain*, in 1998 we have released three full-length albums, *Hope is Important* (1998), *100 Broken Windows* (2000) and *The Remote Part* (2002). During the writing and recording of *The Remote Part* we worked with Stephen Street, renowned for his work with the Smiths and Blur, and Lenny Kaye – sage of the US new wave thanks to his membership of the Patti Smith Group. *The Remote Part* went straight into the UK album chart Top 10 and has so far produced three Top 30 singles.

Usually people expect me to say someone like Bob Dylan, or Kurt Cobain or Patti Smith, when I'm talking about the people who influenced me. But probably the most influence an artist has had over me was seeing the films, artwork and reading the books of Derek Jarman. The way he singlehandedly created his own world, in which to create what he wanted, is something that can be applied to anyone should they be absorbed by what they're doing.

MY ADVICE: *Create your own creative world and if people don't understand it, it's their problem.*

Andrew Yeates
Director General, BPI, Record Industry Trade Association

I trained as a solicitor and qualified in 1981, then joined Thames Television as a Contracts Manager. I moved in 1987 to Phonographic Performance as a company lawyer. In 1988, I joined Channel 4 starting as Programme Acquisition Executive, then Senior Programme Acquisition Executive, and then Head of Acquisitions and Business Affairs. In 1994, I became Channel 4's Corporation Secretary and Head of Rights. In 1999, I moved to BPI as the Director of Legal Affairs and became the Director General in 2000.

Different people have provided inspiration and guidance for me during different stages of my career. All the people who provided particular inspiration provided this through enthusiasm in their work, a flexible approach encouraging others to appreciate why certain goals are important, and obvious dedication. In my case, a family friend, Gerald Thomas, film director, encouraged me to develop my interest in the media industry by working with a film lawyer during my training as a solicitor. This helped to give me background about the way in which legal work is an important and relevant part of so many areas within the media and creative industries. The fact that you could use a qualification in the legal profession to access jobs which would otherwise be very difficult to secure gave my training a real purpose.

The advice given was to have confidence in the desire to be involved in the media industry. It is important to appreciate how flexible you need to be to pick up on career opportunities as these open up. If you are too set in your ways, it is very easy to miss out on an opportunity which may not be ideal when you initially take it up. However, often within the media industry, one opportunity will lead to others.

MY ADVICE: *Be enthusiastic, be flexible in your approach to opportunities that arise. Above all, listen as much as possible to others with experience in the business.*

advertising, PR and marketing

Trevor Beattie
Chairman and Creative Director, TBWA Advertising, London

Let's start at the very beginning. I was born in Birmingham, a late entry into a family of eight children. I have no less than FIVE elder siblings. So, I guess you could say I'm more than qualified to write in support of a charity named Big Brothers & Sisters.

But what of my mentors? When you're neither the eldest, nor the youngest (and you've even missed out on the trusty fall-back of middle-child syndrome), where on earth do you turn for life guidance . . .?

Well, in short, to the Fab Four. Though probably not the ones you have in mind. No, my Fab Four consisted of my mum, my dad, a bloke called John Lowe and a character known variously as 'The Louisville Lip', Cassius Marcellus Clay, The Greatest or, simply, Ali.

As you can probably gauge from the statistics, what my mum and dad didn't know about raising children isn't really worth knowing. And if there was a family trade beyond rearing fine upstanding Brummies, it was the motor trade. Cars cars cars. My childhood witnessed a fabulous procession of Morris Minors, Ford Anglias and Minis of every hue and spec. Sump oil flowed through Beattie family veins.

So wherefore advertising? Well, the first advertisement I ever wrote was perhaps inevitably, a car ad. To be precise, a piece of card taped to the windscreen of a scruffy old VW Beetle parked outside our house, mid-70s. 'FOR SALE' read my copywriting debut. '£60 o.n.o.' Dad promised me a tenner if it sold within a week. He believed in me. And, perhaps, in the power of advertising. Even to flog an old banger. It sold. And I learned the meaning of the letters o.n.o. I was hooked, though not on cars. (I remain the only member of clan Beattie never to have taken a driving test.)

A few years later and my title of Long Haired Sheep of the family was secured, as I became the first person in Beattie family history to study for a degree. The course was Graphic Design, the college Wolverhampton, the weather wet. As I recall, it rained every single sodden day for three long years. The only ray of light in my Black Country adopted home was my course tutor, Mr John Lowe. He had time for me. Time to understand that while I wasn't really cut out for graphics, I might just crack it in adverts. I never knew such a profession existed until he put me up for it. So it's probably safe to assume that I owe him everything. He believed and made a believer of me. Both in myself and the profession we'd sort of chosen between us.

John continues to weave his magic star-spotting spell, now at Birmingham University. Advertising is annually a brighter place as a result of his protégés.

So to Muhammad Ali. And what, you may wonder, could a retired boxer offer me in the way of advice on a career in advertising? Well first of all, to describe Ali as a 'boxer' is akin to dismissing William Shakespeare as a hack. Secondly, Muhammad Ali is the greatest adman the world has ever seen. He is 'The Man Who Sold The World'.

Ali has always been there. A constant in my life for as long as I care to remember. He shaped one of my earliest memories, as controversy raged in our household over (the then) Cassius Clay's notorious split glove in the fight with 'Our' 'Enery Cooper in 1963. Little did we all know then that decades on, I'd be privileged enough to buy that very same glove at auction and house it forever as part of our family's history.

I've seen Ali in triumph, standing tall over the fallen Sonny Liston and George Foreman. The ogres and the world at his feet. I've watched him in abject defeat, jaw broken and wired, The Lip buttoned, to the delight of his many detractors. I studied the video of his demeanour following that fight, the day after my own redundancy. It got me through. He was an even bigger man in defeat than he had been in victory.

And I've held my breath with 3½ billion others as we watched him do battle with his demons to ignite the Olympic Flame in Atlanta in 1996. Parkinson's disease versus superhuman self-belief. No contest. Ali in one.

But most importantly of all, I've been blessed enough to spend some time alone with The Man. An experience I hope one day to record in a book for posterity, and dispel for once and for all the nonsensical adage that one should never meet one's heroes. Turn down a chance to meet Ali? Don't be so ridiculous.

So there we were. Ali and me. Having dinner together following the 1999 Brit Awards. As you do. The Great Man fired me a question across the table. 'You know the greatest thing you can give another person. . . ?' I was floored for an answer, assuming that mere 'love' would not be enough to carry the day. I was right. 'Your time,' he said. 'It's the only thing no one else can give 'em. It's yours for the giving. Give folks your time, you'll go to heaven. Wanna go t'heaven, don'cha?'

Right there, he nailed my theme for this piece.

My simple advice to anyone trying to break through into advertising, or anything else for that matter, is to be patient. To be strong. To never ever ever give up. Then to not give up some more. To hopefully find a figure of inspiration with whom you might spend some time. Their time. Then to pay it back with interest.

Someone once said (it was probably Ali) that life is just a dash between two dates: your birth and your death. And in my profession there seems to be more dashing than most. From meeting to meeting, deadline to deadline. I hope I've learned from my mentors that occasionally pausing between the dashing between the meetings often counts more than the meetings themselves.

That taking time out to give others some of your time isn't time 'out' at all. It's time invested. So thanks for the time that you have taken to read this right to the end. And thank you mum, dad, John and Muhammad, for your very very precious time. I promise you, it wasn't wasted.

Stephen Alambritis
Head of Press and Parliamentary Affairs, Federation of Small Businesses

I am Head of Press and Parliamentary Affairs to the 170,000-strong Federation of Small Businesses (FSB). Prior to joining the FSB, I was Research Director to the Association of Independent Businesses, responsible for a range of reports and studies into the private business sector. I also have practical business experience through my earlier involvement with my family's own business in the West Midlands, and sit on various small business boards. I have a BA in Government, an MSc in Economics and an MA in Business Law. I have been a member of various Government task forces looking at better regulation, disability rights, and work-life balance issues, most recently, and have chaired the DTI's Better Payment Practice Group in 2001. In my spare time I am also a Class I Football Association referee.

The person who inspired and guided me in my career was Lord Weatherill. He was Speaker of the House of Commons between 1983–92 and was subsequently a Convenor of the Cross Bench Peers. More appropriately, he was the Chair of the Industry and Parliament Trust from 1993–2002 and has been a Trustee of the Prince's Trust and the Prince's Youth Business Trust. In 1967, he published *Acorns to Oaks,* a crucial paper on policy for small business. In his earlier working life he had worked in his family's Savile Row tailoring business rising eventually to become President of the company in 1992.

I met Lord Weatherill in 1984 when I began my career in the world of small business and as I moved on to the Federation of Small Businesses I became involved with the Industry Parliament Trust. This seeks to inform politicians about the world of industry and small businesses. Lord Weatherill gave me the guidance and inspiration to maintain a position of independence and credibility required for representing small businesses and raising their fears, aspirations and hopes with Ministers and MPs from all the political parties. His own work in both the business and political world aimed to create an understanding about the pressures on politicians and the aspirations of the business community.

Lord Weatherill taught me the benefit of speaking when you have something to say; of speaking on a small number of topics in order that you become well known for one or two particular issues rather than speaking about all things on all subjects. The best advice he gave me is that in lobbying for change, if you feel you may lose your argument, it is better to withdraw discreetly and respectfully, than to receive the obvious 'no' in public. This gave me the confidence to argue for issues based on merit and research and to know when to withdraw and to fight another day.

MY ADVICE: *For anyone wishing to enter the world of lobbying, learn to ensure that arguments are based on research and that they have merit. It is also important to maintain independence and integrity and to be discreet. It is a good idea to give a particular idea or policy initiative to one side and wait for them to pick it up and run with it, rather than have a scattergun approach. In the world of representation, it is vital to learn when it is, and is not, appropriate to speak. Business people admire those who listen, take information on board and come back later, rather than those who give an instant and rashly thought-out reaction.*

Deborah Bennett
Entrepreneur, Image Builder for Luxury Brands

I started as a merchandising editor at a glossy magazine and later moved to an advertising and public relations agency and then to the press office at Jaeger. My career then changed towards cosmetics and I worked at Fabergé where they had Cary Grant and Roger Moore as their promotional figures. From there I was headhunted to the supreme cosmetic company Estée Lauder and worked for them for ten years in public relations and then in marketing, setting up the Prescriptives brand. I left the corporation to start my own company specialising in marketing and public relations for luxury goods companies and have been lucky enough to have worked with most of the brand leaders. Additionally I am now able to do a certain amount of *pro bono* work and sit on the Board of the English National Ballet School and on the Advisory Council of the Courtauld Institute.

The major influence in my career was the man who headhunted me for Estée Lauder, Roy Harrington. He was my boss and was a totally inspirational figure and a natural leader and teacher. He has sadly recently died and I feel this is a fitting way to remember him. He built the UK affiliate of Estée Lauder and as Managing Director was unsurpassed as a leader and innovator. His energy and personal presence was larger than life and he stood totally by his team and encouraged them both personally and privately. I was recommended to him by a number of people in the industry and I vividly remember my interview with him together with Mr and Mrs Lauder. I was really terrified and he came up to me afterwards and said, 'Don't worry, we will all work as a team and you will succeed.'

Roy Harrington expected high energy and absolute results at all times. His door was always open for help and advice and he gave unstintingly of his time. He had only one standard – perfection – and that is what we all had to achieve. I have never been in a happier work environment. We were all extremely young, but together managed to achieve the most extraordinary results. He gave enormous confidence to his team and I have tried to emulate his management style, with a strict eye to perfection and a happy atmosphere.

MY ADVICE: *Work with something you love doing and that makes you happy. That is a cliché, but so much time is spent at work it is essential to feel fulfilled. Don't give up and keep trying if companies reject you. Try to meet the people concerned. Also ask everyone you know in an associated business for professional advice – it takes just one person to open a door.*

Dominic Fry
Group Director, Corporate Communications, Scottish Power

I help manage my company's reputation in the eyes of important groups of external stakeholders in both the UK and the US. I've done similar jobs for other large companies such as Sainsbury's, the Channel Tunnel and the US phone company AT&T, and before these jobs I used to work for a number of different PR companies doing similar things for a variety of IT companies. I've always had a number of outside interests, in particular the Almeida Theatre, the Royal Shakespeare Company, organic food and farming, and rural action.

Sir Alastair Morton, who ran the Channel Tunnel from its inception through to 1996, was my biggest source of inspiration. He was both my boss and a friend – someone who never gave up, no matter how hard the work, complex the issue or implacable the opposition. He taught me that hard work, attention to detail and the ability to think through the strategies of those with differing views would always win through. He has remained a friend and an inspiration long after our time working together.

Sir Alastair taught me to know myself and be myself: to stick to my guns and trust my own judgement. He always had the knack of being able to see the positives in many seemingly bleak situations, and he created a climate of real and supportive camaraderie amongst his colleagues even in times of the most dire adversity. He made me more confident and harder working, and he helped me to appreciate that one gets out of life what one puts in.

MY ADVICE: *Be yourself and know your limits. Listen hard and attentively to the views of others. Never be afraid to put your case with force and imagination, but appreciate the right of others to opposing views. Put the interests of shareholders first. Be prepared to work very hard over long hours. Keep outside interests to ensure you stay fresh. Never underestimate the power of words. Prize loyalty highly. Don't be afraid to be unpopular. Eschew spin.*

Martin George
Marketing Director, British Airways

I started work at The Boots Company on a sandwich placement in the buying department as part of a Management Science degree course at Loughborough University. Having completed the course, I moved to work in product management for Cadbury's, starting with Flake, Éclairs and Star Bar. At Cadbury, the highlight was the launch and roll-out of Wispa, then the most successful confectionery product launch ever, and winning the National

Marketing Award from the Institute of Marketing. By the time I left in 1987, I was Product Manager for a number of brands at Cadbury. I then joined British Airways as the Brands Manager for Club Europe, responsible for its relaunch in 1998. Since then I have held a range of marketing positions at British Airways with responsibility at different times for the UK Domestic & Super Shuttle, UK/I Sales, a secondment to US Air, and Telephone & Retail Sales. I was appointed Marketing Director in 1997 and am now responsible for an annual budget of over £100 million to look after the airline's marketing, fleet, network, pricing, e-commerce and public relations. This includes all kinds of activities from the new advertising campaigns to the BA London Eye (Millennium Wheel) to BA's support for the England 2002 World Cup Team bid and the British Olympic Association sponsorship.

Looking back to my time at school, Mike Davey was my economics teacher, career adviser, squash player and friend.

A steadying hand is a wonderfully calming influence for an 18-year-old intimidated by the pressures of expectancy. A job? University? College? Which course? Where? Life-changing dilemmas coinciding with the intensity of the most challenging academic year of your life.

Mike Davey was the voice of logic, concern and support, helping me to stay in control and steer a course to a destination that was both desirable and achievable. He knew me as an individual, my strengths and preferences, and was honest about my limitations. He supported me in identifying the right options and closing others down in a sensible way, so that I used my time and emotional resources efficiently. He had seen it all before but showed empathy and, as necessary, the sympathy required by someone at times struggling to cope with a process of both academic and emotional maturing.

When the going got tough there was always squash as a time of much-needed light relief, reminding me that being fit in body helps you stay fit in mind. But, when all is said and done, it's always worth remembering that friendship and family support are surely the greatest assets in life.

MY ADVICE: *Never stop learning. Never give up. Believe you can do it.*

Michael Hastings
Head of Corporate Social Responsibility, BBC
and Chairman, Crime Concern

I was born in Lancashire, and moved at the age of eight to live in Montego Bay, Jamaica. Six years later, my older brother and I returned to the UK to attend boarding school in Lancashire. I went on to study in London, and then Oxford to qualify as a secondary school teacher. After five very productive years, I moved on to work with the Government in 1986 through the Downing Street Policy Unit as a consultant on urban development and employment initiatives following the 1985 city riots across the UK. My remit was to liaise across the UK on behalf of the DTI Inner Cities Unit to build bridges of understanding between black and ethnic communities in cities affected by riots.

This led to many passions, one of which was tackling school truancy by setting up a US-inspired project to link schools and community services together. There followed connections with Bruce Gyngell, then Chairman of TV-AM, who invited me to produce the first-ever television series on absenteeism. This became a mammoth exercise covering three weeks of daily features, a policy book, a video and public campaign. The data collated was used to advise the Government's truancy policy.

After some years of reporting and presenting a live programme each morning, I became GMTV's Chief Political Correspondent, and then went to the BBC as Presenter of BBC2's *Around Westminster* programme. From there I moved to the BBC's corporate head-quarters to become Head of Public Affairs, dealing day-to-day with the political process on behalf of the BBC before moving in 2003 to my current position. I have also developed the BBC's Community Affairs function and enhanced this with a new corporate social responsibility emphasis for the whole BBC. Over the years I have taken on outside roles including having been a Commissioner of the Commission for Racial Equality for nine years.

I became one of the founding Directors of Crime Concern which was created to innovate and experiment with new models for effective crime prevention work and community safety ideas.

Crime Concern has grown to over 350 staff and 1,000 volunteers acting with HRH The Princess Royal as our President. I am now the Chairman and was awarded the honour of a CBE in 2002 for services to crime reduction.

Going back to 1977, Major General Sir John Nelson, who had been a top army leader in the North African Second World War campaign, was leading a group to give young potential leaders inspiration to believe in national change. He wanted to get students excited not by protest but by inspiration to gather others and was detemined to turn wild vision into practice. He taught me to network and to value every person and every contact, not because of what they can do for you, but because creative, intimate relationships transform behaviour. Over 14 years, until he died in 1992, I met him every few months and he shared a new nugget every time. He valued time as an asset to be invested in others to inspire and encourage.

MY ADVICE: *Build friends for that reward: intimacy and support, value and respect, and to hold you through turmoil and pressure. From friendship and warm partnership, great ideas can be resourced, and men and women can elect to put cash, time, passion and effort into doing. Without giving time and intimacy, no one has a stake in making a long-term difference.*

John Hegarty
Chairman and Worldwide Creative Director, BBH

I started in advertising as a junior art director at Benton and Bowles, London in 1965. I almost finished in advertising 18 months later, when they fired me. I joined a small Soho agency, John Collings & Partners, going places. They did – out of town. In 1967, I joined the Cramer Saatchi consultancy which became Saatchi & Saatchi in 1970, where I was a founding shareholder. One year later I was appointed Deputy Creative Director.

I left in 1973 to co-found TBWA, London as Creative Director. The agency was the first to be voted *Campaign* (the UK's leading advertising magazine) Agency of the Year in 1980. In 1982, I left to start Bartle Bogle Hegarty. Four years later, in 1986, BBH was also voted *Campaign* magazine's Agency of the Year, and won the title again in 1993. In addition, BBH became the Cannes Advertising Festival's very first Agency of the Year in 1993 by winning more awards than any other agency. It won the title yet again in 1994. My advertising credits include 'Vorsprung Durch Technik' for Audi, and Levi's 'Bath' and 'Launderette'. Recently I was awarded the D&AD President's Award for outstanding achievement in the advertising industry and chaired the 1999 New York Art Director's Advertising Show.

My father once said to me, 'There's no point being Irish if you can't get lucky.' I, therefore, consider myself fortunate to have had an Irish father.

Three people, something to do with the Holy Trinity, made a difference to my life and career. All of them were teachers.

The first was Colm O'Halpin, who taught me history, geography and English, who, more importantly, taught me learning could be fun.

The second was Peter Green, lecturer at Hornsey Art School, who later became the Dean of Middlesex Polytechnic. Peter brought me to the realisation that I was not going to be the next Picasso. Something of a blow at the time. Instead he saw that I had a gift for ideas and that's what I should pursue as a career

And, finally, the wonderful and remarkable John Gillard, who switched a light on in my head and showed me that advertising with its obsession for ideas could be intelligent, funny, informative and, most importantly, inclusive.

They were, all three, brilliant.

Something else my father said, 'The best thing you can be given is an education, because it can't be taken from you.'

How lucky I was my father thought that.

Dotti Irving
Chief Executive, Colman Getty PR

I run a PR consultancy, Colman Getty, which is an independent consultancy specialising in publishing, the arts, corporate and sponsorship fields. I set the company up in 1987 after a brief initial career as a teacher and then a much more interesting time at

Penguin Books. I started in Penguin's Education Unit and worked my way through a range of jobs to become Publicity Director. After five years in that role – the best possible job in publishing PR – the next logical step was for me to set up my own company, Colman Getty. I've been extraordinarily lucky in my working life in that wonderful opportunities have come along for me that I've been able to grasp – I can honestly say that I am never bored by my job!

Apart from my parents, who inspired me by example and always had a slightly spooky but unwavering confidence in my abilities, the man who has been my chief inspiration is Peter Mayer. Peter whirlwinded into Penguin as the new Chief Executive of Penguin Books in the late 1970s. Penguin was going through a bad time and he had been imported from New York to put it back on its feet. Which he did with a vengeance.

What I learned from Peter is that you have to be brave; you mustn't let the fear of failure hold you back; it's better to try and fail than not to try at all. And if you do fail, learn from that failure and then put it behind you.

It gave me enormous confidence in the way I did my job. Knowing that I had the freedom to be wrong meant that I often got it very right. I also had the fantastic experience of working with a small, creative, energetic team who all felt the same way and all worked towards a common goal. People today often comment on how Colman Getty is remarkable in its lack of office politics, its creative team approach to projects, the fact that we all work together very well – that ethos comes from that time.

MY ADVICE: *It is horribly hard to get into publishing or PR or any combination of the two. So you need to stand out from the crowd. Get a foot in the door; do work experience or be prepared to start from the bottom. But learn as much as you can while you're doing it – ask questions, offer to write stuff, make your enthusiasm obvious. And above all, know that you can do it. I recently came across a quote from Henry Ford which I wished I had had pinned on my board when I was 18: 'Whether you believe you can or believe you can't, you're right.'*

Nicola Mendelsohn
Business Development Director, BBH Advertising Agency

What do you do with a degree in English and drama? A question often asked by elderly relatives during my student days in Manchester. Advertising may not seem the natural bedfellow to my degree course but it did hone key instincts.

Graduating in 1992 I went into the advertising industry via the graduate-training scheme at BBH. I worked on the account-handling side for five years on businesses such as Coca-Cola, Cadbury's and Unilever. In 1997 I moved into the new business role and in 1999 became the Business Development Director. I am also on the executive of Cosmetic Executive Women, a member of the Marketing Society and a director of the Fragrance Foundation UK.

I have been inspired and continue to be inspired by many people aside from my parents, husband and children. From an early age I trained with a drama teacher, Ruby Gold, for many years. She worked with me to develop my creative skills and gave me a wider appreciation of the arts. But most importantly she taught me dedication, the value of hard work and of approaching the task in hand with a clear purpose and full attention.

Ruby instilled me with passion, confidence and, above all, a belief in myself. These are all necessary skills when working with people and looking to inspire others to get the best out of them. She taught me to strive to give the best possible performance and that, even when I thought I was giving the best that I could, deep down it could always be improved upon. This restlessness and constant striving for the best, as well as the need to keep on going, are as valuable in the arts as they are in business. She taught me to practise, practise, practise until the performance was as good as it should and could be.

MY ADVICE: *Advertising is one of the most exciting, fun and dynamic industries to work in. If you are determined, do your homework and have the courage of your own convictions you will succeed. A creative flair and a love of commercials are a necessity. It is an industry that rewards talent, so get in anywhere: at BBH, two of the department heads started out as* *secretaries. Look for any way in, use any contacts that you have or get a work placement, and then it's up to you to prove yourself.*

Chris Powell
Chairman, BMP DDB

After short stints in two advertising agencies, I was involved in the start-up of the agency, BMP, in 1968, which went public in 1980. BMP went on to become the second largest UK agency, with a turnover of £400 million and a particularly strong reputation amongst its peers. I spent a term as the Elected President of the IPA, the advertising trade association, and I am a non-executive director of the FTSE 100 company, United Business Media plc. On a voluntary basis, I'm also the Chairman of the Institute of Public Policy Research, the leading think tank, an honorary adviser to the Board of International Family Health (having past experience as the chairman of a local health authority), and a long-standing school governor and Board member of the Riverside Arts in Hammersmith, London.

When I was at school, I struggled, failed the eleven plus exam, and was heading for a few mediocre 'O' Levels. Education seemed to be about learning facts, which I found difficult to remember, and which I didn't see the point of anyway. Low down in the 'B' stream, I was bemused and depressed by it all.

Then we had this English teacher who seemed interested in my opinions about books and engaged me in arguing for my views. I can't do facts, but I found I could do opinions, and my self-confidence was boosted by his interest. Nowadays I still don't know anything, but have opinions on everything!

The teacher's name has gone (it's a fact, after all) but I heard he went on to be a headteacher somewhere. I'm not surprised.

MY ADVICE: *Enthusiasm (as long as it's not mindless) gives a tremendous edge.*

Amanda Rayner
Event Manager (Proprietor of Amanda Rayner Images)/Novelist

I trained as a graphic designer and started my career in magazine design but discovered an aptitude for organising. I moved into public relations and event management, establishing Amanda Rayner Images in 1992. I organise the annual Race in the Media Awards – RIMA – amongst my various projects and I've also always been a creative writer. Having come up with a storyline for a novel on holiday in 1995 I was encouraged to go ahead and write my first book which was published a year later. My second novel followed in 1997 and my third novel, *The Barbed Wire Tree*, is currently being placed with a publisher.

I attended a very academic/sports oriented school for 'gels' but did not fit into either category, favouring art as my lead subject. An English teacher dismissed me, and in particular my writing, at the age of 15 as 'too imaginative'. (It was intended as a put-down and it worked.) I was demoralised and my self-confidence was severely dented.

However, another teacher in the English department – a wonderful woman called Sheila Woolf – saw beyond my lack of academia and prowess on the sports field and scooped me up. She appreciated my organisation skills and made me editor of the school magazine and a member of the public speaking team (which won prizes at national level). She generally encouraged me in my writing to such an extent that I not only had the courage to finally enter the school's short story competition, but went on to win it.

Thanks to the attitude of that first teacher I left school believing I was perceived as 'being different'. It was thanks to Sheila Woolf that I recognised my own skills as an organiser, which ultimately led me to establish Amanda Rayner Images. This support rebuilt my self-esteem and made me realise that to succeed in life you don't have to fit into a set mould. Belief in yourself is the starting point.

MY ADVICE: *Believe in yourself and your own capabilities. If you need support find your own mentor and don't take 'no' for an answer.*

Jamie Rubin
Foreign Policy and Public Affairs Adviser

I served under President Clinton as Assistant Secretary of State for Public Affairs from 1997–2000 and was appointed by the Secretary of State to be the Department's Chief Spokesman. This meant that during that time I conducted daily on-camera briefings for the state department press corps, represented the administration in print, radio, and television interviews, and served as principal adviser to the State Department and other Government agencies on all aspects of the Department's responsibilities in the conduct of public affairs. I was also a key policy adviser to the Secretary of State. When I left in 2000, I received the State Department's highest honour, the Distinguished Service Award.

Prior to this appointment, I was Director of Foreign Policy and Spokesman for the Clinton/Gore '96 Campaign, and from 1993 until 1996, I served as Senior Adviser and Spokesman for US Representative to the United Nations, Madeleine K. Albright. From 1989–93, I served as a professional staff member on the US Senate Committee on Foreign Relations and Senior Foreign Policy Adviser to Senator Joseph R. Biden, Jr (D-DE). From 1985–89, I was the Research Director for the non-profit Arms Control Association in Washington, DC. I received a Bachelor of Arts degree in Political Science from Columbia University in 1982 and a Masters in International Affairs in 1984. In 1998, I was the recipient of Columbia University's John Jay Award for Distinguished Professional Achievement.

I am currently living in London with my family. I work as a partner at Brunswick and am a Visiting Professor of International Relations at the London School of Economics.

The first real inspiration that I can remember was a professor in graduate school. His name was Morton Halperin, and he had written a definitive study of how decisions are made at the highest levels in the US government. He taught me that governments, like any institutions, make decisions as a result of the personal interests of key individuals, the bureaucratic interests of the civil service, as well as the national interest of countries. By unlocking the way in which the ideas I was learning in graduate school would be affected by those practical factors, a new world opened up to me.

When I moved to Washington after school these practical considerations stayed in the back of my mind. As a result, I think I was better aware of what motivated the political parties, the key politicians and the key decision-makers in government.

MY ADVICE: *Anyone serious about politics and government is to be passionate about some issue, almost any issue. Because when you care intensely about that one issue, you learn about how government policy is really made. You meet the representatives who are interested in it, the civil servants, the outside experts, the journalists and of course get to the root of what members of the public think. There is no better way to be successful in politics and government than to have the practical understanding of how the system works. And once you have mastered one topic, through hard work and determination, you learn that you can move on to other topics in shorter and shorter periods of time.*

Andrew St George
Crisis Management Consultant and Writer

I work as a crisis consultant. My consultancy work involves ideas advocacy and advice for a range of commercial and financial clients in Europe and the USA. I draw on my experiences in finance, PR, law, distribution, information and education. I have also written or edited nine books in history, communications and business. I was educated at Cambridge, Harvard and Oxford Universities and was a research fellow at Christ Church, Oxford.

I met John Scanlon in New York where he was representing CBS, the TV company, in a case against General William Westmorland. John was one of the smartest men I have known, emotionally and intellectually. He developed the area of crisis management for individuals and companies in a mess. I worked for him for 15 years until he died in 2001.

What impressed me about John was that he had come to master several intellectual disciplines using his experience as a seminarian, salesman, spokesman and strategist. He had educated himself, and was a passionate believer in the power of learning and education at all stages of life. The last book he shared with me was a biography of the Nobel Laureate John Nashe (now more popularly known from the film *A Beautiful Mind*). He was always telling me to read more, widely and deeply. He passed on to me an unquenchable thirst for knowing.

John had a powerful capacity to understand complex intellectual and professional issues swiftly and surely. He kept a book of facts and insights for that telling phrase or perception that would unlock a situation or explain a set of beliefs or ideas. And he knew ideas had to be tested, defended, argued over – day or night – usually over a good meal. He would often call early, before the day started, to chat about some piece in the newspapers and how it might affect our business.

John made me realise that life is short and that it is worth taking risks and asking big questions to understand how the world works. He encouraged me to take the long, broad view in everything. He was always supportive, especially when I made mistakes, and used to say when I worried, 'Hey, what's the worst that can happen, Andrew? They can only say no.'

MY ADVICE: *Read widely, never stop learning and don't be afraid to take your own risks.*

Eric Salama
Chairman and CEO, Kantar Group (Information and Consulting Division of WPP Group plc)

In 2002, I was appointed the Chairman and CEO of Kantar, WPP's information and consulting division with revenues of around $1.4 billion. Kantar brands include Millward Brown, Research International, BMRB, IMRB, Lightspeed, Ziment, Center Partners, Added Value, Fusion 5, Icon, Henley Centre, BPRI, pFour, Glendinning and Management Ventures.

Between 1994 and 2002 I was the Strategy Director and served on the board of WPP Group, the largest communications company in the world, and was responsible for developing client businesses, acquisitions and joint ventures, practice development, knowledge sharing, the creation of new offers and of integrated teams for clients and the Group's digital capabilities.

Prior to that I was Joint Managing Director of the Henley Centre, Europe's leading consumer consultancy. And before that I was a researcher and speechwriter to The Labour Party Foreign Affairs Team in the House of Commons. I have a politics, philosophy and economics degree from Trinity College, Oxford and an MSc with distinction in economics from Birkbeck College, London. I am also a Trustee of The British Museum.

I first came across Martin Sorrell, the Chief Executive of WPP Group plc, in late 1987. I was then a very junior partner at The Henley Centre and he was negotiating with my colleagues to acquire the company. Subsequently I moved across to work with Martin at WPP on April Fools' Day 1994 and we have sat in next-door offices and worked together ever since.

Martin has built WPP from nothing to be the largest marketing services company in the world. But it is not this achievement itself which has inspired me. Rather it is seeing at close hand the principles that are important to him and the way that they are applied: that people are all important and that having the right people around you is so much more important than any structure or set-up; that young people have to be nurtured; that individuals and small companies are as potentially valuable to their clients as large organisations.

As a person I think that I've always treated people as I would like to be treated myself. As the son of immigrants to the UK, the words from Exodus, 'You shall not oppress a stranger for you know the heart of the stranger – you yourselves were strangers in the land of Egypt', have unconsciously guided me.

But what Martin has helped me do is to put that meaning for me in a business context. And made me realise that the core of any business has got to be the quality of the people within it and the extent to which those people are engaged.

MY ADVICE: *Make sure you are working in environments in which you can learn from people. The most successful people are not usually the brightest or the smartest. They are the ones who know how to get the best from themselves and those around them.*

Helen Scott Lidgett
Managing Partner, Brunswick Arts

For the last few years I have been working as a Public Relations Consultant, most recently as the Managing Partner of a wonderful group of people called Brunswick Arts which is part of Brunswick PR. We have clients ranging from top institutions like the National Gallery to inspired geniuses like Cameron Mackintosh, restoration theatre projects such as the Hackney Empire and new-build galleries like the Baltic in Gateshead. It's completely varied and never dull.

I have been lucky enough to have had an extraordinary number of different careers – as a teacher, running my own fashion business, and in public relations – each one with inspiring people who have all given me something in new ways of thinking. I spent a wonderful ten years doing the PR and Marketing for Thames & Hudson publishers where Thomas Neurath, the owner and Managing Director, was a fully hands-on boss. The main thing I learnt from Thomas was how crucial it is to hold out for the best and have high standards. He didn't just expect 10 out of 10 from everyone: it was more like 15 or 20. Books, advertising, letters, phone-calls and contracts were all on hold until he felt totally happy with the content. People rolled their eyes and there was a lot of impatience to get jobs done and see books on the press, but he would regularly call a halt, tear things up and make people re-assess their work – annoyingly he was nearly always right. I also remember his unusual letters. They were continental in flavour and always contained words you had to look up; they were elegant and persuasive – an irresistible and effective combination.

Another colleague at Thames & Hudson who taught me something about being non-judgemental was Tim Evans, who was in charge of the Sales Department. He managed to combine effortless delivery with a fabulous sense of humour and an incredible intellectual knowledge of all the subjects we covered. I recall ranting to him about a colleague who had behaved in what I considered to be a wild and unpredictable manner. Tim's response was, 'Everyone's got their own style of doing things; as long as he gets the job done does it really matter if he doesn't do it in your way?' So simple but it made me pause. I like to think it helped me be less judgemental.

In the early 1980s, I worked at the London listings magazine, *Time Out*, for a few years and Lindsey Bareham, now Food writer on the Evening Standard, was in charge of the 'Sell Out' section. She taught me the importance of 'the first sentence'. I was always quite confident with the content and subject matter of my copy but it was often dull and list-like until Lindsey, who was my editor, extracted the one message that gave a kind of emotional direction to the piece. That cleverness has helped me with all kinds of different work and not just writing.

MY ADVICE: *Don't judge others by your own style of delivery but do have confidence in your gut reactions.*

Jan Shawe
Director of Corporate Relations, J Sainsbury plc

I joined the Executive Committee of J Sainsbury plc in June 2000 and was appointed Director of Corporate Relations. Previously I was in a similar position at Prudential plc, and for Reed International, with a two-year period as acting Director of the Tate Gallery's development office. My earlier career included several years working at public relations agencies, although my first job was teaching English in the Bahamas. I am a graduate of Newcastle University, the University of California, Irvine and California State University, Fullerton. I've been a Trustee of the charity Common Purpose since 1990, and still serve on the Friends Council and the Corporate Advisory Committee of the Tate.

My change merchant was a dynamic Californian who challenged me on a series of cop-outs I'd developed over 22 years. His words still echo – a mixture of 'Whoever promised you a rose garden?' with 'If you really want to do it, why don't you?' I went back to university, developed a new skill set and planned a new career which has involved me in a number of issues where I feel I've made a strong contribution.

MY ADVICE: *Be curious; find out how happenings happen and make sure you equip yourself to participate meaningfully.*

Sir Martin Sorrell

Chief Executive, WPP (one of the largest communications services groups in the world including international advertising agencies, J. Walter Thompson, Ogilvy & Mather, Young & Rubicam and Red Cell)

I feel somewhat self-conscious about inclusion in this book, as I don't believe that I've yet fulfilled my dream. My objective would be to create the finest business in our industry and I still feel that we have some way to go, despite the fact that we started only 16 years ago. At the moment, we have a very fine collection of businesses with undoubtedly the best brand names in the industry. However, there is still room to upgrade the quality of what we do, particularly in the creative area, and a consequent need to continually improve the quality of our talent. The other objective is to ensure that all our businesses work co-operatively together to add value to our client's businesses and our people's careers.

As far as the inspirations are concerned, I would list my father as a continuous inspiration and adviser. In addition, as icons, Sir Jules Thorn and Lord Weinstock – both people whom my father worked with in the radio and electrical industries. They were people who had entrepreneurial and managerial qualities, and had to start businesses or develop them from small-scale into very large-scale enterprises.

MY ADVICE: *To succeed in business as Sir Jules Thorn and Lord Weinstock have done, you have to be committed, hard working and visionary with considerable attention to detail. You have to be a macro as well as a micro manager to create a successful new business.*

Bobby Syed

Managing Director, Hearsay Communications and Director/Founder, EMMA Awards

I formed Hearsay Communications as a full-service PR/Marketing agency, which specialises in the UK ethnic market. We've worked with the School of Oriental and African Studies, the Government of Pakistan, Asian Business Breakfast Club, the Yusuf Islam (Cat Stevens) album launch, Black Coral Production (Black People's

Century) and various ethnic media publications.

My burning inspiration towards success started with the love and support of my twin-like sister, who was one year older than myself and died suddenly in 1985 at the age of 23 leaving behind her two baby sons, as well as her unconditional support for my own dreams. Her sad loss made me even more determined to succeed as a testament to her legacy. I went to university at the South Bank in Bradford and the School of Oriental and African Studies, where I later worked. I joined a large PR company and then set up on my own. Having my own company meant I could fulfil my dream to set up the Ethnic Multicultural Media Academy (The EMMA Awards) in 1997. The EMMAs have since honoured legends like Muhammad Ali, Nelson Mandela, Lord Attenborough, Ray Charles and Maya Angelou for this Multicultural Lifetime Achievement Award.

As well as the inspiration of my sister, I was also guided by my friend Donald Woods, a human rights lawyer who was portrayed by Kevin Kline in the film *Cry Freedom*. He made me feel that we can all make a difference to humanity if we try hard enough.

MY ADVICE: *Stay pure and true to your heart, because that is the only real way to make sense of this mad world.*

Hugo Tagholm
Senior Events Manager, Brunswick Arts and Programme Director for PiggyBankKids Projects

After studying French and philosophy at Exeter university I worked in events management for over four years with a wide range of companies including the BBC, the New Statesman, Stonewall and the WPP Group before joining Brunswick Arts and PiggyBankKids Projects in 2002.

As Programme Director for PiggyBankKids I have the chance to work with and meet a variety of inspirational characters, from the staff at other charities, to the stars that kindly donate their time to help our projects.

Outside of work, surfing is my passion. I have been fortunate enough to surf in many countries around the world including the

US, Australia and Indonesia, but where I really learnt about the ocean was France. One of the biggest influences in respect to surfing is my friend Hervé Baranx. We have surfed together many times and his skill, style and attitude in the water were bound to rub off on me in some way. He helped me to push myself more and more – and sometimes, just by watching him catch waves, I would learn something new. There are always personal boundaries that can be pushed further and I try to do this both in the water and at work.

Surfing has given me a positive mental attitude which helps in all areas of life. It has taught me about the environment and about fitness. It has given me more confidence and self-esteem. It has also definitely given me a more responsible mindset – I am ultimately on my own in the water and all the decisions I make, especially when conditions are testing, need to be firm and decisive. Any wavering or panic and I could find myself in trouble.

Saying this, you are also responsible for others in the water – despite the pecking order for the waves, surfers do tend to watch out for one another, and if someone is in trouble, they'll be there. Without the careful help of people like Hervé, I could never have learnt the skills to tackle some of the waves I can surf today.

MY ADVICE: *Whether professionally or in your private life it is essential to have a passion. I am fortunate enough to have a job that I enjoy and also to have a huge passion outside of work. With passion you can find a focus to your life. And remember, what you put in is what you get out.*

Mark Wnek
Chairman, Euro RSCG UK advertising agency

I was a bright working-class boy with a single mother who got a scholarship to a public school in the days when a scholarship meant everything got paid for, otherwise we couldn't have afforded it.

I did the public school and Cambridge thing and, like a lot of people who go into advertising, I had no idea what I wanted to do so I did a lot of stuff: van driving, teaching, journalism. In retrospect, this helps foster the eclectic imagination so crucial to coming up with ideas.

I went into journalism because I thought it was the ultimate creative canvas but from hanging out with my friends in advertising I realised their canvas gave freer rein to the imagination. I did a copy test at Ogilvy (agencies used to have these tests in the old days) and was hired the next day. On my first day I realised I was home.

The person who started my career was the extraordinary Michael Baulk, then, in 1982, Managing Director of Ogilvy Advertising. He put a raw recruit in front of Guinness for the biggest pitch of the decade, showing 100 per cent trust in what others must have said was a huge risk. There is nothing more energising than having someone put their faith in you when you know they are judging you by what is inside rather than your external achievements. The best advice Michael gave me was, 'Always get paid slightly less than you're worth'.

MY ADVICE: *If what you really want to do is be in the film or TV business, go into the film or TV business. The advertising business is no longer a stepping stone to Hollywood. It is about the whole gamut of communications, not only making mini-films in 30 seconds. Unless you're fascinated by this and by the simple art of salesmanship, you'll have no future. Winning creative awards has never ever been less relevant.*

business and finance

Sir Richard Branson
Chairman, Virgin Group

Although people say, one makes one's own luck, I know that I have definitely been very lucky in life. Not only to survive one or two of my experiences, but also the fact that some things that we did in the early years of Virgin just worked against all the odds and gave us the breathing space to build the entrepreneurial companies which comprise the group of today.

One thing I have been lucky in is the people that I have met over the past 35 years. It all started when I was leaving school and working hard to start Britain's first national student magazine in the late 1960s. I wrote to everybody I could think of who was famous in the world, asking them to contribute articles in the magazine or agree to interviews. There was no one more surprised than me when we got positive answers from people as diverse as Gerald Scarfe, John Lennon, Mick Jagger, Dudley Moore, Ted Heath, R. D. Laing, Vanessa Redgrave, Jean-Paul Sartre and David Hockney. I realised the golden rule of being an entrepreneur, namely, 'if you don't ask, you don't get!'

As Virgin developed in the 1970s into a fledgling record company and music retailer, I began to admire the work of entrepreneurs for the first time and one particular character attracted my attention. His name was Sir Freddie Laker. At the end of the decade, he railed against the big state-owned airlines and British Airways in particular for the huge amounts they charged passengers to cross the Atlantic. For a generation who think nothing of going to New

York for the weekend, readers would be amazed that an economy fare to New York in 1980 cost around £4,000 at today's prices. What I loved about Laker was the fact that he put his money where his mouth was. In the winter of 1979 he took on the big airlines and offered fares with his Laker Skytrain to New York for under £200. By the spring of 1980 literally thousands of people queued outside tents at Gatwick every day to fly on his DC10s.

I flew on Laker and realised that it wasn't any better than the big airlines, but interestingly enough it was not any worse either and it was certainly a damned sight cheaper. So I became hooked, but was constantly trying to think of ways that Virgin might do it better if we ever went into the airline business. As it turned out my chance to become an airline boss came quicker than I could have ever imagined and with it my chance to meet Freddie.

In February 1982 Laker went bust and quickly announced that he was considering suing British Airways, Air France, Pan Am and TWA for what were called anti-trust violations. Under these American laws, companies could be sued if they ganged up to put a smaller competitor out of business. Freddie believed that they had and that he had the evidence to get them in court.

Not long afterwards I was approached about buying Freddie Laker's licence to fly between Gatwick and New York and start our own Virgin service; however, the guy who approached me was proposing a business-only airline to replace Laker, which just didn't seem right. I was fascinated by the idea but the first thing I did was contact Freddie himself and ask him for lunch on the house boat which was then both my home and Virgin's 'head office'. It was great to meet him. He sat down, laughed infectiously and immediately got stuck into explaining the mechanics of an airline. He confirmed my own suspicions about the limitations of starting an airline in business class across the Atlantic, 'And you don't want to be all no-frills economy service either,' he pointed out. 'That was my mistake. You'll be vulnerable to the simple cost-cutting attack which put me out of business.'

We began a discussion on the philosophy of the business-class service at that lunch. We talked about offering a first-class service at a business-class fare, and of building in all kinds of extra services for the cost. Two of the best ideas that came out of our lunch were to offer a limousine pick-up as part of the service and offer a free economy ticket to anyone who flew business.

Freddie also warned me to expect some fierce competition from British Airways. 'Do all you can to stop BA,' he said. 'Complain as loudly as possible, use the Civil Aviation Authority to stop, and don't hesitate to take them to court. They're utterly ruthless. My mistake was that I never complained loudly enough. They destroyed my financing and it's too late for me now. I sued them and won millions of dollars, but I lost my airline. If you ever get into trouble, sue them before it's too late. Another thing, Richard, is the stress. I'm not kidding but you should have regular medical check-ups. It is very stressful.'

Freddie then told me that he was just recovering from cancer of the pancreas. I was inspired to see that despite all of his problems, Freddie was still so ebullient. He was unbowed by the experience, and saw me as his successor, picking up the flag where he had left off. I asked Freddie whether he would object if I called Virgin Atlantic's first aircraft 'Spirit of Sir Freddie' but he laughed it off: 'Not the first one,' he said, 'my name's a liability now and you'd send out the wrong signals. But I'd be honoured when you've got a larger fleet.'

That meeting inspired the launch of Virgin Atlantic in June 1984. The following year, Freddie won a final settlement from BA and the other airlines who had put him out of business, and used his massive payout to start another charter airline between the Bahamas and Florida. He had been knighted in recognition of the enormous contribution he had made to the country's aviation industry. This was after all the man who had not only started Laker Skytrain and changed the face of transatlantic travel forever, but had in the 1950s been the pioneer of package holidays by air and even before that, one of the saviours of the western world for his heroic part in organising the Berlin airlift.

As Virgin Atlantic grew, almost everything Sir Freddie said at that first lunch came to pass. We built Virgin Atlantic on quality as well as cost and the concept worked. BA did come after us and we shouted long and hard before in the words of Sir Freddie 'suing the b*****ds' and winning in January 1993. Not long before our court case with BA was due to start I remembered what Freddie had said at lunch in 1983 and named our first plane to fly to Orlando 'Spirit of Sir Freddie', inviting him to be guest of honour on the inaugural flight. We are still friends to this day.

There is no doubt that Freddie became a mentor for me in the 1980s when he gave me good advice which was to help in creating the Virgin Atlantic of today. He has also taught me something, which I would like to pass on. This is a man who inspires you when you meet him and he has clearly never given up. For him, failures are part of life's rich tapestry, to be learnt from but never looked back on wistfully. He has made me realise that whatever world you make for yourself you can keep on embracing new and different experiences over and over again. Most importantly, he also believes that if you don't try you'll never know the outcome and in most circumstances having a go is better than spending all one's time thinking of reasons not to do something.

* * *

Clive Bourne
Life President, CJ Bourne (Asset Management) Ltd, Founder, Seabourne Shipping and Founder Trustee of the Museum in Docklands

I was educated at South East Essex Technical College in Walthamstow until 1958. I then worked for the Regent Shoe Company in Wardour Street in Soho serving 'ladies of the night'. In 1962 I founded my own freight-forwarding business, Seabourne Shipping, and by 1966 started with roll-on-roll off ferries with the first overseas office in Le Havre. The major development and first real break came after eight years, in 1970, with an overnight service between London and Paris, which was followed by other overnight services to European destinations in quick succession.

From this point on the business grew, with the purchase of a civil enclave at Manston Airport, bought on a Friday afternoon in 1982, then a new European head office in 1984 and the purchase of several businesses to add to the growing company between 1984 and 1996. In 1981 and 1988, the business won the Queen's Award for Export Achievement making Seabourne Shipping the first company to win this award twice.

Alongside my business interests, I have been a Newham magistrate since 1990, serving as Chairman in 1995. I am a trustee of various charities including Transaid, an organisation founded and actively supported by HRH The Princess Royal, looking for logistical solutions for poor nations in Africa and Asia. I am also very committed as a sponsor of Mossbourne Community Academy in Hackney, London, one of the leading new city academies due to open in September 2004.

My Uncle Aitch, my father's youngest brother, gave me great assistance when my father died at an early age and when I first started in business.

He gave me the confidence and encouragement to build my business, which actually started from a telephone box in Shoreditch. He was probably the most charismatic person I have ever met and always had the knack, when walking into a room, of making people at all levels aware of his presence. He was fine-looking man, with periwinkle blue eyes and a very large handlebar moustache. He had a certain magnetism and was a born leader, who inspired confidence in all who met him in his business and charity career. He taught me that it was possible to have a successful business career and to combine it with a social conscience to assist people who are not as fortunate.

MY ADVICE: *Be a good listener and never take no for an answer.*

David Boutcher
Corporate Partner, Richards Butler law firm

I qualified as a solicitor in 1981 and have been a partner in the City law firm Richards Butler in London since 1988. I specialise in corporate finance and general corporate and commercial transactions, including mergers and acquisitions, joint ventures and corporate reconstructions. I went to school in Derby and then went to Kent University at Canterbury to study law and economics followed by the College of Law in Chester. I then did my articles for two years and finally qualified. I still love going back to Derby every two weeks to visit my family and watch the football, but I grew up always wanting to move away and do something different. This was partly inspired by my great Uncle Alf.

In so many ways Uncle Alf was as far removed from a City corporate lawyer as it's possible to be. Uncle Alf was always retired. He was a Nottinghamshire miner, but retired when I was only five years old.

There were never enough hours in the day for Uncle Alf. His whole working life was a matter of regret for him, but throughout he anticipated his retirement to be full and long, and it was. Yet there was always an element of sadness, of what might have been. At last he was so happy, but he had spent his entire working life doing something he didn't want to do. Uncle Alf was the first person I ever remember telling me that 'life ain't no dress rehearsal'.

When anyone suggested a career I didn't want to do I would often think of Uncle Alf and his retirement.

MY ADVICE: *Decide what you really want to do, and don't waste time getting stuck doing something you don't enjoy.*

Graeme Cohen
Management Consultant

After graduating with a degree in classics and modern languages from Oxford University in 1996, I have been working as a management consultant based in London. After six years' work with major consultancies, focusing on strategic review and business performance improvement, I have recently joined a smaller consulting firm to take on the new challenge of making a business grow. I have worked as a *pro bono* adviser for Big Brothers & Sisters since August 2002, working on fundraising and the analysis of management information.

I have worked with an extremely diverse and talented set of colleagues and clients over the past years. However, one individual stands out for his role in inspiring me to have the confidence to take risks in order to achieve my personal goals. Simon McBride was officially my 'career adviser' at a previous firm, a senior consultant whose role was to provide me with informal guidance. Since we met in 1997, Simon has become a friend and trusted adviser on many aspects of my life.

I have benefited from Simon's maturity and experience in many ways, ranging from specific project-based issues to insights on other areas of life. In particular, Simon has taught me how to perceive a situation from more than one viewpoint. This has been extremely helpful to me both professionally and personally – empathy for another person and an awareness of their context and agenda is a crucial step in building an honest and open relationship.

Another important thing I learned from Simon is to have the confidence to be myself at work – he showed me that there shouldn't be a major difference between the person you are at work and the person you are with your friends. This confidence has helped me to understand more of what I am looking for in my career, and has been a major factor in my move from a large employer to a much smaller organisation, where an individual can have a greater impact.

MY ADVICE: *As you become more experienced, the person you are will become as important as what you know. The ability to build successful relationships with clients and other colleagues is crucial. The right solution yesterday may not be the right solution tomorrow.*

George Cox
Director General, Institute of Directors

My background is in technology. Starting as an aeronautical engineer, I became involved in computers in the mid-1960s and spent most of my subsequent career in information technology. During my career I have headed up companies of all sizes. I formed a business in 1977, presiding over its growth and international expansion until it successfully floated on the London Stock Exchange in 1990. Before my current role as Director General of the Institute of Directors, I was Chairman of Unisys in the UK and head of all Unisys service-based businesses throughout Europe.

Other roles have included serving on the Management Board of the Inland Revenue and the Boards of LIFFE (the London International Financial Futures Exchange), Bradford & Bingley, Euronext and Shorts.

The individual who probably had the most influence on my career, and many of my attitudes, was David Butler, the colleague with whom I formed, and later floated, a company.

He taught me two things in particular. One was to step back and see a situation in perspective. It is one of the most important qualities an executive can develop. As a consequence, our company back in the mid-1970s was one of the first to recognise that *computing* was about to develop into something far bigger and broader than almost anyone had realised.

The other thing was vision. Too many people – in business, sport or politics – set their aspirations too low. Setting your sights high doesn't guarantee you'll reach the heights; but setting them low guarantees you won't.

MY ADVICE: *In any job – or prospective job – ask yourself two questions. Am I genuinely learning anything from this? And, when it comes to Monday morning, do I really want to do it? If the answer to either is no, do something else.*

Adam Crozier
Chief Executive, the Post Office

I set out on a career in advertising and marketing, and got my first job in this area at Pedigree Petfoods in 1984. After two years, I moved on to the *Telegraph* newspapers, and then to a job in 1988 at Saatchi & Saatchi Advertising agency. In 1990 when I was 26 I was made a Director, and in 1995 I was appointed Joint Chief Executive of the agency. After five years running the agency, I wanted a new challenge and moved to the Football Association serving as its Chief Executive from 2000 to 2002. During this time, I was responsible for the appointment of the new England Coach, Sven Goran Erickson. I am now embarking on a new organisational challenge as the Chief Executive of the Post Office.

I was inspired by David Kershaw who was Chairman of Saatchi & Saatchi Advertising. He lived and breathed the philosophy that ran through the agency of 'nothing is impossible' and challenged everyone to live up to this. David was my ultimate boss at the agency, but had the happy knack of being available and accessible to everyone, whatever their role.

This period in my career inspired me to believe that the greatest challenges lay in tackling the issues that no one else wanted to, for fear of not succeeding. The motivation and satisfaction that comes from achieving a result that no one thought possible far outweighs the fear of failure.

MY ADVICE: *Push yourself to the limit, never be afraid to fail and at all times treat everyone as you would wish to be treated.*

Sir Howard Davies
Chairman, Financial Services Authority (the UK's single regulator)

I previously served for two years as Deputy Governor of the Bank of England. Prior to that I spent three years as Director General of the Confederation of British Industry. I was educated at Manchester Grammar School, went to Oxford University and then on a scholarship to Stanford Graduate School in California. My career started in the Treasury and the Foreign and Commonwealth Office. In 2003 I am moving from the FSA to a new appointment as Director of the London School of Economics.

The key influence on my career was a master at Manchester Grammar School, called Brian Phythian. I was not exactly a shy boy at school, but I had not taken any kind of leadership role until Brian told me one day that there was going to be a school newspaper, and that I was going to be the editor. He also told me that I could play trombone in the school orchestra, which was never a happy experience, particularly for the audience. But he gave me the confidence to think that I could take on responsibility and lead others, a confidence which has stayed with me ever since.

MY ADVICE: *Now I have the task of regulating the financial services sector – which is rather like herding cats. But, like any others, financial firms need* *ambitious people with a clear idea of their goals, and a willingness to work with others to achieve them.*

Tony Freudmann
Company Senior Vice President, and Trustee, Big Brothers & Sisters

I manage a growing network of international airports. My principal responsibility is to create and oversee the complex public-private partnerships necessary to achieve this. I began my career as a lawyer and then moved into politics. For seven years in the late 1980s and early 1990s I was a county council leader. I was a founder Trustee of Big Brothers & Sisters, and in the 1980s I became a founder Trustee of a successful hospice project.

One of my most inspiring influences was an English master at my grammar school in Wrexham. His name was Nathan White, known privately to the boys as Natty. Like all heroes he was shy and unassuming. His was a private world of rules and structure, of spelling and syntax, pronunciation and parsing. A world where a preposition was a word you just did not end a sentence with. And a world where to casually split an infinitive or to begin a sentence with 'and' was a felony and not just a misdemeanour.

However, this was not pedantry for its own sake. Mr White's point was that all those rules were just a means to an end; and the end was the developed skill of clear and concise communication, both spoken and written.

Mr White was no fan of Charles Dickens, whose prose he regarded as wordy, overblown, nineteenth-century journalese. Similarly, and very important in a Welsh grammar school, he had no time for the Celtic tendency towards the windy and the prolix. Dylan Thomas rated very low in the White popularity stakes.

In my day it had not reached the curriculum but my guess is that Mr White would have held Hemingway's prose in high regard. Spare and economical with short sentences, good grammar, uncomplicated syntax and no affectation: these were the qualities that Mr White advocated and admired.

I have spent a working career in communication: as a lawyer, politician and businessman. I have made a living from talking and writing, most recently in international aviation where speaking English to non-English speakers or to amateur interpreters calls for an ability to communicate complex ideas simply but accurately and clearly.

I have many shortcomings, but when it comes to communicating I consider myself to be up there with the best. Whenever I am congratulated on a well-received speech or a well-drafted report I say a silent thank you to Mr White.

MY ADVICE: *Understand that good communication is one of the key elements in all successful human relationships.*

Rt Hon Sir Edward George GBE
Governor, Bank of England

I joined the Bank of England in 1962, working initially on East European affairs. I was seconded to the Bank for International Settlements in 1966 and held several other posts within the Bank before my appointment as Governor in 1993. I have been a governor of Dulwich College (where I went to school) since 1998 and was made a Privy Councillor in 1999. I was appointed a Knight, Grand Cross of the Order of the British Empire for services to the economy in the 2000 Queen's Birthday Honours.

Throughout my life, from early childhood right up to the present day, I have been blessed in finding around me – at school, in my cub pack and scout troop, in my sporting activities, and later at work, as well as in my family life – people I could look up to and turn to when I didn't understand or had got into a muddle. More often than not I found that they would go to great lengths to help.

MY ADVICE: *In my experience the world is full of wonderful people if you only have the courage to seek their help, the good sense to listen to their advice, and if you are really trying your very best to do the right thing in whatever it is you are doing.*

Anthony Goldstone
Chartered Accountant and Company Secretary

My father was a great inspiration: my grandparents were immigrants and my father went out to work by necessity at the age of 14. He succeeded in setting up a family clothing company, still in existence 72 years later, and he became President of Manchester Chamber of Commerce, the High Sheriff, and received the CBE.

That was my inspiration, but it was Lord Lesley Lever, Lord Mayor of Manchester and Member of Parliament for Ardwich, who took me out for lunch knowing my interest in wanting to put something back into the community. He knew my wish in order to both acknowledge my father's achievements and to help others who had not had the same chances in life. The lunch resulted in my joining the Labour Party and the rest is history.

I became Councillor in the area in which Lesley Lever had been the MP serving as a senior regional politician. I then followed my father 25 years later in not only becoming the President of Manchester Chamber of Commerce, but the national President of the British Chambers of Commerce serving from 2000–02. I have also been Chairman of the Regional Tourist Boards, the Regional Water Regulation Authority and now the largest Learning and Skills Council in England. I was honoured to receive both the MBE and OBE, the first for work with young people and the second for tourism.

Fate takes a peculiar route: if my father had not been determined to make something of his life and if Lesley Lever had not instilled his political view in my direction would I have instead been a successful accountant and never had the satisfaction of being part of new and changing regions?

MY ADVICE: *Work hard. Look for every opportunity and take advantage. You only get one chance. Be kind to everyone: you never know when you're going to meet them again.*

Michael Green
Chairman, Carlton Communications plc

I am the founder and Chairman of Carlton Communications which was floated on the London Stock Exchange in 1983. Carlton is a leading UK media company with businesses in free to air television, programme making and distribution, interactive television and cinema advertising. Carlton is a major part of the

ITV channel and broadcasts to 26 million people. I am also a Non-Executive Director of ITN, GMTV and Thomson in France and the Chairman of the Trustees of the charity, The Media Trust.

The late Lord Weinstock was Britain's most successful industrialist in the post war period. For 33 years, until 1996, he was Managing Director of GEC, one of the UK's leading industrial companies. At its height the company employed over one quarter of a million people and when he stood down in 1996, GEC had sales of over £10 billion, profits of more than £1 billion and cash reserves of some £3 billion. To me Arnold Weinstock was a friend, a mentor and an inspiration.

Arnold showed me that you could succeed in business through a combination of common sense and hard work. He believed in building businesses and rejected fads and fashions, concentrating instead on the basics of satisfying customers and controlling costs. Arnold was deeply sceptical of management consultants, loathed long committee meetings and understood the importance of employing talented people and giving them personal responsibility. I have always tried to emulate his approach and talked to him at every stage of my business career; I cannot remember a major deal or move that Carlton made when I didn't talk to him first. He taught me to read the notes to the accounts and not just look at the glossy pictures.

MY ADVICE: *Trust your instincts, but make sure you get the basics right. Businesses are supposed to make profits and that means understanding your customer's needs and controlling costs. Make sure you get some shares. Hard work is immensely rewarding and it must be fun.*

Brian Griffiths (Lord Griffiths of Fforestfach)
Vice Chairman, Goldman Sachs and Conservative Peer

As I look back on my career I owe an enormous debt to Oliver Barclay, who became a personal mentor to me, showed me at a time when I was searching, the relevance of my faith to my life and introduced me to a group of politicians who profoundly influenced me.

I came to London as an undergraduate to study at the London School of Economics in 1960, the first person to go to University from my family. Very few had been able to go to University from Fforestfach, a village on the outskirts of Swansea, which had grown up as a coalmining community, and where the chapel still had a very strong influence on the culture. When I came to London I was a little lost, but very interested in politics and economics. I met Oliver Barclay, who was then the general secretary of a Christian student organisation, a scientist with a PhD from Cambridge and someone who had a first-class mind.

Although I was not interested in science, he helped me in three ways:

First, he took a personal interest in me. He invited me to lunch and tea. We discussed books and ideas. Later, he introduced me to people who I would otherwise never have met. He started to take an interest in me when I was a student, but continued for many years after, in fact until his retirement.

Next, he showed me how and why the Bible should be taken seriously. He argued that it was relevant to all areas of life, including politics and economics, which is something I have never forgotten, and have in fact wrestled with ever since. This profoundly influenced my approach to political life and to the market economy and has since been seminal to my thinking, initially at the London School of Economics, then at 10 Downing Street (working with former Prime Minister, Baroness Thatcher), the City and the House of Lords.

Third, he introduced me to the work and writings of the Clapham Sect: a remarkable group of people who were very influential in political life in the first half of the nineteenth Century. If they had a leader, it was William Wilberforce, whose campaign against slavery is well known. Oliver himself was a descendent of one of the families of this group and his political thinking not dissimilar to theirs, reforming Conservatives but with a radical flavour. This vision and commitment these people gave to public life has been with me ever since.

For all this I shall be forever grateful to Oliver.

Ffion Hague
Executive Search Consultant

I am a Director of Hanson Green, and have been a headhunter for three years. I specialise in work at main board level, both executive and non-executive, across all sectors.

I was previously a Director of the business–facing charity Arts & Business. Before that, I spent six years in the Civil Service, joining the Welsh Office in 1991 as a fast-stream civil servant and leaving in 1997 after three years as Private Secretary to the Secretary of State for Wales.

I graduated from Oxford University in 1989 with a BA in English, and from the University of Wales in 1993 with a MPhil in Welsh Literature.

In pursuing a fairly varied career over the past decade, I have been inspired by people at the top of their professions who have spent time guiding and advising young people on their way up. It is so difficult to single any one individual out, since they have all played immensely important roles in my career, but they have spanned academia, the civil service, the arts and, of course, business. It has been a constant source of encouragement to me that busy and successful people are prepared give of their time and experience to help someone else up the career ladder.

I am truly grateful for all the advice I have been given over the years, but most of all perhaps to my very wise English teacher at school who taught me early in life to ask for help when I needed it.

MY ADVICE: *To anyone setting out now, I would just say — ask for advice and you might be well rewarded. I know I have been!*

Stelios Haji-Ioannou
Founder and Chairman, easyGroup

I was born and grew up in Athens, and moved to London in 1984 to study at the London School of Economics. I also studied at the City University Business School graduating with an MSc in Shipping Trade and Finance in 1988.

After graduation I joined my father's shipping company, Troodos shipping, and then in 1992 I founded my first venture Stelmar

Tankers in the shipping industry and this was listed on the New York Stock Exchange in 2001. Stelmar has a fleet of 36 tankers that are either in operation or on order.

In 1995 I founded easyJet, a low-cost, no-frills, point-to-point airline that is taking advantage of the deregulation of the European airline industry. The company was listed on the London Stock Exchange in November 2000.

In 1998 I formed the easyGroup, a holding company to explore new ventures to extend the 'easy' brand and capitalise upon the expanding use of the Internet. The first such venture, easyInternetCafé, the chain of the world's largest Internet cafés and the cheapest way to get online, started trading in June 1999 and currently has 21 cyber cafés across Europe and one in New York. Other brands now established include: easyCar, a car rental service that sells 95 per cent online; easyValue.com, impartial comparisons for online shopping; easy.com, a free web-based email service and easyMoney, online financial services. We are now looking at several new industries including easyCinema and easyDorm.

Richard Branson has been a good example to me. It was Richard who first gave me the 'airline bug' when there was an opportunity to invest in the Virgin Atlantic Athens route. In the end I opened up the route myself with easyJet. He has also influenced me through brand extension. Seeing the Virgin Group move into more and more industries with the Virgin brand helped persuade me to start the easyGroup which now operates in a number of areas.

MY ADVICE: *When you see an opportunity, go for it. And when you have established some success, don't be afraid to take it further.*

Paul Harbard
Chartered Accountant and Chair of Trustees,
Big Brothers & Sisters UK

When I first sat down to identify a mentor in my life, I couldn't immediately think of anyone, other than my father. But the more I thought, the more I realised that I had been privileged to know a number of people who had taken an interest in me over the years.

I particularly thought back to growing up in Canada and

graduating from university there and not knowing what career to choose. I was doing a summer job leading a youth programme for the local authority. My boss, Alex Midgley, encouraged me not to take the easy road but to challenge myself and choose a career where I could achieve my full potential.

After three decades as a chartered accountant, mainly as a finance director of a housing-related organisation, I'm glad I took his advice. I can look back over some major achievements and I look forward to many more. My rewards over the years have not been just financial; I have gained a great deal of satisfaction too.

I believe that it is important to give something back, which is why I was instrumental in bringing Big Brothers & Sisters to the UK and why I spend so many hours in a voluntary capacity as Chair of the Board.

MY ADVICE: *When thinking of giving advice to a young person, I realised that the lessons I have learned revolve around the concept of integrity. No matter what you do, or achieve, your reputation is important and should not be sacrificed for short-term gain, because that is just what it says it is.*

In conclusion, I must add that one of the most valuable assets you can nurture is a sense of humour. Wherever possible have fun!

Les Hinton
Executive Chairman, News International plc

After attending British Army schools in Egypt, Ethiopia, Libya, Germany and Singapore, I left secondary modern school in Liverpool and began working for Rupert Murdoch in Adelaide, Australia, as a 15-year-old copy boy. I have worked for the News Corporation for more than 30 years as a journalist and manager in Australia, the United States, and the United Kingdom. In 1976 I moved from London to New York as a foreign correspondent for the group's newspapers in Britain and Australia. I was appointed President of Murdoch Magazines in 1990, two years later becoming President and Chief Executive Officer of News America Publishing, responsible for the company's US publishing operations. In 1993 I was appointed Chairman and CEO of Fox Television Stations, returning to London in 1995 as Executive Chairman of

News International plc. I am a member of the News Corporation Executive Committee. In 1996 I joined the board of the Press Association in Britain. In October 1998, I was elected Chairman of the newspaper and magazine publishing industry's Code of Practice Committee, which sets the code implemented by the Press Complaints Commission. In October 1999 I was appointed a non-executive Director of British Sky Broadcasting.

Sometimes one person can unlock and inspire another. Other times, lives are shaped piece by piece, person by person.

For me there was an editor willing to sit with a 15-year-old schoolboy off the street and give him his first job; a woman who is utterly true, completely without pretence, or malice; a man whose unrelenting energy and boldness dazzles those around him; a working-class couple whose son is ashamed ever to have thought himself deprived, knowing finally the wealth of having parents who care.

In them I saw generosity, goodness, raw determination, and love. But they shared another quality in abundance − self-worth. These people taught me long ago that with self-worth all life falls into place.

Tom Hunter
Serial Entrepreneur, West Coast Capital

My start in life came following completion of my degree at university − the degree prepared me very little for business, something I'm pleased to say is changing these days.

Simply put, no one would employ me, so, having seen an opportunity to sell sportswear, I took it selling trainers from the back of a van; I exaggerate not.

My fledgling business grew into one of the UK's premier sports retailers and I guess if I were being honest I pioneered the concept of out-of-town shopping. It paid dividends in the end.

I sold Sports Division after 18 years of very hard graft for £290 million − at the time we had 7,500 employees and 250 stores. It was unexpected and I really wasn't that prepared for what to do next, other than knowing that retirement at 38 or really any age wasn't an option.

So I dabbled in investment for a couple of years until finally realising my new ambition of creating a new private equity firm, West Coast Capital. Since we started this in 2001 we've made investments of £850m. We take a different approach to most, adding, I hope, real value through expertise as well as cash to our investments.

However, making money is only the half of it for me and giving back through effective philanthropic investment both with time and money is extraordinarily important. In 2001 I gave £5m to my old university, Strathclyde, to establish the Hunter Centre for Entrepreneurship; I guess it's my attempt to make sure students don't leave like I did, without any clue. Of course the Centre does a lot more than prepare students: they have a leadership position in policy influence around entrepreneurship.

I'm often asked what inspired me to build one of Europe's premier sports retailers. The answer may not surprise you – with no job and the encouragement and support of my dad, Campbell Hunter I started selling trainers.

He inspired me in so many ways not least by introducing me to two exceptional individuals – Sam Walton, the founding father of retailing as we know it today and Andrew Carnegie, the inspiration for modern day philanthropy. We never met them, of course. My dad just gave me their books.

Today I continue to build businesses and attempt to make a difference in education and enterprise through charitable giving – and I still read those books.

MY ADVICE: *Find your inspiration and remember YOU CAN DO!*

Digby Jones
Director-General, CBI

I studied law at University College, London, and after some time in the Royal Navy, I started my career with the Birmingham corporate law firm Edge & Ellison in 1978. I made Partner in 1984 developing a specialisation in corporate affairs, and becoming Senior Partner of the firm in 1995. I facilitated alliances with law firms in Europe and the USA and helped develop the London office. In 1998 I joined KPMG as Vice Chairman of Corporate

Finance where I acted as close adviser to many public companies across the United Kingdom. I also worked on the development of KPMG's global markets. I have also been a non-executive director and chairman of several companies, covering sectors as diverse as quarry aggregates, local radio and automotive component manufacture.

I sit on the City of Birmingham Symphony Orchestra Development Trust. In 1998, as Chairman of the Birmingham St Mary's Hospice Appeal, which raised £1.5 million, I personally raised £218,000 towards their target by cycling from John O'Groats to Lands End.

I became Director-General of the CBI on 1 January 2000 to serve a five year non-renewable term of office. As the Chief Executive of the UK's 'Voice of Business', I regularly and repeatedly visit businesses around the UK and also the CBI offices in Brussels and Washington DC, taking their views back to those who make the rules within which UK business operates throughout the world. I constantly campaign for an environment where prosperity and jobs can be created in the UK.

Other than my parents, there are two people I would single out as having played an important and inspirational role in my working life.

John Webber was the Headmaster at my junior school. John gave me a sense of fun in learning and told me that I should ALWAYS ask 'why' if I didn't understand something and not be ashamed of doing so.

The second person was John Wardle. He was the Senior Partner of Edge & Ellison during my time there as a young lawyer and taught me a number of lessons: that a reputation can take a lifetime to build and five seconds to lose, that you should NEVER risk your personal integrity, and that being 'professional' means putting your clients' interests ahead of your own – always.

MY ADVICE: *My advice is formed from my own experience of working with many people across a broad spectrum of disciplines, backgrounds and personalities. I have chosen three messages and I try to heed each of them during my day-to-day business and at home:*

1. *No matter how talented one may be there is NO substitute for damned hard work.*
2. *ALWAYS treat others as you would like to be treated.*
3. *No matter how dark things seem, the sun WILL come up in the morning – positive vibes work wonders!*

I wish you all the very best of success with your own careers and if you have any personal tips that have worked for you then I would love to hear them.

Sir Terry Leahy
Chief Executive, Tesco plc

I grew up in Liverpool, and went on to study management sciences at the University of Manchester Institute of Science and Techology (UMIST). I joined Tesco in 1979 as a Marketing Executive and was promoted to Marketing Manager in 1981 and then became Commercial Director of Fresh Foods in 1986. I was appointed to the Board of Tesco plc as Marketing Director in 1992. I became Chief Executive of Tesco plc in 1997, when I was 40. I am also a Director of the Liverpool Vision Regeneration Board, and Chancellor of UMIST.

I owe everything to my mum and dad, but in looking at someone outside my family, I'm going to choose a schoolteacher, Tony McCann.

I had a great education, through Catholic schools in Liverpool that took me from a prefab to a red brick university, and Tony was perhaps the outstanding example of the many dedicated teachers who, between them, finally (and without much cooperation from me) pointed me in the right direction.

Tony had a natural authority and gift for teaching that made it easy to listen – I can still remember some of the lessons. The striking thing, when I look back, is how often he made connections to the big world beyond the council estate and broadened my horizons, without me realising it at the time.

Sandy Leitch
Chief Executive, Zurich Financial Services (UK, Ireland, Southern Africa and Asia Pacific)

I grew up in Dunfermline, Fife, and, at an early age I decided to pursue a career in computers. I joined Allied Dunbar (then Hambro Life) in 1971 as a systems designer and took over as Chief Executive in 1993. Allied Dunbar was taken over by BAT in 1985, and in 1996 I became responsible for all financial services businesses outside North America. I took up my current post in 1998 when the financial services businesses demerged from BAT and merged with Zurich Insurance. I was also the Chairman of the Association of British Insurers from 1998–2000.

As a passionate advocate of corporate social responsibility, I am Deputy Chairman of Business in the Community and Chairman of Cares Incorporated, a major national initiative to increase volunteering by 100,000 people, working closely with business, community and Government. In 1999 I won the Prince of Wales Ambassador's Award for outstanding achievement in charitable work. I am the Chairman of the National Employment Panel and Deputy Chairman of the Commonwealth Education Fund.

One of the most important people in my life was a brilliant man called Gary Davies. Gary was a Church of England vicar-turned-business consultant and, as such, saw business through an unconventional lens. Through the years, Gary became my personal adviser, my mentor, and most of all, my friend. As a result of his constant inspirational guidance, I discovered new parts of myself that I didn't know existed. He had an enormous influence on me and he opened new doors for me in my career and my emotional and spiritual development. Through him I grew to experience and see new aspects of life and I will forever be grateful. I was devastated when he died a couple of years ago after a long illness – but his wisdom endures.

Although I qualified for university, I chose not to go. I was in too much of a hurry to get out there and make my mark on the world. At 17, I borrowed £30 from my sister and headed for London – enthusiastic and determined to be successful. Looking back, I did miss something. Education is the best preparation in life and the world will still be there when you finish.

Why, then, did I succeed? I must have competed against tens of thousands of very able people, many of whom were brighter, better qualified or better connected than me. One simple word – enthusiasm. I now look after all of Zurich's business across the UK, Ireland, Southern Africa and Asia Pacific, with more than 20,000 people and across 17 countries. I am also a member of Zurich's Group Executive Committee, and oversee all of the Group's life businesses.

MY ADVICE: *People like working with enthusiasts. Enthusiasm is infectious – it motivates people and gets things done. Enthusiasm makes all the difference. It is the enthusiast who succeeds.*

Heather McGregor
Director, Taylor: Bennett, executive search company

I am a director of, and shareholder in, Taylor:Bennett and my focus is exclusively on investor relations appointments. I joined Taylor:Bennett in November 2000 from ABN Amro Bank where I worked for eight years, originally as an investment analyst and latterly as a senior manager within the equities division. During this time I had been posted to Hong Kong, Singapore and Tokyo, and worked in both debt and equity capital markets and corporate finance. Prior to ABN Amro, I worked in-house for five years in Investor Relations (IR) and Corporate Communications for a public company, and completed my MBA at the London Business School. I have also at other times worked in financial PR and set up an IR practice in a full service consultancy. I continue to work as a financial journalist, and am retained by both *The Times* and the *Financial News* as well as writing the monthly advice column in *Investor Relations* magazine. I have a PhD from the University of Hong Kong and am a visiting lecturer in finance at Cass, City University's business school.

Many people have inspired me in the course of my career. When I was 13, I started studying economics for 'O' Level and had an incredibly inspirational teacher who also taught me at 'A' Level. Her name was Alison Thring and I wish I knew where she is now. She made the world of economics and finance come alive, and from the moment she described the inverse relationship between the rate of interest and the price of bonds, I was completely hooked. She was young, newly married and spent her weekends learning to fly planes and doing aerobatics. I desperately wanted to do well in my exams, both at school and university, in order to say thank you to her for the wonderful example that she gave me.

My career has been a mixture of financial PR, investment banking, financial journalism and now the privilege of owning a large proportion of the company for which I work. Different people have inspired me and mentored me at different stages of that career, right from my first job at the age of 23 in an advertising agency, where I met Fiona Brierley, now one of my greatest friends, who showed me how to vastly improve my personal presentation and bother to use some make up, through to Airdre Taylor and Annita Bennett, the women who founded the company where I am now a proud shareholder. The biggest thing I have learned in all this time is that I have something to learn from everyone, and that there is never an end to the journey of learning and development.

Equally, it is very important to give back as well as to take. The people who have mentored and inspired me over the years have my undying gratitude, and I make sure that I always prioritise the return of their telephone calls, and their invitations to join them at events. My 'second career' as a journalist had always bumbled along quite nicely until in 1999 Julia Cuthbertson, then the editor of the *Weekend FT*, invited me to write a weekly column about my life and family. Her leadership and guidance, her support on ideas and development of these, plus constant encouragement and praise, led me to develop a long-running column and ultimately a book. She remains my first port of call on all things related to journalism.

In my late twenties I studied for an MBA at the London Business School and was taught economics by David Currie, now Lord Currie of Marylebone, Dean of City University Business school and Chairman of OFCOM. Ten years later, as I was struggling through a PhD in finance, he encouraged and supported me to finish and, more importantly, pointed me in the direction of the work of other people that had a direct bearing on my chosen subject for research.

Many other people have touched my life and my career but both Julia Cuthbertson and David Currie are the embodiment of the type of mentors that I believe are important for all young people today as they grow up and pursue careers.

MY ADVICE: *If you are lucky enough, as I have been, to be given considerable amounts of time by people who are leaders in their field, treat those opportunities with the respect they deserve and try and learn as much as possible when they occur. Even now, at 40, I believe there will be more people who will mentor me and develop me in the years to come and I'm sure I will still be looking to other people for inspiration even when I'm 60!*

Jim O'Neill
Head of Economic Research, Goldman Sachs

I am Partner and Head of Economic Research for Goldman Sachs, a major global investment bank. I lead a team of around 80 people worldwide in providing the firm's views about the world economy.

Other than my parents' encouragement, I was guided by many different people during my education. Teachers at school who encouraged me to pursue sports as well as formal education were especially influential. These teachers included John Dowty from my days at Burnage High School, and Mr Whitehead from Crossacres Junior School. From Sheffield University, Professor Jim Ford deserves a mention as he made me believe that I was capable of independent research and completing a PhD.

He also gave me the confidence to believe that I was capable of studying alone and developing my own thoughts. Within the economics profession, I always found Rudi Dornbusch to be a great inspiration, as he had a simple ability to combine wit with his academic talent, and never stood behind an academic façade.

MY ADVICE: *Be Yourself. There is no need to behave in any particular manner that you are uncomfortable with. I would like to think that my own career has proved that so long as you achieve results, you can succeed. Don't deceive yourself or anyone else. Inspire yourself to succeed.*

Swraj Paul (Lord Paul of Marylebone)
Chairman, Caparo Group and Labour Peer

I was born in India and educated at Punjab University and the Massachusetts Institute of Technology (MIT), USA from which I graduated with a Masters degree in Mechanical Engineering in 1952. I came to the UK in 1966 and in 1968 founded Caparo, the UK-based industrial company which specialises in the manufacture and supply of steel-based engineering products for industry. I am an Ambassador for British Business, Chancellor of the University of Wolverhampton, Co-chairman of the India-UK Round Table, a member of the UK Industrial Agency and a member of the Foreign Policy Centre Advisory Council. I became a member of the House of Lords in 1996 and sit on the House of Lords Select Committee on Economic Affairs. I am also Chair of Trustees for the PiggyBankKids charity.

My view of life has been inspired by many people, but especially so by the poor man in India. I admire the courage with which he has struggled against huge odds and yet still manages to smile and be content. This has always made me aware that the world needs to pay greater attention to the eradication of poverty, and that we all have a part to play in that.

The three most important things I have learned in my life are, first, from my father that there is dignity in all work; second, from MIT, always to strive for excellence; and third from Mrs Indira Gandhi, the former Prime Minister of India, never to abandon hope. My own experience has taught me that hard work and integrity have no equal.

MY ADVICE: *My advice to the next generation would be to enjoy what you do. You will encounter adversity, but it is part of life and makes you a better person. You should not be discouraged by it.*

Susan Rice
Chief Executive, Lloyds TSB Scotland plc

I studied first at university in the United States, then at the University of Aberdeen, Scotland. I worked for a long time in the US, as a medical researcher at Yale University then as Dean of one of the Yale colleges. I continued to work in academia moving to become Staff Aide to the President of Hamilton College, and then Dean of Students at Colgate University. In 1986, I moved to banking to run the community development programme for National Westminster Bancorp as Senior Vice President and stayed for ten years. I moved back to Scotland in 1997 and joined the Bank of Scotland working as Director of Business Projects, then Head of Branch Banking, and then as Managing Director of Personal Banking. In 2000, I had the opportunity to run a bank and was appointed Chief Executive of Lloyds TSB Scotland with responsibility for a workforce of 2,300 people.

Beyond my family, inspiration comes from many people. Some of them I've known; some not at all, for instance some writers.

I think of Beryl Markham, an Englishwoman in Africa who was the first person to fly across the Atlantic by herself from east to west. She wrote a book called *West with the Night*. Or John Buchan, a Scots writer who wrote thoroughly entertaining tales of intrigue.

Whether his characters, or her real-life story, what I admire is people who have a zest for life, who jump into the unknown, who are willing to take a risk. People who go somewhere even though they don't know how they will get there or what they will find at the end. People who achieve something against all expectations.

I find myself running a bank, the first woman ever to do so in the UK. I wasn't brought up to expect to be a banker and indeed started my professional life in a different industry. In my career, each change has been a step into the unknown. It's been exciting, interesting and fun.

MY ADVICE: *Don't ever feel limited by what you already know how to do. Every person has far more potential than they realise. Whatever you want to do, dream it, picture yourself there, and then go for it.*

Irwin M Stelzer
Senior Fellow and Director of Regulatory Studies, Hudson Institute

Prior to joining the Hudson Institute in 1998, I was the resident scholar and director of Regulatory Policy Studies at the American

Enterprise Institute. I am also the US economic and political columnist for *The Sunday Times* (London) and the *Courier Mail* (Australia), a contributing editor of the *Weekly Standard,* a member of the Publication Committee of *The Public Interest,* and a member of the board of the Regulatory Policy Institute (Oxford). As a consultant to several US and United Kingdom industries with a variety of commercial and policy problems, I advise on market strategy, pricing and antitrust issues, and regulatory matters.

I founded National Economic Research Associates, Inc. (NERA) in 1961 and served as its president until a few years after its sale in 1983 to Marsh & McLennan. I have also served as a managing director of the investment banking firm of Rothschild Inc. and as a director of the Energy and Environmental Policy Center at Harvard University.

My academic career includes teaching appointments at Cornell University, the University of Connecticut, and New York University, and an associate membership of Nuffield College, Oxford. I am a former member of the Litigation and Administrative Practice Faculty of the Practicing Law Institute. I served on the Massachusetts Institute of Technology Visiting Committee for the Department of Economics, and have been a teaching member of Columbia University's Continuing Legal Education Programs.

I received my Bachelor and Master of Arts degrees from New York University and my doctorate in economics from Cornell University in the United States.

Like many others, I found that a great teacher set me on my professional path. Alfred E. Kahn, now professor emeritus at Cornell University, then presiding over the economic department's most stimulating seminar, fanned my interest in the branch of economics that deals with government policy towards business. It is not so much the specifics of what he taught, but the style of thought – an almost Talmudic 'How do you know that?', 'What is your source?', 'Have you considered the other point of view'?

He taught, too, there is no substitute for hard work – native intelligence and intuition are fine, but only when supplemented by research, reading and, in the end, committing thoughts to paper: the latter the ultimate proof that writing maketh the exact man. Note, too, the teaching method: not exhortation, but example. In the office early, leave late, lunch at the desk, weekends not very different from weekdays.

But with it all, fun. Enjoy the learning process; the cut and thrust of civilised debate; the company of exciting colleagues; and all of the diversions from work, from square dancing to reading for sheer pleasure.

This made an enormous difference. Both what I learned and how I learned stood me in good stead during my stints as an academic, during my business career, and since then in journalism and in policy work.

My advice to a young person is so simple as to be trite: find something you love, and work at it. If you make a mistake, do what that great philosopher Frank Sinatra advised: 'Pick yourself up, dust yourself off, and start all over again.' Failure is no disgrace; failing to try, and to dare, is.

MY ADVICE: *Refuse to accept what passes for received wisdom, or for what is merely popular, and sing your song your way. Stay a bit outside of the conventional consensus, not so far as to tromp on the rights of others, but far enough to remain your own person. And never, ever, forget an outstanding IOU. Many people will help you along the way; find ways to reciprocate, even if not asked.*

John Taylor (Lord Taylor of Warwick)
Company Chairman and Barrister-at-Law

I am Chairman of World Sports Solutions plc, a marketing company which represents stars from the Sports World. I am also Chairman of Warwick Communications Ltd, a PR company which has a number of prestigious companies amongst its clients.

My mother (who came from Jamaica) was a single parent and for a time was homeless in England. When I was two months old, she had nowhere to sleep and nothing to eat; she prayed in desperation that her newborn son would one day make her struggle worthwhile. She was in the public gallery of the House of Lords when I was elevated to a peerage. Enid Taylor was her name and she died at Christmas in 2001.

My mother's faith inspired me and made me determined to do well at school. She taught me never to give up and to maintain my Christian faith. When I was five, she helped me with extra reading at home.

MY ADVICE: *If you want to make your dreams come true – Wake Up! If you do not know what your target is, you will not achieve it.*

James D. Wolfensohn
President, The World Bank

I am the World Bank Group's 9th President since 1946. I established my career as an international investment banker with a parallel involvement in development issues and the global environment. I am currently serving my second five-year term as president. Since becoming President in 1995, I have travelled to more than 100 countries to gain first-hand experience of the challenges facing the World Bank, and its 184 member countries. I have visited development projects supported by the World Bank, and have also met with representatives from business, trade unions, media, non-governmental organisations, religious and women's groups, students and teachers. In the process, we are forming new strategic partnerships between the Bank and governments it serves, the private sector, civil society, regional development banks and the United Nations. In 1996, together with the International Monetary Fund, we initiated the Heavily Indebted Poor Countries Initiative (HIPC) as the first comprehensive debt reduction programme to address the needs of the world's poorest, most heavily indebted countries, and have continued to review and improve this programme.

The person who most influenced me was Sir Siegmund Warburg, founder of the UK banking house of S. G. Warburg which contributed as much to the development of London as the international financial committee during the last 50 years. He was an immigrant to the City from Germany prior to World War II, leaving his distinguished banking business in Germany as a consequence of Hitler's rise to power. He was a friend and I never worked for him. I worked with Schroders under the remarkable leadership of Lord Richardson who had faith in me and gave me example, opportunity and support.

Warburg combined courage, entrepreneurial spirit and great intellect. He inspired me by his example. He established a firm where teamwork was paramount. Standards and quality were the basis of the business. Professionalism, hard work and commitment to the clients and their interests characterised the firm.

But there was something else that set him apart. He had enormous outside interests in literature, philosophy, and the arts. He was charitable to many causes. He looked for colleagues who were not just businessmen, but interesting and involved people.

This sense of balance, this involvement in culture and the world-at-large gave me confidence to try to balance my own life, to try to be the best in my profession, but more importantly, to do so with a commitment to my family and to society and with an active interest in humanity, culture and the arts.

MY ADVICE: *I would advise any young person to seek mastery of his trade or profession but to balance this with concern for others and with a parallel interest in some other field, whether it be literature, the arts, sport or public service. The life of a one-sided individual cannot be as rich as that of a person with balance in life.*

politics and government

Rt Hon Michael Martin MP
Speaker of the House of Commons

I f I had been told, while still a teenager, that I would one day serve as Speaker of the House of Commons, I would have regarded the suggestion as a joke.

Growing up in the poverty of Glasgow, although I had a very happy childhood, I didn't have many advantages . . . certainly not in terms of wealth, family influence or educational achievement. Like many boys and girls of my generation, I was short of confidence.

Over the years I have been able to take on roles for which I have felt unworthy, mainly due to the encouragement and guidance of other people; people who saw in me some potential and did all they could to develop it.

As a school leaver my greatest ambition was to get an apprenticeship. My mother had vivid memories of the depression years and was anxious that her four sons and daughter should have a trade or skill – something on which to fall back should times get bad. Her father was seven years unemployed during the great depression and my father was forced to take a job at sea – the only available work at the time.

I left school in the summer of 1960 and the following Monday found myself in Pinkston Road, in the north of Glasgow, walking from factory to factory looking for an opening. Since my father was a seaman, job-seeking was a lonely task. Even then I received encouragement, often from the factory gatekeeper who would tell me there were no vacancies at his place but to try next door.

Even these simple words helped build my confidence. I finally found an apprenticeship in sheet-metal working, two miles and ten days after I started looking, at an electrical engineering business in Lomond Street, Possilpark. Little did I know that I would meet my wife, Mary, there and one day represent the area in Parliament.

Almost immediately I came face-to-face with injustice.

I recall my horror seeing a man of 60, a loyal employee all his life, threatened with dismissal simply because he had brought a valid complaint to the firm's attention. In those days apprentices were often used as cheap labour, being asked to work in dangerous conditions. We were exposed to asbestos and asked to work cutting machines without proper protection . . . all quite illegal.

The loss of a job would have meant loss of the apprenticeship.

At that stage I resolved to do something about such injustices and joined the sheet-metal workers' union – I'm still a member of its successor organisation, the engineering union AMICUS.

As the years passed, I realised I wanted to do more for the community in which I lived and worked – injustice and poverty were not confined to the factory floor, and so, as a young married man of 21, I joined the Springburn Constituency Labour Party. I felt that I wanted to listen to debates, get to know more, help in whatever way I could (mainly, I recall, by putting election leaflets through letter boxes in the tenement buildings of the area. I was much more physically fit in those days!)

It was at this point that I began to be helped by people who could see in me a potential which I didn't recognise in myself. I recall the minute taker, a certain Jack McGuinness, a veteran of World War I announcing that he was too busy to carry on in the role that he had held for 16 years. I was unanimously proposed to take over. Later I realised the older members of the party had press-ganged me into the job as a means of educating me in the skills of writing I would later need in public life.

Agnes Arnott, a veteran ally of the suffragettes and member of the Co-operative Movement then asked me to become branch treasurer. Despite my protestations, I was duly nominated, and gained more experience that was to serve me well later.

As the years rolled on, the same story was repeated. People helped me to find new roles of which I would never have felt capable. In 1973 I was asked to stand for election as a councillor. I loved that role – helping people I knew and cared for, and I certainly had no expectation of ever advancing further politically. It was an added bonus to represent the community in which I lived.

Three years later I was asked to become a full-time officer with NUPE – the union representing hospital workers and other public sector employees. Again I felt unequal to the task, but with encouragement I took on the role. It was a big jump from being a lay shop steward in Rolls-Royce, Hillington to being a full-time professional.

In 1978, quite unexpectedly the local MP Richard Buchanan announced he was retiring and I was asked to stand as his replacement. I was one of five nominees, all of them local. I won through and in the election of 1979 I was elected to Parliament.

I remember quite vividly that first year at Westminster. I kept thinking that someone would come up to me, put their hand on my shoulder and say, 'Sorry, Michael. Remember you're the son of a merchant seaman/stoker and a school cleaner. This isn't a place for people like you!'

Of course, I was wrong, and no matter what background one comes from I am ever more convinced that Parliament is the place for people who have a strong belief in what is right and a desire to help others.

The first priority of any aspiring politician should always be to help others, not the self-fulfilment offered by the Westminster scene.

On 23 October 2000, after 21 years in Parliament, I was elected Speaker of the House, a long way from the tenements of Anderston where I set out in life.

Looking back I realise that in Parliament, hard work is essential. I had made the right decision in accepting Speaker Weatherill's invitation in 1987 to become a Chairman of Committees. This meant long hours, sometimes through the night and into the early hours of the morning, chairing meetings of standing committees and the Scottish Grand Committee. These long hours of hard work prepared me for the task I was now to fulfil as Speaker of the House.

If I could draw any lesson from those years it would be this: all the encouragement in the world is not enough unless it is combined with hard work and self-discipline.

However, encouragement there was, and plenty of it.

Firstly I salute the heroic efforts of my mother and grandmother. Both had larger than average families and thus developed a deep appreciation of the midwifery service; women who cared for mothers in the family home. I recall hearing how, when my mother was eight, her tonsils needed removing. In those pre-NHS days as soon as the operation was completed, my grandmother had to carry her daughter home in her arms, still under the influence of chloroform. This young girl was carried across the busy city centre streets of Sauchiehall and St Vincent Street. There were no beds and no real aftercare. In fact to call out a doctor in those days, a fee had to be paid.

It's no surprise, then, that both my mother and grandmother deeply appreciated the arrival of the free National Health Service in the 1940s. They knew it would revolutionise the health of the nation. At a very early age I learned from them that political decisions made by people I would never know had changed my life and my family's life for the better. It was a crucial lesson.

A teacher who changed my life was Patrick McLaughlin at St Patrick's school in Anderston, Glasgow. He refused to write off the class of boys before him, as many others might have. Instead he demanded a lot of us. It worked. I went from 25th to 2nd in the class in one year.

I was so proud to be able to welcome Patrick and his wife to the House of Commons many years later. He complimented me on my knowledge of the Stuart and Tudor periods. I retorted that it was all due to his good teaching!

Later I learned an even more profound lesson from this man. He had a brilliant wartime record in the Royal Navy as a liaison officer based in Russia to help assist the famous Russian Convoys. These convoys brought assistance and relief to the Russian people in their darkest hour. Patrick could have risen to the highest echelons at the Admiralty, yet he chose to give all that up and come back to teach in a humble school in Glasgow. Why? Because Patrick McLaughlin's father, a builder's labourer, had scrimped and saved all his life to give his son an education, and Patrick felt it was only right that he should offer others the chance he had had through devoting his life to teaching the disadvantaged. What better example of public service could there be?

Tommy McKenna was another great hero who helped me on my way. He was my first shop steward, a highly intelligent man who saw it as his vocation in life to help others improve their lot – at no gain for himself. His wife Becky often went without wages because Tommy's unflinching commitment to justice led to him being blacklisted by some employers. As I started out as a shop steward, Tommy was always there for me – at any hour of the day or night. I will never forget his kindness and commitment. He stayed just round the corner from my house and when I knocked the door, Becky would always invite me in for a cup of tea.

Another great influence in my life was Bill Hatton, the NUPE organiser who convinced me to work as a full-time union official – a post I didn't feel up to! He told me he had watched me over the years and knew I could make a valuable contribution. I later learned he had submitted one of the most glowing references imaginable on my behalf to union HQ. Bill taught me that anyone in public life is constantly under scrutiny. We all have our effect on others, be it for good or ill. I'll always be grateful to Bill for believing in me and teaching me that valuable lesson.

Of course, it is not only those who share the same political sympathies who can teach us valuable lessons. And so I should like to put on record my admiration and gratitude to two former Prime Ministers – Harold Wilson and Ted Heath.

Harold Wilson always impressed me – especially in his use of the medium of television, then in its infancy. It was a great honour for me when, within days of entering parliament, I was able to hear this man speak on the floor of the House. Ted Heath, on the other hand, impressed me in his dedication to the House of Commons, and to the democratic process. Listening to him was a great joy — his oratory was magnificent. Even those who didn't agree with what he said could admire the way he said it! He taught me a profound lesson — that you can put your case much more effectively if you really listen to the opposing point of view. It's a lesson I hope any young person entering politics bears in mind.

I could not end this brief summary of the influences on my life without mentioning my wife Mary. She has given up a great deal to allow me to advance in political life. She is also a great judge of character — far better than me — and as such has been a wonderful adviser — especially since I became Speaker.

Speaker's House can be a lonely place. But Mary decided to come with me to London. That meant seeing less of the family, especially our son Paul, our daughter Mary and our grandson Ryan — the joy of her life — but it helped me settle to my new role.

We both worked in the factory in which I served my apprenticeship. She married a sheet-metal worker, not a politician. It's a tribute to her that she has been able to adapt so well. She jokingly chides me that I once promised my mother that I would never take a job that meant being away from the family for long periods. It's not a promise I've been able to keep!

As Speaker I have had to lay aside all previous political affiliations. That is a hard thing for a committed politician to do, but I take great pride in fulfilling my role as Speaker with total impartiality. In return I have received whole-hearted support from all sides of the House.

It is typical that, following my election as Speaker, the first Member of Parliament to visit Mary and me in Speaker's House, to offer me support, was William Hague, then Leader of the Opposition, followed rapidly by Alex Salmond, Westminster leader of the Scottish National Party.

In conclusion I can only say that I am deeply grateful to many people who have helped me along the way of life. I can honestly say that I never dreamed of high office when I entered the world of politics and my ambition now is to continue serving the people of Glasgow Springburn and the great House of Commons.

MY ADVICE: *is this: Never allow anyone to say you are incapable of achieving all that you aim for, and never under-estimate your own abilities.*

* * *

Wendy Alexander MSP
Member of the Scottish Parliament for Paisley North

I studied at Glasgow and Warwick University, worked in management consultancy for several years and completed an MBA at the Insead Business School in France. In May 1999, I was elected as a Labour Member of the new Scottish Parliament for the Constituency of Paisley North. I served in the Scottish Executive as Minister for Communities, then Minister for Enterprise and Lifelong Learning, and most recently until May 2002 as Minister for Enterprise, Transport and Lifelong Learning.

The person who inspired me was Jessie Alexander. She was my aunt and she was very glamorous. When I was five, she possessed the best dressing-up box in the world. At twelve, she treated me to my most coveted present, an overnight stay in a hotel. Jessie also knew where she came from; what she believed in and whose side she was on. She was a social worker and I often accompanied her on family visits where I learned right from wrong first hand.

I saw the conviction of a Barbara Castle leavened by the occasional wickedness of Ab Fab's Patsy in my Aunt Jessie. I learned to abhor snobbery, have a strong sense of justice and to enjoy the Scottish countryside at the weekend.

MY ADVICE: *For a life in politics — trust your instincts, know your own mind, think big and have the courage of your convictions. Try and accumulate some life experience first. And don't forget family and friends: they will be around longer than any career!*

Ed Balls
Chief Economic Adviser to HM Treasury

I studied economics at Nottingham High School, Oxford University and Harvard University before writing about it at the *Financial Times* and doing it at the Treasury. I have been lucky enough to learn from and work with so many people who have been hugely influential in my life – Larry Summers at Harvard, Martin Wolf at the *FT*, and, of course, Gordon Brown.

But I would never have started out on the career path I have taken without the influence of Peter Baker. Peter was my assistant personal tutor at school. Together we ran the school politics society. And he taught me 'A' Level economics between 1983 and 1985 – in the shadow of the by then collapsing monetarist experiment of the first Thatcher government. As unemployment rose above three million, we studied John Eatwell's book, *Whatever Happened to Britain?*, and debated how we would do things differently if only we could.

I guess many people have had a particularly inspirational teacher at school – someone whose commitment and intellectual excitement continues to influence you throughout your life. Peter Baker was, for me, that teacher. His enduring influence was to embed in me the belief that a government could run the economy both competently and at the same time pursue progressive goals – delivering full employment, tackling poverty, promoting regional equality, investing in public services.

Peter died early and tragically three years ago. I was proud that he lived long enough to see me appointed Chief Economic Adviser to the Treasury working under a Labour Chancellor of the Exchequer. I only wish he had lived long enough to see us showing that government can advance both economic prosperity and social justice. He always believed it could be done.

MY ADVICE: *When you meet those rare and generous people who want to teach and inspire as well as just do their jobs, take full advantage: stay late, ask too many questions, keep saying 'Why?', learn from them while you can, and demand that they show you how.*

Anne Begg MP
Member of Parliament for Aberdeen South

I was elected Member of Parliament for Aberdeen South in 1997. Previously, I had been an English teacher for 19 years, and in 1988 won the award for Disabled Scot of the Year. (I was born with the genetic condition Gauchers Disease and have used a wheelchair since 1984, the year after I joined the Labour Party and became active in local politics.) I've always regarded my wheelchair as 'liberator' and believe that disabled people should not be excluded from society. My political interests include civil rights for disabled people, social justice and broadcasting: I'm Secretary of the BBC Group in the House of Commons amongst many other activities.

My parents were my greatest inspiration. They were an ordinary working-class couple who wanted the best for their children. They always encouraged me to 'do my best' and didn't wrap me in cotton wool when I was diagnosed with a degenerative disease. They have been the rock in my life, always supportive, taking pride in everything I have achieved. I'm sure I have inherited my strength of character from them.

MY ADVICE: *Always do your best and then no one, least of all yourself, can ask for more.*

Rt Hon David Blunkett MP
Member of Parliament for Sheffield Brightside and Home Secretary

I was first elected to Parliament in June 1987, representing the Sheffield Brightside seat. I held a number of Opposition posts in Environment (Local Government), Health, and Education and Employment. After a Labour Government was elected in May 1997, I served as Secretary of State for Education and Employment. I was appointed Home Secretary in June 2001.

I was educated at the Manchester Road School for the Blind, Royal National College for the Blind, Shrewsbury Technical College, Sheffield Richmond College of Further Education, the University of Sheffield and Hollybank College in Huddersfield. My early political career was spent in local government, on the South Yorkshire County Council from 1973–77 and on Sheffield City Council from 1970–88, where I became chair of the Social Services Committee and then Leader of the Council from 1980–87. I have a National Certificate in Business Studies as well as 'A' Levels, a degree and Post Graduate Certificate in Education. I also have advanced RSA typing and 100 words per minute Braille shorthand.

What we make of ourselves is, of course, down to ourselves. Self-determination and self-reliance are the foundations on which dreams can be made, modest or outrageous!

But those of us who have – in one form or another – made it, know that we would never have done so without the help and inspiration of others.

Raising our expectations, but providing a leg up the ladder that makes achieving them a reality, is what mutuality, friendship, or mentoring, is all about.

Some have a family member – my Mum certainly taught me all about responsibility – whilst others, as I did, have people outside their immediate family to help.

From a teacher that inspired me to read history and to believe in the future, through to the Leader of Sheffield City Council in the early 1970s, I learnt that both the example of others and the encouragement of others made all the difference.

Ron Ironmonger (Sir Ron as he became known) taught me as a young Councillor, 30 years ago, that hard graft as well as confidence and inspiration were needed. He also taught me, by taking me down a peg or two and challenging me at key moments, to learn about how to cope with the hard knocks and at the same time about picking myself up, dusting myself down, and starting all over again.

MY ADVICE: *It is someone to encourage you, someone to support you, and someone sometimes to tell you the truth, that makes the difference in life. That is why I think this collection of thoughts by Sarah Brown is so important in enabling others to get it right for the future. We are independent, but only truly so when we recognise our inter-dependence, one with another.*

Rt Hon Nick Brown MP
Minister for Work and Member of Parliament for Newcastle upon Tyne East and Wallsend

After studying history and government at Manchester University, I first worked as an advertising executive for Proctor & Gamble in Newcastle during 1974-75. And later as Legal Officer, in the

Northern Region of the General and Municipal Workers Union from 1978–83. Since 1983, I have been the Labour MP for Newcastle upon Tyne East, and my constituency includes Wallsend since 1997. I have held the following posts in Parliament: Opposition Spokesman on Legal Affairs 1984–87; Opposition Spokesman on Treasury and Economic Affairs 1987–94; Opposition Health Spokesman 1995–96; Deputy Chief Whip 1996–97; Government Chief Whip 1997–98; Minister for Agriculture, Fisheries & Food 1998–2001; Minister of State for Work since 2001.

When I was five years old, I had started at the village infant school in Hawkhurst, Kent where I grew up. The school was on the other side of the main road through the village. I was too young to walk home on my own and so I used to go across to granny and grandad's house until my dad finished work and called to take me home.

One day after school I came to tell grandad all about the day's events. 'Grandad,' I said (remember this was 1955), 'we've been told at school all about how Mr Churchill won the Second World War!' He sat me on his knee and solemnly said, 'Nicholas, Mr Churchill tried to kill your grandad and your Uncle Hubert.'

The enormity of this slowly dawned on me. Why would a national hero, the British Prime Minister and war leader, try to kill grandad and Uncle Hubert?

Grandad told me that he, and his brother Hubert, had been sent by Mr Churchill to fight at Gallipoli in the First World War. He told me, at some length (I was only five), in vivid detail, about the awfulness and futility of the campaign. He hated Churchill for sending him to this hell hole, and had a grudging admiration for the Turkish soldiers who fought bravely in even worse conditions than the British and Commonwealth troops.

I learned two things from this that have stayed with me ever since. Firstly the official version of events may not be the only one. Secondly, it is possible to respect the other side (the Turks, not Churchill) even in a hard-fought conflict.

Dawn Butler
London Regional Organiser for the GMB trade union

I was initially inspired to go into the field of computers by my computer teacher, Mr Taylor. He was the only teacher actually to show an interest in teaching me as an individual, not prejudging, and I can still remember his inspiration.

I did eight 'O' Levels including Computer Studies and an 'A' Level in maths, and then did various courses including a BTEC National Diploma in computer studies. My first job was with Johnson Matthey as a systems analyst/programmer. I then moved to work as a staff trainer with the Employment Service and did voluntary work at the African Caribbean Centre of Waltham Forest helping their fundraising by organising various shows and plays. My first trade union job was National Recruitment Officer at the PTC (Public Services Tax and Commerce Union, now PCS) and I was the first National Black Woman's Officer helping to increase membership. After two years, I moved to the GMB as London Regional Organiser and Race and Equality Officer.

I am now inspired by my desire to eradicate racism and inequality in society. In the trade union movement, I was inspired by a black woman called Mrs Padrika Kennington, an amazing lady. Actually I don't think I ever told her.

MY ADVICE: *It is very difficult as a young person to be successful in the trade union movement as it is predominantly run by white middle-aged men. I would advise anyone to keep on going, don't give up and seek out people like me who will help you along the way.*

Louise Casey
Director, Homelessness Directorate, Office of the Deputy Prime Minister

I am the Head of the Government's Homelessness Directorate in England which is responsible for reducing the use of B&B accommodation. By March 2004 no family with children should be placed in B&B accommodation except in an emergency, assisting local authorities with the implementation of the Homelessness Act and sustaining the two-thirds reduction in the number of people sleeping rough.

Previously I was the Head of the Government's Rough Sleepers Unit, a cross-sector Unit established in April 1999 with the target of reducing the number of people sleeping rough by two-thirds by 2002. This target was met in December 2001 – the numbers of people sleeping rough fell from nearly 2,000 in 1998 to around 550 in 2001. Between 1992 and 1999, I was Deputy Director of the charity, Shelter, and between 1990 and 1992 was Deputy Director and then Director of Homeless Network in London.

Sister Ita was the Deputy Headteacher of the school (Oaklands RC Comprehensive School in Waterlooville, Hampshire) I attended from age 11 to 18.

She did not directly teach any subject, but taught me much about life and how to always push yourself to do better. She was a constant presence during the tough years from 14 to 18 and always provided support and help.

When we did school plays or events she was always the person behind the scenes that held it all together. This was very similar to the way she held together the school and many of the pupils within it.

At that age we all sometimes do wrong things like smoking in the town centre or bunking off school. When we got caught, Sister Ita would always find out. She would never tolerate it, and you always felt ashamed that you let her down. But every time a lesson was learnt.

The biggest thing I learnt from her was that I was worth something and that I had something to give society. She also taught me that justice and goodness were worth fighting for and that would be the advice that I would pass on to anyone starting out in life. I keep fighting for these things every day and I will always be grateful for the guidance, inspiration and love she gave me.

Michael Cashman MEP
Member of the European Parliament

I am one of the 28 British Labour Members of the European Parliament and I was first elected in 1999 for a five-year term. In the Parliament I specialise in Justice and Home Affairs, Human

Rights, Minority Rights and Freedom of Information. Getting elected was the achievement of a long-held ambition stretching back to the late 1980s. I first sought the Labour Party nomination to stand for the European Parliament in 1993 but I came second. In the meantime I continued working as an actor and continued to campaign and support the Labour Party. Then in 1998 I stood for election to the controlling body of the Labour Party, the NEC, and was surprisingly elected. This was to be one of my many lucky breaks.

No one single person inspired me but the person who gave me my love of language, and through it I suppose my communication skills, was Miss O'Sullivan from my primary school in East London. She encouraged me to read and often got me to read aloud to the class – in order to keep them quiet. My other teachers like Miss Donkin and Miss Plant encouraged me to write short stories – called compositions. And I was lucky because I enjoyed telling stories and using my imagination. So I suppose the stimulation of the imagination is what set me on the path to be an actor and ultimately to become a politician. To imagine is to be able to offer another option, another way; it is the ability to change the world, even change places in your imagination with another human being. There really is nothing more powerful than the imagination.

Later at stage school, and as a child actor from the age of 12, I began to develop confidence skills and total awareness that any job needs to be done properly and that deadlines have to be met. The discipline that I learnt as an actor and as a writer has stood me in good stead. You have to have the courage to work alone and the courage to be unpopular. In this respect having the love of your family steadies you when things begin to hurt. The love of my partner Paul also gives me amazing strength and courage.

MY ADVICE: *The advice I would offer is gain some confidence and communication skills, perhaps by doing some acting with an amateur group or some role-playing in teams. Be prepared to work hard, stimulate your imagination and picture yourself in other situations, other places and as other people. Join a political party and at the same time get lots of experience outside of politics, remind yourself of what is wrong with the world and give* *yourself the courage to be part of changing it for the good. And above all else don't go into politics thinking it is a job for life. Go in determined to do the work, determined to make a difference, and with the courage to leave before you've lost that spark. Finally, listen to some of the speeches of Neil Kinnock. They are truly inspirational.*

Barbara Follett MP
Member of Parliament for Stevenage

I cut my political teeth in apartheid South Africa – a tough apprenticeship which came to an abrupt end in early 1978 when my first husband was shot dead by right-wing extremists in front of our two young daughters. With my own life under threat I returned to Britain with my young family.

A month later I joined the Labour Party. After fighting two hopeless seats in the 1983 and 1987 General Elections I contested the selection for the marginal seat of Dulwich. I lost by three votes. So, the run-up to the 1992 General Election found me feeling rather hopeless about my own political future.

Despite Nelson Mandela's recent release I was not all that optimistic about South Africa's political future either. Coincidentally, I made my first trip back to South Africa at this time with Glenys Kinnock on behalf of the charity One World Action. Armed policemen and surly officials at Johannesburg airport made me seriously question why I had come back to this beautiful but awful country.

My discomfort showed on my face. As she greeted me outside the airport, Adelaide Tambo said, 'Cheer up Barbara, I have got a surprise for you.' She bundled us into a waiting car and drove us to a walled house in Soweto. As we drew into the drive a tall, grey-haired man came out to greet us. It was Nelson Mandela.

I had not seen him for over thirty years. But he made no reference to the passing of time or to the horrors he had lived through. In the two hours we spent with him, drinking tea and eating cake, he talked about the future. About the country he hoped to help to build. About the people he hoped to build it with. Many of them were his jailers. But he was looking at the bigger picture. Not at himself.

I felt ashamed. I had been feeling sorry for myself. Here was a man with a great deal more to feel sorry for himself about and there was not a trace of it in his speech or demeanour. He was not letting the past rule his life. He was making the best of the present. I vowed, there and then, to always try to do the same.

I returned to Britain with renewed vigour. This carried me through Labour's 1992 General Election defeat and helped me get selected, and elected, as the Member of Parliament for Stevenage in 1997.

MY ADVICE: *Anyone thinking of going into politics should bear Mandela's example in mind. Stay focused on your goals, not yourself. Do not dwell on the hurt and mistakes of the past. Look to the future. It is yours to shape.*

Philip Gould
Political Strategist

I work as a political strategist trying to help progressive parties win elections. Mostly I work with the Labour Party, but I have also worked in elections in other countries including the USA, Germany, Holland, Israel, Sweden and Norway.

I started working with the Labour Party in 1985 with Neil Kinnock and was involved in two losing election campaigns in 1987 and 1992, before Labour won in 1997 and 2001. I studied politics at the University of Sussex and the London School of Economics, and worked in advertising before starting in politics. I am now a visiting professor at the LSE.

I was such a failure at school, and I mean really not successful at all. I failed my 11 plus and did, as I remember it, no homework at all until I went on to fail almost all my GCSEs (or 'O' Levels as they were then). There was one teacher, however, called Mrs Sharp, who had faith in me and got me to believe in myself. She taught Geography, the only 'O' Level I passed, and instilled in me, from an early age, the power of mentoring.

I struggled through to one university, then another university, and finally ended up at the London Business School of all places, desperate to get into politics. I didn't want to go into business – I wanted to do politics. But again I was saved, this time by Charles Handy, a professor there who taught my course. Charles is one of those people who is genuinely transforming, looking at everything and seeing it differently. He recreates the world with his ideas, and through his ideas goes on to change the world. He certainly changed me, giving me the confidence finally to live life on my own terms. He persuaded me to believe that if you have a mission, a burning desire to change things, then everything will, in the end, fall into place. If I ever forget this, my life stalls; if I don't, things always sort themselves out. This is a big lesson, perhaps the biggest lesson there is to learn. I will never forget Charles for changing my life.

MY ADVICE: *Be determined to make a difference. Never ever give up. Never lose sight of the values and mission that drive you.*

Mary Goudie (Baroness Goudie of Roundwood)
Labour Peer

From the time I went to secondary school I began to understand about injustice and colour prejudice.

When I was 16, I joined the Young Socialists in Wembley South. The area of London that I lived in was a suburban residential area with a large amount of private housing and some excellent council housing. Early on, as an active member of the Labour Party, I understood that for those of us who believed in change and equality we had to win elections. It was no good sitting in meetings and going to the pub and just talking.

I decided that campaigning was important and it should not be unfocused nonsense. Every single vote mattered and to do this we had to change, so I started going to assist in local by-elections in Wembley and Willesden, which were later to become the London Borough of Brent.

During this period I made two long-standing friends, Frank Brooker, a retired railway worker from Wembley, and Johnny Hutton, a postman and treasurer of his union. I fought my first Council seat in the election for the new Borough and lost. Labour lost control in Willesden as well, and deservedly so as the Councillors had taken their positions for granted. The conditions that people, in that part of Brent, were living in were appalling – they should have been paid to live there, not the other way around!

I discussed the housing and other issues day after day with Johnny and his friends. We talked about how Labour could win control again, and influence people of vision to stand for the Council and take on and take out the old guard. We wanted new Councillors who would not just attend functions, but who would push the Government, the voluntary agencies and the press for this change. Johnny and his friends gave me every support at the Labour Party meetings in the Borough. Little did I know that Johnny had decided that, so far as he was concerned, I would be the next Councillor for his area, Roundwood Ward. This was an area that had the highest unemployment, a prevailing culture of truancy from school, the highest number of cot deaths in the Borough and one of the highest levels of depravation in London. I won the seat as the youngest Councillor in Brent.

With Johnny's support I started a campaign for change in Roundwood that no one there had really tried before without the officers of the Council putting them down. I was not prepared to put up with prejudice; Johnny gave me support at meetings, helped with my speeches and newsletters, and worried about me going on demonstrations (not in case I was arrested, but in case I was hurt). He supported me when I was invited by the joint Chairmen of the Labour Solidarity Campaign to become the Secretary of this organisation for change in the Labour Party.

I was very sorry that he died just before I was invited by the Prime Minister to become a Labour Peer and to see me take the name of the Roundwood Ward in the House of Lords.

MY ADVICE: *Never be afraid of campaigning to change things for the better. It is well worth the hard work and setbacks to bring greater justice and social equality for people.*

Patricia Hewitt MP
Member of Parliament for Leicester West
and Secretary of State for Trade and Industry and
Cabinet Minister for Women

I was born and grew up in Australia, then came to Britain to do a degree in English literature at Cambridge. I joined Liberty (then the National Council for Civil Liberties), as Women's Rights Officer before becoming General Secretary. After standing unsuccessfully for Parliament in 1983, I worked for the then leader of the Labour Party, Neil Kinnock. In 1989 I became Deputy Director of a new think tank, the Institute for Public Policy Research. Between 1994 and 1997, I was with Accenture, the global business consultancy, as Director of Research.

In 1997, I became one of the 101 Labour women MPs elected in our landslide victory, representing Leicester West. A year later, Tony Blair appointed me Economic Secretary to the Treasury – where I helped deal with pensions mis-selling and made radical reforms to the tax treatment of charities – and in 1999, I became Minister for e-commerce and small business at the Department of Trade and Industry. I was appointed to the Cabinet after the 2001 General Election.

The person who has most supported and inspired me is my closest friend, Adrienne Burgess, who, like me, grew up in Canberra, Australia. We met on our first day at secondary school, 43 years ago, and we've been best friends since.

We both came to Britain as students, and both married for the first time just after we left university. The day after my wedding, my younger sister, Antonia – who was in the same class as Adrienne's sister – plunged into a devastating nervous breakdown. Adrienne was one of the few people to whom I could talk about Antonia's illness and gradual recovery.

My marriage didn't work out, and nor did Adrienne's, and, again, it was Adrienne who supported me when I left my first husband.

When I was 25, Antonia, who was by then working in Brussels as a simultaneous interpreter, had a second breakdown, engulfed by terrifying psychotic hallucinations. I flew out to Brussels to rescue her, getting her to safety in a hotel and – after Antonia had finally fallen asleep – telephoning Adrienne for comfort and advice. She had already supported another friend through a breakdown and through the psychiatrist she recommended I found a wonderful consultant who supported my sister – and me, and the rest of the family – through the treatment that followed. Antonia suffered from hypermania, the 'up' half of manic depression – with the result that this gifted, witty, energetic person would get on with her life for two or three years and then, as the stress built up, and the lithium wore off, she would descend into another breakdown. Gradually, partying and social drinking turned to alcoholism and – after 15 years of crises, hospitalisation and treatment – she finally had to give up work and returned to Australia where she drank herself to death. I don't know how I would have coped without Adrienne's strength, wisdom and patient support.

MY ADVICE: *Believe in yourself – and don't believe anyone who says you're too young. Find a mentor who also believes in you, a friend, a teacher or school mentor, a business coach, whoever will help you work out your own way. Don't think of politics as just another career option: it's a vocation and you need to believe passionately that you can make a difference.*

We have some terrific 20-something Labour MPs, thanks to the 1997 election. But in general, I would also recommend getting some experience and expertise in the wider world – whether it's in business, the voluntary sector or public service. It will be invaluable when you become an MP and even more so when you find yourself a Minister!

John Hume
Member of Parliament for Foyle in Londonderry and
Member of European Parliament
Winner of the Nobel Peace Prize

As leader of Northern Ireland's Social Democratic and Labour Party, I was jointly awarded the Nobel Peace Prize with Ulster Unionist leader David Trimble, in 1998. I have been Foyle's MP since the constituency was created in 1983 and a member of the European Parliament since 1979.

I was a teacher of French and history, and became involved with the civil rights movement in the late 1960s. I was a founder of the Social Democratic and Labour Party in 1970, and became its leader in 1979. Most of my political working life has been focused on attempts over the last 30 years to resolve the Northern Ireland problem.

One of the major influences in my thinking, particularly about conflict resolution, has been my European Union experience. When I first went to Strasbourg in 1979 to the European Parliament, I went for a walk across the bridge from Strasbourg in France to Kehl in Germany. I stopped in the middle of the bridge and I meditated. I thought that if I had stood on this bridge 30 years before, just after the Second World War, and if I had said, 'Don't worry, its all over. In a few years' time all these countries will be in a united Europe,' I would have been sent to a psychiatrist.

The first half of the last century was the worst in the history of the world − two world wars and millions of dead. Who could have foreseen that in the second half of that century those same peoples would be united? Yet they were and it is the duty of all areas of conflict to study how they did it. And that is what I did. The principles at the heart of the European Union are the principles at the heart of the Good Friday Agreement in Northern Ireland.

The first principle is respect for difference. All conflict is about difference, whether it is religion, nationality, or race. Difference is an accident of birth, therefore it is something that we should respect.

The second principle is institutions that respect differences. All the institutions of the European Union − Council of Ministers, Commission and Parliament − fully respect and represent all countries.

The third principle is the most important − the healing process. They worked together in their common interests − economic development − and by spilling their sweat and not their blood they have broken down the barriers of centuries and the new Europe has evolved and is still evolving.

The philosophy of these principles should be sent to all areas of conflict in the world and I look forward to the day when the European Commission has created a Department of Peace and

Reconciliation that sends and takes the philosophy to such areas.

MY ADVICE: *Let us work to achieve a new world in the new century in which there will no longer be any areas of war or conflict.*

Rt Hon Charles Kennedy MP
Member of Parliament for Ross, Skye and Inverness West and Leader of the Liberal Democratic Party

I've been extremely lucky to have had several mentors at key points in my life. Without them I could not have achieved my hope of entering politics.

My grandfather, a West Highland crofter, taught me standards and values – by example – as a youngster. At high school, my English teacher encouraged me in public speaking and debating. At university my professors broadened my mind and opened my eyes to a wider world than I'd ever known before.

All had two things in common: the gift of good teaching, based on high standards and ethical principles, and respect for other individual human beings.

MY ADVICE: *We all gain by having someone, somewhere, to look up to.*

Horst Köhler
Managing Director, International Monetary Fund

I became the Managing Director of the International Monetary Fund in 2000 after being selected unanimously by the Executive Board of the IMF. Prior to taking up this position I was the President of the European Bank for Reconstruction and Development, after working as the President of the German Savings Bank Association. I had previously served in various positions in Germany's Ministries of Economics and Finance including Deputy Minister of Finance from 1990–93 during the time of the Maastricht Treaty negotiations.

I had studied at the University of Tübingen where I earned a doctorate in economics and political sciences, and was a scientific research assistant at the Institute of Applied Economic Research.

In 1953, when I was ten years old, my family and I lived in a refugee camp in Southern Germany. Often there was friction between the local children and the refugee children. I was not afraid of standing up for myself, including in school. Once, in class, I practised my whistling. A piercing whistle earned me a punishment and an hour's detention. I was surprised when my teacher, Mr Balle, came and sat beside me during detention. He told me that he knew that refugees were not always treated in a friendly way. However, I should look on school as a place where everyone had the same opportunities. From then on, I paid much more attention in school than I had done before.

A few weeks after this conversation, my family was moved to another refugee camp. An invitation already awaited my parents to attend a discussion with the new education authority: subject – Horst Köhler. My mother went with mixed feelings. To her amazement, the head of the education authority recommended sending me to grammar school, Germany's highest secondary education institution. In doing so, he passed on some strong advice from Mr Balle. My mother followed this advice.

This was, perhaps, the most defining moment for the future course of my life.

MY ADVICE: *Make the most of school as this opens up the way for your own opportunities.*

Jack McConnell MSP
First Minister, Scottish Parliament and Member of the Scottish Parliament for Motherwell and Wishaw

I grew up on a sheep farm in Arran, attending the local high school in Lamlash, and went on to train as a teacher at the University of Stirling. While at university, I also served as the President of the Students' Association. After I graduated, I worked as a maths teacher, and was also a member of Stirling District Council, serving in my time as Treasurer and Leader of the Council.

In 1992, I stepped down as both a teacher and as Council Leader, to take up an appointment as General Secretary of the Scottish Labour Party. During my six years in this position, I managed the 1997 election campaign in Scotland, and co-ordinated Labour's 'Yes Yes' referendum campaign to achieve a Scottish Parliament in 1997.

With the creation of the Scottish Parliament I stood for election, and was appointed as Scottish Labour Environmental Spokesperson for the 1999 Scottish Election. As an MSP, I have served first as Minister of Finance, and then as Minister of Education, Europe and External Affairs. I was elected First Minister by the Scottish Parliament in 2001.

While our lives are influenced by many people, our values and ambitions can be formed at an early stage. I was extremely lucky to have four first-class teachers at Lamlash Primary School. Isobel Craig, Mary McNicol, Margaret Boyce and Joyce Scott taught standards, ambition, skills and discipline in an all-round education which left a lasting impression.

Lamlash was a small rural school, at the heart of the community. We were encouraged to work hard, respect others, learn about Scotland and the world, develop talents and 'be all we could be'.

I was fortunate to meet Mary, Margaret and Joyce again when I reopened my old school in new premises a year ago. They had changed little, reminding me of those age-old basic values – honesty, respect and ambition – which young Scots today should value in whatever career they pursue.

David Miliband MP
Member of Parliament for South Shields and School Standards Minister

I am the Minister of State for School Standards at the Department for Education and Skills. I have been Labour Member of Parliament for South Shields since 2001. Previously I was Head of the Prime Minister's Policy Unit (1997-2001), and Head of Policy in the Office of the Leader of the Opposition (1994-97). Before that I was a Research Fellow at the Institute of Public Policy Research, and Secretary of the Commission on Social Justice. I was educated at a comprehensive school in London, and went to Oxford University to study philosophy, politics and economics, followed by a Masters' degree in Political Science at The Massachusetts Institute of Technology where I was a Kennedy Scholar.

I edited the book, *Reinventing the Left,* in 1994 and co-edited

Paying for Inequality that same year. I was a founder of the think tank, the Centre for European Reform. I am President of the South Shields Football Club and a member of the Whiteleas and Cleadon Social Clubs.

I went to a friendly, family-oriented primary school near Leeds. One teacher stood out – he had an unusual foreign name, and his brother occasionally appeared on television playing rugby league for Keighley. Harry Pieniazek was also an inspirational teacher – not that I was ever in his class, but he devoted himself after school and at weekends to running the school sports teams. My parents were always worried that I was never interested in books, and only seemed to care about football. Harry Pieniazek was partly responsible. I played in goal at the time with devotion and commitment, but although I hoped to be the next Gordon Banks I was more of a Gary Sprake. Mr Pieniazek's teams played hard but learnt – through a lot of practice – to be good losers. He was all that a good teacher should be: kind, informed, and completely committed to getting the best out of children, by putting a lot in. I have not seen him for over 25 years, but the memory of his professionalism and devotion is still vivid. I owe him, and many teachers like him, an awful lot.

Bill Morris
General Secretary, Transport and General Workers Union

I came to Birmingham in 1954, at the age of 16, to join my recently widowed mother. After two short spells of employment, I joined an engineering company, Hardy Spicers, attending a day-release course in engineering skills at a local technical college. I joined the Transport and General Workers Union in 1958, and was elected Shop Steward at Hardy Spicers in 1963. I then became a member of the governing body, later joining the staff, until I was eventually elected General Secretary in 1991 and later re-elected in 1995.

I have held office in a wide range of organisations in the trade union and Labour Movements and in the country's life generally. I am currently a non-executive Director of the Bank of England and was a member of the Royal Commission on the Reform of the House of Lords and the Commission for Racial Equality. I am Chancellor of the University of Technology in Jamaica, involved at various levels on the Governing Bodies of six universities and colleges in the UK. I have been awarded eleven honorary degrees in the UK and Jamaica.

I take an 'I can do it' approach to life which was inspired by three people. My grandmother was the most influential person in my life as I was growing up. She never took 'no' for an answer and saw no challenge as unachievable. Her attitude was simply 'everyone can do it'. So you did!

My second inspiration was Miss Sewell, my teacher at junior school in Jamaica. She was a strict disciplinarian who did not suffer fools gladly. Her attitude was simple. If you did something incorrectly, you re-did it until you got it right.

In England the Chair of the Joint Shop Stewards Committee at Hardy Spicers, Graham Gould influenced my behaviour. He taught me the importance of clarity; he had the ability to express complex issues in simple terms, and he would work at the solution. His dedication to the task in hand inspired me to work until the task was completed.

These influences gave me the determination to prove wrong all those people who doubted my ability to win and my vision to succeed.

MY ADVICE: *Don't worry about the next task; concentrate on doing the one in hand to the very best of your ability.*

Gus O'Donnell
Permanent Secretary, HM Treasury

'Yes!' I punched the air with delight. 'I've got tenure.'

'What's that?' my soon-to-be wife Melanie asked me.

'It's a letter from Tom saying I've got a job for life.'

'Sounds more like a life sentence,' she replied.

'Tom' was Professor Thomas Wilson, holder of the prestigious Adam Smith Chair of Political Economy at the University of Glasgow. A few years before he had heard me give a seminar at

Nuffield College, Oxford where I was finishing a postgraduate course and offered me my first job. Since then he had helped me as I struggled to learn how to teach and do research.

So when I got the letter the obvious next step was to go and ask Tom what I should concentrate on, now I was 'tenured'. His advice was clear. 'You should leave,' he said. 'You're a good applied economist but you're not exactly Nobel Prize material. Use your economics to make the world a better place. Join the government.'

I was gobsmacked. 'Become a civil servant? But Tom, you know that "Advisers advise and Ministers decide". I'll never change anything.'

'Yes, but if Advisers advise better then Ministers decide better. Go and persuade them to reduce trade barriers, untie aid, cut taxes (this was 1979 and the top rate of tax was 83 pence in the pound). Leave the world a better place than you found it.'

Tom, as ever, was right. I left Glasgow University, joined the Treasury and worked my way up to be Permanent Secretary and the Head of the Government Economic Service. I owe it to Tom who was an ideal mentor, offering a guiding hand so gentle I didn't know it was there; giving praise when it was due but not afraid to pass on some home truths about my failings. Tom died over a year ago. My regret is I never said any of this to him when he was alive. But if I can leave the world in a better shape he'll be pleased. I'll try for the Nobel Prize next time around.

MY ADVICE: *My advice to young economists and civil servants is the same advice Tom gave to me: don't use jargon, do use evidence; be honest and be influential; above all use your professional skills to make a difference.*

Rt Hon John Prescott MP
Deputy Prime Minister and Member of Parliament for Hull East

I was born in Prestatyn, Wales, in 1938, the son of a railway signalman. I was educated at Ellesmere Port Secondary Modern and, at 15, began work as a trainee chef. In 1963, after working for 10 years as a steward in the Merchant Navy, I gained a diploma in economics and politics at Ruskin College, Oxford, which specialises in courses for union working people. I later went on to gain a BSc in economics and economic history at the University of Hull.

Maritime safety motivated my decision to work as a full-time official for the National Union of Seamen between 1968–70. I was elected Labour Member of Parliament for Hull East in 1970. I was a member of the Council of Europe between 1972–75, EEC Parliamentary Delegate in 1975 and then Leader of the Labour Party Delegation to the European Parliament between 1976–79. I held a series of Shadow Cabinet posts dealing with regional affairs, employment, energy and transport and, in 1994, was elected Deputy Leader of the Labour Party and appointed to the Privy Council.

Following the Labour Party's election in May 1997 I was appointed Deputy Prime Minister and First Secretary of State for Environment, Transport and the Regions and following the election in June 2001 a new Office of the Deputy Prime Minister was established in the Cabinet Office. The Office of the Deputy Prime Minister was established as a department in its own right in May 2002.

There are many individuals who I think have influenced my personal development and character. In my 16 years at sea, six in adult education and 32 as an MP, I owe debts of gratitude to many. I also owe a debt of gratitude to my union, the National Union of Seamen, who taught me the value of collective action on behalf of others in a democratic participatory process.

However, I feel my tutor, the late Raphael Samuel, and the Labour Ruskin College experience taught me everyone was of equal worth and you shouldn't feel inferior to anyone. He taught me how to mould my raw passion and anger into disciplined and cogent arguments. Raphael's legacy was to give a lad with my background the confidence to believe he could make a difference – I have tried to do just that.

Meta Ramsay (Baroness Ramsay of Cartvale)

Labour Peer

I studied at Glasgow University and was the first woman President of the Scottish Union of Students. I was then elected to the Co-ordinating Secretariat of the International Student Conference, in the Netherlands, and this opened up the world of international politics for me. I had a successful career in HM Diplomatic Service, with postings to Stockholm and Helsinki during the Cold War.

I retired from Government service in 1991 and became Foreign Policy Adviser to the late Rt Hon John Smith QC MP, Leader of HM Opposition 1992–94. I became a member of the House of Lords as a Labour Peer in 1996.

An inspiration in my life was Agnes McKendrick, Vice-Principal and Head Classics teacher at Hutcheson's Girls Grammar School, Glasgow. Rome and the Romans came to fascinating life in her classes. A formidable figure, she would boom out at any unfortunate unable to answer, 'At least look intelligent, girl, and you might never be found out.' She inspired us with a confidence that we girls could do anything we wanted, and drilled into us a sense of social responsibility to the community.

She said that her ambition was to have taught a woman prime minister, but she would settle for a Cabinet member if that was the best we could do. I thought of her in 1997 when I became a Government Whip, which was the best I could do for her.

MY ADVICE: *Strive to do the best that you can, and remember, as you succeed, to give back whatever you can to your own local community.*

George Robertson (Lord Robertson of Port Ellen)

Secretary General, NATO

I have been Secretary General of NATO since 1999. Before that I was the Defence Secretary of the UK from 1997–99, and the Labour MP for Hamilton and Hamilton South from 1978–99. I entered Parliament in 1978 after almost 10 years as a trade union official looking after Scotch Whisky workers. As an MP I worked for the first 18 years in opposition, mainly doing Foreign Affairs, and was elected to the Shadow Cabinet in 1993, and then appointed Shadow Scottish Secretary.

I was inspired by a teacher, Archie Blair, at my secondary school Dunoon Grammar, who died last year. He was a history teacher but one with a special care for the subject and a unique way of getting it over. He made me appreciate the richness of the past but also the potential of the future – you learned from history. He had a party political view, though probably was not in a party, but apart from his passion, the view never affected the objectivity of his teaching.

He calmed my teenage enthusiasms which were taking me into politics even then and urged a more balanced, studied look at the world and issues. At the same time his own strength of conviction and his transparent decency were an example of how to live a life of political and public involvement.

MY ADVICE: *Believe in yourself; if you don't, you can't expect others to do so. Be confident but not arrogant. Be informed but not impossibly opinionated. Be clever. Be lucky.*

Wilf Stevenson
Director, Smith Institute

I am the Director of the Smith Institute, an independent think tank, which currently centres its work on issues that flow from the changing relationship between social values and economic imperatives. Recent programmes have included reviewing which aspects of equality should inform social and economic policy; an investigation into the roles of creativity and entrepreneurship in the new economy; a programme on women in the new economy; work on pensions and savings; and a seminar series on competition policy. Before joining the Smith Institute, I was the Director of the British Film Institute, the national agency that develops the arts of cinema and television and conserves them in the national interest; and before that I was an educational administrator.

Neil Kinnock came to Edinburgh at the invitation of Gordon Brown MP, in 1987, just after he had been elected Leader of the Labour Party. He could have done a straightforward 'stump' speech, but he gave a passionate, funny, committed and honest oration, which moved everyone present and left many in tears. Everyone in the audience that day came away feeling that they had reconnected with the heart and not just the business of politics.

Listening to Neil Kinnock, and meeting him and other politicians subsequently, convinced me that we all had to do what we could for society and that I should try to find a job which contributed in some way to the political process – which I eventually did – by offering ideas and policies derived from firm principles.

MY ADVICE: *Take your time – and wait until you find a job that suits you and your interests. It can be done and the synergy that it creates is worth all the waiting and wondering if you've made the right choice.*

Matthew Taylor
Director, Institute of Public Policy Research

I am the Director of the Institute of Public Policy Research, Britain's leading centre-left think tank. Until 1998, I was the Assistant General Secretary of the Labour Party. During the 1997 General Election, I was Labour's Director of Policy and a member of the Party's central election strategy team. I was appointed to the Labour Party in 1994 to establish Labour's rebuttal operation. My activities before then included being a county councillor, a parliamentary candidate, a university research fellow and the director of a unit monitoring policy in the health service.

I am a regular broadcaster and contributor to newspapers and journals. I have written pamphlets and book chapters on issues including the record of New Labour, democratic renewal, the role of local councillors and family-friendly working. My first book *What Are Children For?* was published in January 2003. I have a first class honours degree from Southampton University and a Masters degree in industrial relations from the University of Warwick.

Councillor Gordon Jones was a Conservative councillor in Warwickshire when I joined the Council in 1985. I was an aggressive left-winger with a sizeable portion of chips on my shoulder. Over four years we worked together to reform special school provision. He taught me to judge people by their thoughts and actions rather than by what 'side' they might be on. He taught me to respect different views if soundly based and to be patient and clever rather than angry and impetuous in seeking change.

MY ADVICE: *Listen as hard to your opponents as your allies. Judge an idea or person by what they are, not where they come from.*

Sir Andrew Turnbull
Cabinet Secretary and Head of the Home Civil Service

I went to school at Enfield Grammar in North London and studied economics at Cambridge University. I joined HM Treasury in 1970, having spent two years working as an economist in Zambia. After 30 years in the Treasury, Number 10 Downing Street and the Department of the Environment, I am now Cabinet Secretary and Head of the Home Civil Service for the British Government.

When I arrived at Christ's College, Cambridge in 1964, I told my brother, who was already there, who my tutor was to be: Dr Chris Bliss who went on to be Nuffield Professor of Economics at Oxford University. 'They say he's the next Keynes,' my brother told me. Well, he wasn't the next Keynes. His talents were in theoretical economics rather than public policy. What Chris Bliss was and is, is a brilliant teacher, someone who could inspire young men and women to think more ambitiously, to tackle problems in greater depth and with greater rigour.

Success at Cambridge made me realise I could aspire to work in one of Britain's most important organisations, and gave me the confidence to work on some of the most difficult policy issues of today.

MY ADVICE: *Hard though we try through adult education to give people a second chance, the best opportunity is still at school and college. Look on your teachers as a resource and try to transfer as much of their knowledge, experience and intellect from their heads into yours.*

Simon Woolley
National Co-ordinator, Operation Black Vote

I am the National Co-ordinator for, and one of the founders of, the Operation Black Vote Campaign. OBV is the first comprehensive campaign that addresses the Black political democratic deficit. My interests and expertise stretch across issues of political empowerment, Black civil rights, policy research and development, campaign strategy, fundraising, public speaking and the implementation of citizenship programmes within the community. I am called on to advise many government departments such as the Home Office, the Electoral Commission and the Lords and to take part in their International Visitors Programme. I was recently voted onto the Grassroots Power-list 2002, which was published by the *Big Issue*.

Two people have inspired me: my mother and Muhammad Ali. My mother because she taught me how to be a good person; to care about others, and also be the best I can be. Muhammad Ali because he was the best in world at what he did and he was the smartest, fastest-talking black man I ever heard. As a black kid in a nearly all white school, Muhammad Ali made me feel proud to be black.

MY ADVICE: *There is nothing wrong with being ambitious or having a sense of self-pride, but only if it is coupled with how your achievements can help others too. Ambition or success for success's sake serves only an inflated ego.*

Believe that a purposeful success is your destiny. You'll constantly be faced with obstacles, but these are there to test your character.

media

Rebekah Wade
Editor, The Sun

The only time success comes before work is in the dictionary. I bet many of the successful men and women in this book will testify you can't have one without the other. But hard work is only the basic component: the magic ingredients that ultimately weld them into one are ambition, self-belief, support . . . and luck.

From the age of 14 I was lucky. I knew without question that I wanted to be a journalist. Not in magazines, television or radio; nothing but newspapers would do. I speak to many successful young journalists and have come to realise that 14 is quite early to be so certain. And though it helped me, it certainly isn't vital in making a success of your life.

Look at JK Rowling, the author of the Harry Potter novels. Jo Rowling was 32 before she published *The Philosopher's Stone*. Now, of course, she is one of the most successful British authors of our time. But the most important lesson to learn from her well-deserved success is that once she sat down at her kitchen table to create the magical world of Harry Potter, it was her sheer hard work and self-belief that led her to achieve her goal. All writers need inspiration and even before the beginning of every novel you'll usually find the author's acknowledgements to those who precipitated or inspired their success, plus a dedication to one special person.

Well, at 21, I arrived at the *News of the World* for my first reporting shifts. Ten years later I returned to the paper as editor. And I'm sure that without certain people in my life, I wouldn't have achieved nearly that. It's impossible to list them all without turning this article into a traditional Oscar speech. But for my own acknowledgements I'd like to thank: Ross for constant love and pride; Judy for ten years of real friendship; Les for always and remarkably still believing in me; Piers for making me believe in luck; and Andy for always being true; Charlie for giving the sandwich girl a break; and Pete for ignoring my CV. Sue for the second chance; Colin for the first chance; and, of course, Mystic Meg for the prediction.

Without them all, I'd still be making the tea, and for those great gifts they all deserve thanks. But if I was writing a book, my dedication is to Deborah: a beautiful, 59-year-old woman who continues to be the greatest of inspirations in my life. Her unequivocal support, her total unwavering belief in me, and her fantastic, if rather eccentric, sense of humour in times of trouble, have all been essential to any success I may have achieved. Deborah has many great qualities. But it is her strength and courage that have taught me the lesson we all forget at our peril: on the path to success you will sometimes fail. How you cope with that failure and rise above it determines your future.

I remember, early on in my career, the *News of the World* had budget cuts. I was a freelance, not a permanent member of staff, and the features editor very regretfully told me I wouldn't be needed the following week as they were cutting down on the amount of work available. I was devastated and rang Deborah for instant advice. Her response was immediate. 'Why don't you just turn up at the office as normal and see what happens. They can only tell you to go home again.'

So I did. I turned up for work on Tuesday morning, which, on a Sunday newspaper is the day a number of the staff begin their week. I simply sat at the desk – there was certainly plenty of space!

I waited, almost holding my breath, for the stinging rebuke: 'What are you doing here? I thought I told you . . . '

Then it came 'Rebekah . . .' It was pure luck that the desk was extremely busy . . . because, of course, all the casual staff had been fired. Me included! The call was to send me out on a job: my reappearance wasn't even being questioned. And I never looked back.

Deborah is a great believer in, 'What's the worst that can happen?' You have to take chances if you're going to succeed. Playing safe is sometimes not an option and if you deeply believe you are right and you've calculated the risk – do it.

When we launched the *News of the World*'s anti-paedophile campaign I relied on this piece of advice and we published our now-famous 'Named & Shamed' issue in which we identified a large number of attackers.

Yes, there was uproar in some quarters. And yes, there was a risk – as there is in every issue of any newspaper – that our public might not agree with us. All that Sunday the *News of the World*'s campaign was plastered across every news bulletin, with critic after critic pulled out to complain, effectively, that we had no right to warn mothers and fathers of the dangers in their midst. For hour after hour that Sunday it looked like the odds were stacked against us. I phoned Deborah. 'Well, you knew it was going to be tough,' she said. 'Do what you know is right and never do what you believe is wrong.'

Readers have a habit of telling papers what they think in two ways: they vote with their feet and either buy us or shun us; or they write letters to the editor. On Monday the first e-mails came in. On Tuesday I arrived at the office early to check the post. It arrived in mailbag after mailbag, hundreds upon hundreds of letters from mothers and fathers pouring out support, many detailing their own long-suppressed horrors at the hands of paedophiles. The e-mails were the same. It was impossible to read some of them without weeping. If more inspiration were needed, this was it.

Deborah phoned; she knew I had been waiting for the post. 'Well?'

I could hardly answer, but I didn't need to. She understood.

Recently the *News of the World* missed out on a great story and, even more irritating, the interview went to a rival paper. Great stories are the lifeblood of all newspapers and I was deeply depressed. To rub salt in the wound, news of their exclusive scoop was all over television and radio.

But it wasn't long before Deborah was on the telephone. 'Why didn't you get the story?' she asked. 'Not like you to lose out. I hope you're going to come back with something better next weekend.'

Another lesson from Deborah. Never dwell too long on a failure. Learn from the mistake, pick yourself up and do even better.

Everyone who meets Deborah feels the same. There's something quite extraordinary about this lady. Certainly, I've never met anyone with such kindness and generosity of spirit.

When my friend Sarah Brown asked me to write this Media introduction, I was at first uncertain. Again, I sought Deborah's advice. 'You just can't say no to Sarah,' she said simply.

Deborah and I have known each other a long time and I know I'm very lucky to have her in my life. I can only hope you all find that special person who'll spur you on to realise your dreams.

So back to my dedication. For Deborah, my mother. Thank you.

* * *

Dawn Airey
Managing Director, Sky Networks

I have worked in television for 18 years. I first joined Central TV as a Management Trainee in 1985, in 1986 I was appointed Channel 4 Liaison Officer, and a year later Associate Producer of *Classmates*. In 1988, I became Controller of Programme Planning, and the next year joined the Central Broadcasting Board as Director of Programme Planning.

In 1993, I was appointed ITV's first Controller of Network Children's and Daytime Programmes, in 1994 Channel 4's Controller of Arts & Entertainment, and in 1996 Director of Programmes for the new Channel 5 which went on air on 30 March 1997. I became the Chief Executive of Channel 5 in October 2000, and then moved to Sky Networks as Managing Director in 2003.

Andy Allan, Director of Programmes at Central TV, appointed me as a graduate trainee. Throughout my nine years at Central, he was my mentor. His advice was simple, and I have followed it throughout my career. He told me to enjoy what I did; never forget working in television is a privilege; always be enthusiastic and sincere; don't give up if tasks are difficult, just roll up your sleeves and keep going and always employ the best people around you. This was just copper-bottomed advice that has proved invaluable time and time again.

MY ADVICE: *Follow exactly the same advice as Andy Allan gave to me.*

Christiane Amanpour
Journalist

I am CNN's Chief International Correspondent and I am based in London. I have reported on most crises from many of the world's hotspots including Afghanistan, Bosnia, Iran, Israel, Pakistan and Somalia. I have interviewed a wide range of people from Jordan's King Abdullah to Hillary Rodham Clinton to President Musharraf during the war against Afghanistan. I have been fortunate to receive a number of awards for journalism for my work

I was at school in England and then returned to Iran with a plan to go to medical school. The Iranian revolution of 1979 turned life upside down for all my family and friends, and I returned to England, took up a place at a small journalism college on Fleet Street in London. I then went to finish my education at the University of Rhode Island in the United States, and got a job as an assistant on the foreign desk of the then new cable station CNN in Atlanta. After a period of time, I moved up from assistant to writer, then senior writer and then finally landed a foreign assignment to Germany. The timing was such that I landed at the time of the Gulf War and soon found myself reporting from the front line. As a journalist I still work for CNN and work on foreign assignments around the world.

My earliest inspiration came from my horse-back riding teacher. His name was Colonel Shaki and ever since I started riding at the age of five, he taught me courage, perseverance, hard work and how to endure pain! Every time my horse threw me off Colonel Shaki picked me up and plonked me back on again. This was an invaluable lesson for life, and when it came to starting out in my career I used the discipline I had absorbed to work very very hard, rise up the ladder at CNN and achieve my goal of becoming a war correspondent. Colonel Shaki taught me to reach for the stars and importantly, to get there by working hard, learning from mistakes and having the commitment and courage of my convictions always to persevere despite setbacks and disappointments.

MY ADVICE: *My advice is to find something you love doing, set your eyes on the prize and don't give up until you get there. It will be so rewarding when you do.*

Jackie Ashley
Journalist

I have worked as a political interviewer and columnist for the *Guardian* newspaper since January 2002. I am also a freelance broadcaster making regular appearances on programmes such as *The Week in Westminster, The Talk Show* for BBC4 and *Powerhouse* for Channel 4.

After school in Epsom, I went to St Anne's College, Oxford and joined the BBC News Trainee programme after I graduated. I then worked as a reporter and producer for *Newsnight* for five years, then moved to become Political Correspondent for ITN for 12 years. I became the Political Editor of the *New Statesman* magazine in 2000 working there for two years before moving to the *Guardian*.

I have three inspirations: my father, Jack Ashley, a former Labour MP; my English teacher, Kathryn Huggett, and Harriet Harman MP. My father gave me a love of politics and current affairs, and, as a campaigning MP who often dealt with the media, an insight into how newspapers and television worked. My English teacher conveyed her enthusiasm for words and for language. Harriet Harman taught me that women can play an important part in the workplace, even with children, and encouraged me to fight for part-time work and job-shares during the years that my children were very young. Without any one of these three inspirations, I would probably not have pursued a career in journalism, and certainly would not still be here now.

MY ADVICE: *Don't be afraid to pick up the phone and ask to speak to* *people who may be able to help. Everyone remembers their first years in a new career and are usually happy to share experiences and suggest ways forward. Be persistent, and, in the early years at least, be prepared for long and gruelling hours! Stick around in August, when everyone else is on holiday – there are lots of opportunities to show what you can do then.*

Lisa Aziz
Broadcaster, Sky News Presenter

I am currently one of the main anchors at Sky News and also present documentaries for BBC2. I started my television career with BBC Television West, moving on in 1985 to co-present HTV's award-winning current affairs programme, *The West This Week*. In 1988 I moved to the breakfast news programme *TV-AM* as a reporter, becoming the main daily news presenter by 1989. After *TV-AM*, I worked with BBC World Service TV, *Financial Times* Business Daily TV and NBC Super Channel before joining Sky News ten years ago. I also work all over the world as a corporate presenter for multinational companies.

I feel honoured, privileged and flattered to have had 'visionary' bosses throughout my career who were all willing to give me a chance regardless of any academic abilities or huge experience. One man, my boss at *TV-AM*, Bruce Gyngell, was my guiding light throughout. From the day he hired me as main newscaster – he told me to push myself further and not to be afraid of 'jumping in at the deep end'. He became a great personal friend and my greatest 'fan'.

I felt that, knowing that I had the backing and support of such a man and boss, anything was possible. He instilled great confidence in me and taught me to have presence on screen. He was known to be quite 'wacky' and 'offbeat' but he inspired great loyalty because he was so different. Sadly he died a couple of years ago. I miss him greatly.

MY ADVICE: *The media is a very, very different animal now – it's horrendously tough and competitive. I fear for all those young people emerging from higher education with media degrees as there are only limited jobs actually available in the business. Choose your media course wisely and don't be put off at the first sign of rejection. Keep on trying, keep getting work experience and keep on applying!*

Floella Benjamin OBE
Broadcaster

One of six children, I was born in Trinidad but was brought up in England. After leaving school I spent a short time working for a bank, but this didn't suit my personality and I soon found my way into the theatre. I appeared in several West End shows, and then moved to television drama. Then fate took a hand and I found my place as a presenter of the BBC's legendary children's programmes, *Playschool* and *Playaway*. Since then I have appeared in drama, comedy, current affairs and magazine programmes and in films, pantomines and on radio. I have written books and scripts, and have set up my own production company with my husband Keith Taylor. We have produced hundreds of programmes for the audience I love best: children. I also sit on many boards and charity and advisory committees, including a role as Vice-President for NCH Action for Children, and have run the London Marathon four times, raising money for Barnado's and the Sickle Cell Society.

The main inspiration in my life has been my mother who told me every day during my school years that education was my passport to a successful life. She instilled confidence in me and my five brothers and sisters. In my working career Cynthia Felgate, the Producer of *Playschool*, was my mentor. She made me aware of how to communicate to an audience, and especially how to see things from the child's point of view. This enabled me to approach things as though I was seeing them for the first time and to have empathy with others. It also taught me not to be afraid to try things I'd never done before even though I might make mistakes. I just had to learn from them.

MY ADVICE: *Don't ever compromise yourself. Believe and have confidence. Study hard and you will reap the benefits long term. Keep the faith and don't lose your sense of humour.*

John Bird
Founder, *The Big Issue*

Frederick Rosskelly was a journalist on the *West Briton* newspaper in Truro, Cornwall in 1934. He was a club reporter. Later he became a poet, writer and social activist, joining the Labour Party in the 1940s.

I met him when I was 21 and he was 50. He was an inspiration. Married with three children, he inspired youth and the uninformed in a way that was a joy.

Alas he died recently at the age of 83, but was active and game to the last.

MY ADVICE: *Look around for people you can learn from; the young, the old, the rich, the poor; those at the top and those at the bottom.*

Leslie Bunder
Co-founder, Publisher and Editor-in-Chief, Jewish Media Trust and Founder of Park Royal Media

Over the past ten years, I have worked in new media and online publishing for a number of leading organisations including the BBC, Teletext and InfoSpace in roles ranging from journalist and reporter to project manager. With all the skills I acquired, I have, since 2002, focused on building up my own media ventures in print and online. Like many, I have a desire and thirst to see my own ideas developed and the only way to do this is to branch out on my own and employ the skills and talents of others to help make the ideas a reality. This is being achieved with the help of my wife, as well as working with some very talented and ambitious people who also share the same thirst for success.

Over the past five years, I have built up jewish.co.uk and jewish.net into leading independent Jewish-focused websites and now they form part of the Jewish Media Trust, a venture in which I will also be looking to branch out into other media outlets including print. As well as the Jewish Media Trust, I am a founding partner of Park Royal Media which develops and publishes print and online ventures in niche-focused areas both aimed at business-to-business as well as consumer.

When not busy developing the Jewish Media Trust and Park Royal Media, I, along with my wife Caroline, write and develop Jewish comedy ideas and scripts for TV and radio and hope one day to write a Hollywood blockbuster.

What inspired me? The determination of turning rejection into something positive. Many people will try and put you down; many people who have fewer skills than you will try and make it difficult for you to do well. So it is always a question of getting someone to give you a break. Somebody you can trust and somebody who knows they can trust you and be able to spot your potential which will not only help them, but also help you at the same time.

The big break for me was in 1994 when I saw the potential of the Internet and new media but didn't have any connections or ideas on how to get into it. I have always been a journalist writing about technology, but had been on the fringes of success, rather like a footballer being in division three and knowing they have the ability to make it to the premier league.

So, I thought, how can I move forward as a journalist? I knew that Teletext (on ITV and Channel 4) was a leading service, so decided 'on spec' to contact the editor of the service, Graham Lovelace. I sent Graham a fax asking, 'Can you give me a break?' And he did. Graham is a very switched-on person who has a wonderful knowledge of new media and the Internet and the potential it offers. I spent five great years working at Teletext and working with Graham and in this time, Graham gave me the opportunity as a journalist not only to write about the subject of new media and Internet, but also to play a part in the development of the Internet in the UK.

Working with Graham also taught me some great skills and insight into being a better journalist. From better keeping of notes and files to areas such as getting more out of interviews I did with people.

Through this, I learnt much about the Internet and in time other associated areas such as digital television. And importantly for me, all these skills could then be applied to my other ventures which included jewish.co.uk and jewish.net and more recently, *Project Berg*, a Jewish lifestyle and entertainment magazine for 20–40-year-olds.

Without Graham taking me on at Teletext, I wouldn't have been able to get involved in as much as I have done. And I wouldn't have been able to gain access to all the information and knowledge that I now have. Graham gave me my first real break and that has now given me the opportunity to progress further.

MY ADVICE: *Have confidence in yourself. Don't be afraid of rejection. Learn from rejection and, indeed, learn from others. Follow your dreams, and don't let others put you down. If you know what you are talking about, others will also want to know and share in your knowledge. And above all be respectful to others and never ever make any assumptions about anything. Enjoy your work, enjoy life, and share.*

Bill Campbell
Managing Director, Mainstream Publishing

I am Managing Director of Mainstream Publishing, one of the few independent publishing houses in the UK based in Edinburgh. I trained and worked originally as a journalist and writer. I started in publishing as the Publications Manager at Edinburgh University Student Publications from 1975-78 before setting up Mainstream Publishing in 1978.

What inspires you as a young person is not so much one person as one, hopefully communal, idea. As a working class kid in the 1950s, I was fortunate to be open (or opened) to so many new ideas – musically, socially and politically. I had Cuba, CND, the assassination of JFK, the Beatles, a Labour Government and, most importantly, the realisation that I really could play a part in this society and in my own destiny. Various teachers, lecturers and friends were very important in shaping my character and my beliefs, but none more so than the written word and a good friend, or friends, to discuss it with.

MY ADVICE: *From Dickens and Dostoevsky to Lenin and Lennon, books and ideas are the key to your life. Read them, debate them and learn that the world is within your grasp. Nothing is unattainable!*

Peter Cox
Editor, *Daily Record*

I started as Assistant Night Editor on the *Sun* in 1983. I was promoted to Assistant Editor and then worked as Deputy Editor of the *New York Post*. I came back to the UK to join the *Daily Mirror* as Executive Editor, moving to Scotland as Deputy Editor of the *Daily Record*, then Editor of the *Sunday Mail* (the *Daily Record's* sister paper). I became Editor of the *Daily Record*, Scotland's bestselling tabloid, in the year 2000.

Roy Pittilla, doyen of the Fleet Street night editors inspired me. He worked both on the *Daily Mirror* and the *Sun*, where I met him. He taught me that every word in tabloid journalism counts; that a youngster from the provinces can night-edit a national newspaper; and that the only way to wake up a dozing copy-taster is by pouring a cup of coffee on his or her head.

Today I make every word count, I edit a national newspaper and I always keep a cup of coffee handy!

MY ADVICE: *You must be different from the pack and have total self-belief, or to put it in tabloidese: Be An Ego-Driven Adrenalin Junkie.*

Susan Crosland
Author and Freelance Journalist

With virtually no experience in journalism, I moved to England, desperate for a job. John Junor, famous Editor of the *Sunday Express*, then Britain's most influential broadsheet, was, at 41, 'The Old Monster' to his staff. I wrote to him (always go to the top) asking to see him to discuss writing features from an American viewpoint. Happily, Junor wasn't interested in CVs: he made judgements by instinct. He saw me and sized me up. A trial feature was commissioned and published. Six days later I was on the staff as Susan Barnes. Under Junor's guidance, I began my career of interviewing public figures.

MY ADVICE: *You need enterprise and good luck; neither is enough alone.*

Paul Dacre
Editor-in-Chief, *Daily Mail*, *Mail on Sunday*, *Evening Standard*, *Metro*

As well as being Editor-in-Chief of our group, I have been Editor of the *Daily Mail* for ten years and before that was Editor of the *Evening Standard* for two years. I started in journalism as a reporter and then feature writer on the *Daily Express* which appointed me New York correspondent at the age of 26. Subsequently I joined the *Daily Mail* as American Bureau Chief, returning eventually to London where, over the next few years, I was in turn News Editor, Foreign Editor and Features Editor. I can honestly say there are very few jobs on the paper I haven't done and very few days in my career when I haven't worked a 12-hour day.

My inspiration was, as a ten-year-old, seeing the glorious red, black and gold blazer belonging to a friend's brother. He went to a North London direct grant school called University College, and from that moment I knew I had to go. In those days the State gave scholarships to schools like UCS and I remember at my interview having to read out an essay I'd written on 'The Day That Everything Went Wrong'. The headmaster, a man called Mr Vogel, seemed to find what I'd written enormously funny and he gave me one of their coveted places.

A devoted Christian and lover of the classics, Mr Vogel taught me Latin. In those days, before adolescence wreaked its havoc, I was a terrible swot and would write long essays on classical Rome and Greece in my holidays. God knows where he found the patience, but Mr Vogel would mark them and talk them through with me, gently teaching and correcting as he went. He was possessed of divine patience and through Latin taught me, I believe, the power of clear and simple thinking – something I find lacking in many young journalists today. He also believed in absolute standards of right and wrong, combined with enormous compassion, and that everybody in the school, whatever their intelligence, had something to offer society.

Some years ago I read that, in retirement, he had joined the Church. I wrote a long letter to him to say how much he had influenced my life but, in the end, felt too embarrassed to send it.

MY ADVICE: *I'm afraid all the media studies courses in the world won't help if you don't have an instinct for journalism. If you do have that instinct and love words, then go for broke but accept that there will be a lot of disappointment and rejection on the way. Once you have made it on to a newspaper, never cease striving for perfection but remember, when you believe* *you have achieved it, you have become complacent. If you become an executive, never bear a grudge against anyone. And if you are lucky enough to become an editor (which, actually, is a very lonely job) never forget that you're finished if you believe yourself to be more important than your product – and that all too many people who befriend you do so because they want to get something IN your paper – or, more pertinently, keep it OUT.*

Greg Dyke
Director General, BBC

Currently in charge of the BBC, I started in television at the age of 30 as a researcher in current affairs. In between I was a Producer, Programme Editor, Director of Programmes and Chief Executive at a range of different television companies.

Having been a failure at school, and only going to university in my mid-twenties I was driven by a desire to achieve in my field. My inspiration was the desire to overcome things I found difficult. However, once I had overcome a particular challenge, I was always keen to take on a new one, to test myself once again. I was inspired by Professor John Kotter who I met in 1989 at Harvard Business School. He convinced me that leadership was more important than management. The effect Kotter had was to give me the confidence to simply be myself and not to ape the language and actions of traditional management.

MY ADVICE: *Be determined, never give up, have good ideas. Treat people you work for, with, or who work for you with dignity and respect. Be a real person.*

Sir David Frost OBE
Television and Film Producer and Presenter, *Breakfast with Frost*

Only one person comes to mind who can be considered a mentor in my life: Geoff Cooksey. He was my English teacher from the time I turned 15 until I was 18.

In 1954, I had just moved to a new school because my father was a Methodist minister and we travelled a lot. Mr Cooksey was a remarkable human being whom I encountered at this very formative time of life. He ignited my interest in words as well as my passion for them. He made words irresistible to me.

One particular assignment comes to mind. Mr Cooksey was concerned about the difference between a 'loaded' article and an accurate one, between fiction and the truth. For that reason he told us to read two newspapers instead of one, so we could learn to decipher this difference. He taught us to investigate in order to find the truth, and not to be afraid to question what was going on or what was being said.

When the 1956 war over the Suez Canal occurred, it caused great turmoil throughout the country. England, France and Israel attacked Egypt after its President, Gamal Nasser, nationalised the Suez Canal. This was the beginning of a great division in England between those who supported the Suez invasion and those who were opposed. At this time, Mr Cooksey had us reading the *Observer*, a Sunday newspaper, so that we could keep informed of the current situation. We were urged to observe and to heed the great changes that were only just beginning to shape England at that time. This was happening when it was still run by the 'old school' style of rule – when our leaders insisted that their way of operating was best and proper. Also, about this time Mr Cooksey took us to see a play by the brilliant playwright, John Osborne. That play was called *Look Back in Anger* and it was staged at the Royal Court Theatre in London. The main character was Jimmy Porter, about whom the phrase 'angry young man' was originated.

This play, and Mr Cooksey, taught me to be more aware of the outside world, to observe the changes that were now going on in the country and to question the nature of things, particularly words. He also taught me how to relate what I was learning in English class, concerning literature and words, to the world around me. He explained that English is not just an important subject to which I must pay attention, but that the lessons I learned would serve as paradigms for life experiences.

My Cooksey gave me a new view of the future. He was an inspiring man who offered valuable lessons about the world. He taught me not to be afraid of change, but to confront it head-on and look past an initial impression. His teachings were instrumental because they inspired me to think for myself. He helped me to see the sheer pleasure in words and to learn from them. And he stimulated my mind. He was truly my mentor.

Philip Graf
Chief Executive, Trinity Mirror plc

My first inspiration was Jack Sayers who was editor of the *Belfast Telegraph* in the 1960s. Northern Ireland was at the beginning of its long and painful road of the last 30 years or so. As Editor, he established the paper as a champion of non-sectarian unionism and sought to lead the Unionist community into a much more open relationship with the Nationalist community and Northern Ireland's southern neighbours.

He showed me the importance of newspapers and the value of editors taking a stand, however difficult or unpopular it might be at times.

I enjoyed and respected the newspaper so much that I simply wanted to have the chance to be involved in running a newspaper or newspapers like it.

I worked with Thomson Regional Newspapers for 13 years (including six years with the *Belfast Telegraph*), and then became Assistant Managing Director for the *Liverpool Daily Post and Echo*, part of Trinity International Holdings, moving on to become Corporate Development Director of the Group, and then Chief Executive. I was appointed Chief Executive of Trinity Mirror plc in 1999.

MY ADVICE: *Show you can make a difference, not simply that you have a relevant academic record. Show that you can write, you can take responsibility, or that you can create something new.*

Dylan Jones
Editor, British *GQ* Magazine

Before editing *GQ*, I was an Editor at *i-D* magazine, the *Face* and *Arena*. I also ran *Arena Homme Plus*, and was Senior Editor at the *Sunday Times* and the *Observer*. I won the BSME Magazine Editor of the Year Award for *Arena* in 1993 and again for *GQ* in 2001.

I was initially inspired by a girlfriend of mine who worked at the BBC: Helen Gallacher. She encouraged me to start writing, so I did, immediately. Before that I had been a rather unsuccessful photographer, but as soon as I started to write I fell in love with it. The first person to give me a break was the editor of *i-D*, Terry Jones. Within a year I was editing the magazine. Terry taught me that anything is possible. But he encouraged me to be ambitious in my aspirations. So I was.

MY ADVICE: *Approach everyone until you get a job, and when you do, work harder than everyone else. Be nice, be eager, be positive. If someone asks you to do something, never ever tell them it can't be done. And never stop learning.*

Diane Louise Jordan
TV and Radio Presenter and Motivational Speaker

My television and radio career began back in January 1990 when I became the first black presenter on *Blue Peter*. I am currently a regular face on *Songs of Praise*. However, over the last 12 years I have presented such a variety of programmes that I've been described as 'a presenter across boundaries'! I also work closely with a number of charities, all of which reflect issues close to my heart. I am a Vice President of NCH and Patron of many other organisations. I was asked to sit on the *Diana, Princess of Wales Memorial Committee*, and am also very proud to be one of the trustees for the BBC's long-running and hugely successful *Children In Need Appeal*. My underlying passion to encourage, motivate and inspire all people to be the best they can possibly be, coupled with the many requests to speak at corporate and charity events, inspired *me* to launch my corporate speaking company, *Chronicle21*.

My career in the media can be traced back to a schoolmate's challenge to apply for drama school. At the time I was hugely self-conscious and uncomfortable with the thought of even reading out loud in class! So the prospect of a career reliant on speaking publicly was near anathema to me! However, always being one to rise to a challenge, my acceptance eventually resulted in constant work as a professional actress for seven years before joining *Blue Peter*.

For me, relationship is the key to success, both in life and work. There have been some remarkable relationships in my life that have had and continue to have a significant impact on me. My 16-year-old daughter inspires me – when I'm getting flustered about work this relationship reminds me what my true priorities are. I have also always known the unconditional love of my parents – their utter belief in me as a person, regardless of merit, has underpinned my sense of self-worth. My late grandfather was a very wise man whose steady principles and strong values are imprinted on my heart. For example, my determination to do my best and 'see things through' is a principle based on these wise words imparted from him – 'No matter what you do, whether you're running the country or cleaning it, always do it with at least 100 per cent of your ability.'

There's a saying that 'behind every successful man is a good woman'. Well I believe that behind every successful and fulfilled person is an inspiring teacher. My inspiring teacher is Mrs Morton who believed in me when I didn't even believe in myself. She was tough, exacting and fearsome. She expected high results from her pupils, and worked with and encouraged us to achieve them – which with her kind of support, we did.

A less obvious source of inspiration came in the form of 'advice' from my drama school course director. On leaving college he praised my acting ability but assured me that acting work for me would be thin on the ground: he reasoned that my skin colour would prevent me being cast in any major Shakespearean role; my (too) youthful looks would hinder a convincing portrayal of any leading lady; television would also be elusive as I am five inches shorter than the apparent standard five-foot-five required for that particular medium. Not exactly encouraging advice (!), but rather than being defeated I decided to challenge it – to test if these genetic characteristics were indeed obstacles to my future success. Upon graduation, although I hadn't had the opportunity to fully test all the alleged obstacles, I was the only student in my year to leave with a substantial acting contract and the all-important Equity card!

One of the most significant influences in my life is my best friend

Sue. She's seen me at my worst and has loved me through the difficult times. Ours is a friendship built on trust, respect, accountability and a commitment to stick at it for the long haul.

The greatest influence in my life is God – knowing how much He loves me, no matter what, is liberating!

MY ADVICE: *I am so often asked, 'How do I become a television presenter?' If I am honest, I really don't have a simple answer. However, I do believe that becoming a 'success' at anything involves beginning to know and accept who you are. Start with the inside out! I've learned that the most important thing in life is to VALUE yourself. We all have an intrinsic 'worth' – something special about us, something valuable to offer – to make a difference to the world. Approach all you do with integrity and tenacity; have the courage to live your dreams.*

Mark Leishman
Head of Public Policy, BBC Nations and Regions

I started out as a press assistant for the National Trust for Scotland, and then took on various posts including police training in Kent. Next, I worked for three years at the United News Service in Edinburgh learning the job of a press reporter. Since then, I have worked as Reporter and News Editor with a local newspaper and local radio, a national newspaper and as a presenter on *Good Morning Scotland*, the flagship radio news programme.

I joined the BBC in 1995 as Head of Corporate Affairs and then Secretary and Head of Public Policy for BBC Scotland, working at an interesting time with the establishment of the Scottish Parliament. I was appointed Head of Public Policy for BBC Nations and Regions in 2002 where, amongst other things, I oversee relationships with the devolved institutions across the UK.

Back when I first started work, George Millar was the owner of the press agency United News where he offered me an apprenticeship in journalism. Although unpaid, it provided essential experience in court and council reporting. He also taught me how to make contacts and to develop relationships with politicians. Although he is now dead, his name is legendary in Scottish journalism.

One of the most significant lessons from George Millar was about the importance of professional integrity. Although he was steeped in a rough, bruising profession he always urged truth, accuracy and respect for those who were being written about. He used to say to me, 'Never lie about anything. Cultivate a reputation for straight talking and it will take you a long way.' I've tried to stick by it in journalism and in management.

MY ADVICE: *Play straight and work hard at building lasting relationships. Journalism is in many respects devalued and needs good people whose only agenda is to tell the truth about public life.*

Catherine MacLeod
Journalist/Political Editor of the *Herald*

I am the first woman to be political editor of the *Herald*, a long-established Scottish newspaper. I did not have a career plan, and my career followed a rather haphazard course. After leaving Edinburgh University I edited a magazine in the Highlands before working on the *Press & Journal* in Aberdeen. In the eighties I worked in the BBC in Scotland before moving south to join my husband. After a spell busily freelancing in London, I worked for Grampian television on a part-time basis, an almost ideal arrangement when my children were young – a good salary, parliamentary holidays, and a three-day week.

Now I have to juggle constantly my work and home commitments, but a supportive husband and understanding children make it possible.

I have been incredibly fortunate to meet many people who influenced me and broadened my horizons. Probably the first woman was Morag MacDonald, my primary seven teacher in Mallaig school. She passed on her passion for literature and reading, and greatly encouraged me to read books and work hard. Eddie Hutcheon, my English teacher in Inverness Royal Academy, was another inspirational teacher, whose love of his subject made his classes a pleasure.

James Grassie, my first boss in the Highlands and Islands Development Board, was an exemplary manager – he was imaginative, kind, encouraging, and wise. Never dogmatic, he empowered his staff, extended their experience, and produced wonderful work.

The West Highland Free Press, and the ideals for which it stood, was incredibly important. The journalism was courageous, of a very high standard, often funny and a beacon of decency.

The *Guardian*'s women's page was another great inspiration – women like Jill Tweedie and Polly Toynbee bravely pushing out the boundaries.

My mother, who was a teacher, impressed upon me the value of economic independence – when I was very young she rather shockingly told me that she lived with my father only because she liked him!

MY ADVICE: *Be confident and determined. Don't waste time, make up your mind what you want to do and go for it.*

David Mansfield
Chief Executive, Capital Radio plc

I was appointed Chief Executive of Capital Radio, the largest UK commercial radio group, in 1997. Prior to this, I was the Managing Director, having joined the company in 1993 as Commercial Director. I have spent over 20 years in media, starting my career as a Marketing Executive at Scottish Television and Grampian Sales in 1977. Following a number of management roles, I left in 1985 to join Thames Television as Marketing Controller. At Thames, I became responsible, as Deputy Director of Sales and Marketing, for the day-to-day sales operation of the company until leaving to join Capital Radio.

Since 1993, Capital Radio has expanded its operation from two to twenty analogue radio licences and has over eight million listeners. In preparation for the future transfer of radio broadcasting from analogue to digital, Capital has significantly invested in digital radio. Capital Radio is now a leading digital radio broadcaster owning a network of 42 digital licences in all major UK conurbations, including one national licence.

Twenty-five years ago, before my first media job, I began as a trainee confectionery salesman for Terry's of York. In the early months I succeeded in being the worst performer in the region. I was ready to give up. Luckily I gained a new manager, Mike Orchard, who trained me, gave me confidence and helped me use my fear of failure as a positive force. I became one of their most successful representatives and it launched my selling career in media.

Lack of self-belief and fear of failure hold many people back from realising their true potential. Mike was one of several people who taught me how to move forward.

MY ADVICE: *Persistence and determination triumph*!

Terry Mansfield CBE
President and CEO, The National Magazine Company

When I left school at 16, I began my career with London advertising agencies and then served two years in the RAF, being stationed on Christmas Island in the Pacific. When I returned I worked in advertising sales for a number of magazines. I then joined *Queen* magazine as Senior Sales Representative and went on to become Advertisement Manager there. I joined The National Magazine Company in 1969 as Advertisement Manager on *Harpers & Queen*. I moved up to Associate Publisher, then Advertisement Director, and then Publisher. In 1980 I became the Deputy Managing Director of The National Magazine Company, then Managing Director two years later where, as well as *Harpers & Queen*, our magazine titles include *Cosmopolitan, Company, She, Zest, Esquire, Good Housekeeping, Prima* and *You & Your Wedding*. In 1985 I also became Chairman of COMAG, the largest magazine distribution company in the UK. Today I am President and CEO of The National Magazine Company and Vice President of our parent company, The Hearst Corporation.

There have been three people who have influenced my life dramatically outside of my own family. The first is Stephen Raven of DH Brocklesby Advertising who, when I was just 16 in 1954, said, 'As you are the only one who has applied for the job, I will give you a chance, but if, at the end of the month, you are hopeless, you will have to go!' And that was the beginning.

The second was Jocelyn Stevens who, at that time, was the proprietor of *Queen* magazine. He asked me at an interview, 'Have you ever been to school, as I like to employ people who have been to school at least once!' It was Jocelyn who recognised I was not only good with people but had creativity in me, and that creativity he encouraged.

The third was the extraordinary Betty Kenward who, for 47 years, created Jennifer's Diary and we had a very close relationship. She always gave me this advice: 'Darling, you can lose your money, your relationships and your position, but what really counts in life are your contacts. Contacts constantly change and without them you can never get going again.' Such sound advice that has stayed with me and I use it daily.

MY ADVICE: *Develop and look after your own contacts.*

Sir Trevor McDonald OBE
ITN Newscaster

One of my biggest slices of good fortune was to meet, even before I left college, a man who was programme manager of a radio station which I hoped to join and from where I hoped to launch myself into the big and exciting world of journalism. The man was Ken Gordon and he did everything to assist me. In fact he did much better than that. Whenever I had a very limited vision of what was possible he saw much more clearly what I could do and not only encouraged but pushed me into doing it.

My first big break with him was when I was elected to cover an important political conference in London, an assignment the like of which none of my colleagues, much higher up than me, ever got close to. I learned how formidable the competition was for this assignment but Ken Gordon put his faith in me and I managed to survive. I probably did a little better than that because I befriended one of the members of the Trinidad delegation and got my first journalistic scoop.

Ken Gordon didn't stop there. He pushed me into learning a variety of media disciplines. So not only did I read the news on radio but I was for a time a disc jockey, and a commentator at special events like the opening of Parliament and the broadcasting of sporting events like cricket, football, tennis, horse-riding and, most extraordinarily, water polo. I shall never forget when I went to do my first horse-riding broadcast, it was the first time I had ever been near a track. I came to be quite competent at it.

Ken Gordon is one of those people – I see him still today on my visits to the West Indies – blessed with the vision of what young people need to do to succeed. He inspired me and I have absolutely no hesitation in saying that it made me.

MY ADVICE: *My advice to anyone seeking a career in the media or in any other profession is to embrace the help offered by others, of course, but to remember there can be no substitute for hard work and individual effort. In the end how well you do in any job depends on the work you put into it. Aim to reach the top; never settle for mediocrity and never sell yourself short.*

Piers Morgan
Editor, *The Mirror*

To some, Kelvin Mackenzie is a monster, to others a hero. To me, he's just Kelvin. A raging, cackling, mischievous, passionate tornado of a man who defies all convention or rational explanation.

I worked for him on the *Sun* for five years from the age of 23 to 28, and can honestly describe it as the most exhilarating, despairing, fascinating, terrifying, stimulating and inspiring time of my life.

Kelvin was, and is, a whirlwind of energy and ideas – a creative violent force that barely sleeps, and tolerates mediocrity as a leopard tolerates a nosy antelope.

Yes, he could be brutal – I still have nightmares of his eye-bulging, neck-popping, ball-breaking bollockings over minor transgressions.

But he was a genius too, producing some of the most anarchic, hilarious newspapers this country's ever seen.

If you had talent, balls, a developed sense of humour, and a ferocious work ethic then he invested his time and brilliance in you. Wasters, the weak and the humourless were dismissed to the dustbins of Wapping.

When I left to be editor of the *News of the World* at 28, Kelvin said simply: 'Don't get drunk during the week, you can't edit on a hangover, and if you get in the s★★t, get out of it a million miles an hour.' Both sound pieces of advice.

He remains a loyal, wise, amusing and occasionally desperately dangerous mentor.

Kelvin taught me that living on the edge is more fun, that loyalty has to be earned, that apathy is the enemy – and that there is nothing more important in business than good people and good ideas.

MY ADVICE: *My advice to wannabee journalists is to work hard, play hard, and constantly seek better ideas.*

Cristina Odone
Deputy Editor, New Statesman

I am the Deputy Editor of the *New Statesman* weekly current affairs and arts magazine and a columnist on the *Observer* newspaper. I contribute regularly to *Thought For the Day* on BBC Radio 4 and frequently broadcast on television and radio. Previously I was the Editor of the *Catholic Herald* from 1990–94.

The words 'Work hard, and you can do anything', spoken in a French accent, were the leitmotif during my most formative years. They were repeated, day-in, day-out, by my sixth form French teacher, Andrée McCallum – a small, red-cheeked beacon of vitality who used to stride up and down the classroom, hands waving to emphasise her point. And the point was always the same – no challenge was too big, no task too arduous for her students. 'A' Levels? 'A cinch.' Oxbridge? 'A doddle.' And so forth. In the end her tremendous faith in us all proved infectious: we began to believe that, from prescribed texts at school to news reporting in Fleet Street – anything was, indeed, possible.

MY ADVICE: *Find something you're passionate about. Immerse yourself in it. Become an expert in at least one area of this subject and then talk about it to everyone.*

Jeremy Paxman
Journalist and Broadcaster

I started out by writing the occasional essay or review for school magazines, then editing the university newspaper. For three years, I was based in Northern Ireland where I covered the Troubles for the BBC. I then became a roving reporter for the *Tonight* programme, followed by five years as a reporter on *Panorama*, where assignments took me to Beirut, Uganda, Zimbabwe and Central America.

I learnt the craft of studio presenting by anchoring *Breakfast Time*, and since then I've been presenting *Newsnight, University Challenge* and for several years I presented *Start the Week* on Radio Four.

It is really only by looking back that you can see a pattern to your life. I had no idea how things would turn out when I was at school. I was a very rebellious teenager, and think that if my housemaster at school, Tony Leng, had not had the wisdom to see beyond my behaviour, I'd have drifted nowhere.

I learned that if you are persuasive enough, you can make people change their minds. But to be persuasive, you need to think before speaking.

MY ADVICE: *The world is an immensely complicated place. But it is run by human beings. Never be afraid to ask the question 'Why are things like this?'*

Raphael Rowe
Senior Broadcast Journalist, BBC Radio 4 *Today* *Programme*

If you had said to me just over two years ago, 'You're going to be a reporter on the BBC's flagship news and current affairs programme' I would have smirked, shaken my head and walked off. You see, I was in prison just over two years ago. I had been there for 12 years and had no date for release. I was a wrongly convicted prisoner. That was eventually acknowledged by the Court of Appeal in July 2000. On that day my convictions were quashed and I was set free. I was freed with a grant of £47 and nothing else.

After a year of adjusting to society, in June 2001 I met the person that helped transform my life. His name was Rod Liddle, then

Editor of the Radio 4 News and Current Affairs programme, *Today*. After a brief conversation he offered me a four-month contract on his programme as a producer/reporter. He arranged for me to attend some intense training courses, helped guide me through the steps to becoming a reporter and gave me the self-belief that I would be a good reporter. At the end of my four-month contract he offered me another six-month contract and now I have a permanent job as a senior broadcast journalist for the BBC. I did not attend college or university and have very few qualifications.

MY ADVICE: *Be positive and be yourself. Don't be afraid to ask questions even if you expect the answer to be 'No', because you will never know unless you ask.*

John Sergeant
Political Editor, ITN

I have been a professional broadcaster for more than 30 years. I started as a reporter on the *Liverpool Echo*.

Robert Bolt was one of the most successful British playwrights of modern times. He wrote *A Man for All Seasons* and a host of West End hits, but his greatest triumphs were in the cinema: he was responsible for the screenplays for two of the most highly regarded films of all time: *Lawrence of Arabia* and *Dr Zhivago*. He was also my English teacher. He taught me that you could achieve real success, however difficult your circumstances seemed to be. My parents had separated, and I was only at Millfield, a very expensive private school in Somerset, because my father taught there. He paid £100 a year for me to attend.

In the year that Robert Bolt taught me he also became famous for a play called *Flowering Cherry*. He was rigorous and obsessive. When I wrote, 'the war clouds were gathering' in my first piece of work, at the age of 13, he put a line through it. 'That's a cliché,' he growled. Only years later did he admit that he had been a little harsh. The most important lesson was that writing is a craft, which you can perfect with practice; and even writing comedy should not have to wait until you are in the right mood. After more than 30 years in journalism I am still trying to put that lesson into effect.

Jon Snow
Presenter, Channel 4 News

I started work as a reporter with LBC radio and, since 1976, have worked with ITN who make Channel 4 News. I have been the anchor of Channel 4 News since 1989. I am also the Chair of New Horizon Youth Centre since 1986, having worked there as its Director from 1970–73. I also work with a number of other charitable and arts organisations: I am Deputy Chair of the Media Trust, a Trustee of the Stephen Lawrence Trust, a Trustee of the National Gallery in London, and of Tate where I am Chair of the Tate Modern Council.

I was sent down from Liverpool University for demonstrating against the University's investments in South Africa, and so never finished my degree. I was introduced to Lord Longford by a friend of a friend. He needed a Director for a teenage project he has running for homeless young people in London: I was at a very low ebb and fairly traumatised by being sent down. Frank Longford believed in me, encouraged me, treated me as an equal and constantly expressed his belief that I would succeed and make something of my life. We remained friends for 30 years until he died.

MY ADVICE: *Believe in yourself. Know what you want and go for it. The media is a rare field in which your own personal commitment and drive can make the difference. Keep going and you will get there!*

Carole Stone
Radio Producer and Journalist

I left grammar school at 17, trained as a secretary at Southampton Technical College, and joined the local hospital broadcasting and debating society. I then joined BBC South as a secretary and went on to produce Radio 4's *Any Questions?* programme. When I left the BBC, I became the director of a small independent radio and television production company. Recently, I also published my book, *Networking: the Art of Making More Friends*.

For me my mentor was my mother. She was ever interested in other people – curious but not envious. She encouraged me to give my full attention and energy to whatever I set out to do. She made me understand that stretching myself to the full, and enjoying doing so, was more important than reaching the top. She suggested that I work towards becoming a journalist. Mama made me feel I could have a go at anything at all. I had the freedom to fail – that was learning. She told me, 'Take life by the scruff of the neck.' Her example proved to me that you can gain something from most experiences. It's your 'attitude' – how you cope with what life throws at you – that matters.

MY ADVICE: *Join organisations concerned with your profession – become an active member. Read newspapers, listen to radio, watch TV and then form your own opinions. Seize the moment and take a chance on a new direction. Make friends with a wide variety of people and be generous with your contacts.*

Parminder Vir
Television Producer/Cultural Diversity Adviser, Carlton Television

At Carlton Television I advise the Chief Executive, Clive Jones, on how to make the company more ethnically diverse. This is both in terms of the programmes we make and the people we employ. I also produce a variety of films, dramas and documentaries which are all vehicles for Black and Asian talent. I have worked with such talent as Meera Syal, Nina Wadia, Felix Dexter, Marcus Powell and Mandish Pendey.

Not long ago I was asked in an interview with *Eastern Eye* to name the person I admire most. I said Muhammad Ali. As a kid growing up in Southampton, aged ten or eleven, when he was boxing, he was the only real person who made me feel proud. He really made me feel as though nothing could defeat me and I would sit up late at night to watch whenever he was boxing. His inspiration guided my self-belief in my own perseverance and stamina, and my passion for what I do.

MY ADVICE: *Follow your passions, find your niche and steer your career. To succeed in the film and television industry, you have to be tenacious, deter-mined and develop the right attitude. You have to endure a lot of rejection, and simply move onto the next project and generate more ideas. It is essential, whatever you want to do – act, write, produce, direct, costume design, casting –*

*that you develop a wide range of contacts with people in other areas as you will
find all these different perspectives interesting and useful.*

Tina Weaver
Editor, *Sunday Mirror*

I edit the *Sunday Mirror* and oversee the *M* titles at the *Mirror*. I did
an NCTJ course to enter journalism. Worked at South West News,
a Bristol news agency, for 18 months before coming to Fleet Street
in late 1988.

I worked on the *People* for two to three years, and was their chief
reporter at the age of 24. I moved to the *Mirror* for a year and then
to *Today*. I won the Reporter of the Year award in 1993 and became
Features Editor. When it closed in 1995 I moved to the *Daily Mirror*
becoming Deputy Editor two years later in November 1997. I've
been Editor of the *Sunday Mirror* since April 2001.

It was old Fleet Street that first inspired me, the buy-ups, the cat
and mouse chases against your rivals, the bar room tales of boozed
up old hacks and even dodgy characters like monstrous Robert
Maxwell juddering menacingly through the news room. It was a
day of great characters, outrageous behaviour and an unbridled
hunger for breaking stories.

Two editors who were my greatest inspiration were Richard Stott,
who I worked for on three different papers, the *People*, *Mirror* and
Today over five years. He had huge conviction in his beliefs; he was
and is a great champion of the little person, and exposer of greed and
corruption. He was also a great believer in women in the business at
a time when female hacks were regularly consigned to the 'womb
trembler' interviews, or rubbish like being 'fired out of a circus
cannon in a gold bikini.' (Yes – I did tell the then news desk to stuff
it.) He became mentor and friend and is now a columnist for me!

In 1995 I got a call from Piers Morgan to work for him on the
Mirror when the *Today* newspaper was closed down, first as features
head then his deputy. He was motivating and hilarious and of course
there were many times I'd have happily strangled him. His advice
was actually quite sensible: 'Um, how are you going to defend that
on the *Ten O'Clock News*?' he'd call in from holiday and ask, when I

was trying to push through a particularly legally fraught splash.

MY ADVICE: *For any young people who are trying to get into the business, it is the most frustrating, rewarding and exhilarating job you can do. Stick with it, it's a hard old slog but worth it when you get there.*

Caroline Westbrook
Film and Entertainment Journalist and Co-Founder of Jewish Media Trust

I began my career in 1990 as a Staff Writer on the teenage title *TV HITS*, where I spent four years. In 1994 I joined the film magazine *Empire* as a Staff Writer, spending seven years there and moving up the ranks to Reviews Editor and News Editor before leaving in the summer of 2001 to pursue a freelance career. I am still a Contributing Editor to *Empire* and my work appears regularly in the magazine. I have also written for a string of publications and media outlets including *BBC News Online* and Ceefax, *BBC History Magazine*, *The Times*, *Eve*, *Web User* and others. I am co-founder (along with my husband Leslie Bunder) of the Jewish Media Trust which publishes the websites jewish.co.uk and jewish.net as well as *Project Berg*, a Jewish lifestyle magazine for 20–40-year-olds.

I have appeared on a number of TV and radio shows commenting on films and film-related issues, including *Liquid News*, *BBC London*, *ITV News*, *LBC* and *CNN*. I have authored two books on the actors Brad Pitt and Leonardo DiCaprio and am currently working on further projects with my husband, with whom I want to write a best-selling novel!

Like the majority of teenagers in the 1980s, I was an avid reader of the music magazine *Smash Hits*, which I admired greatly for its irreverency and sense of humour. At the time, I didn't want to work anywhere else.

As it happened, I didn't make it to *Smash Hits* but to *TV HITS*, a teenage title covering TV, film and music. I spent two years there working with the magazine's first editor Lesley O'Toole, whose support and encouragement proved invaluable when I was finding my feet in journalism.

I left *TV HITS* in 1994 and during a brief period of freelancing

I approached Phil Thomas, who at the time was the Editor of the film magazine *Empire*, a magazine which I loved for the fact that its approach to film was as irreverent as *Smash Hits'* approach to music. My letter to him, which began with the headline 'Can You Give Me A Break?', resulted in my landing two weeks' work a month on the magazine which eventually turned into a full-time job. It was a very different market to *TV HITS* – but Phil turned out to be an excellent manager, teaching me a lot more about the profession, offering me new journalistic challenges (such as editing an entire section of the magazine!) and always on hand for both constructive criticism and positive feedback (something which is all too rare in this industry).

Phil Thomas allowed me to take the next step in my career, further developing my skills and my sense of responsibility and increasing my confidence. He gave me my second big break – the one which allowed me to establish myself as a film and entertainment journalist, from which came my books, my radio and TV work and many other things too numerous to mention!

MY ADVICE: *Get as much experience of writing as you can, for a school magazine, student newspaper or local paper, and read as much as you can as well – the more newspapers and magazines you read, the more you'll get an idea of what area of journalism interests you. An endless stream of ideas for features or news stories on your chosen subject always helps (a magazine like Empire, for example, receives thousands of letters from prospective writers each year and the ones who tend to succeed are those who come up with interesting feature ideas rather than those who just want to review films); also boundless enthusiasm, a willingness to work unorthodox hours and a sense of perspective – journalism might look glamorous but it's very hard work!*

Many publications take on students for unpaid work experience, and this is a really good starting point (I did it myself so I should know!) – while you might not get to do any writing it's a brilliant insight into how newspaper and magazine offices operate. And if you show enough enthusiasm and willingness to tackle any job, no matter how menial, you may even be asked back!

Be honest and always deliver your best. Finally, don't give up – it's a very difficult profession to get into but those who are determined enough will get there in the end.

charity and voluntary sector

Victor Adebowale (Lord Adebowale)
Chief Executive, Turning Point

The task I was given was to write a thousand words on how I've managed to get to the dizzy heights of Chief Executive of Turning Point, which is a social care charity, and to become a Peer of the Realm.

For those of you reading this, I should tell you that I'm doing it exactly one hour before I'm supposed to be meeting Sarah Brown, the Editor of this book.

It's difficult to write on something that we know nothing about, but this book is for charity, and so, since Turning Point is a charity, and saying 'no' to Sarah is something I've never done, here goes my contribution. The title of my piece is Success and How to Avoid It.

The first thing to say is that I've failed. I've failed more exams than I've passed. I would like to be able to write a smooth academic history, powered by encouraging affirmations, for those afflicted by 'A' Level results, degrees, etc. But I can't. School was a disaster and I was something of a slacker. My mother believed that it was the system and while the system did me no favours – it was also me. Calculus evaded me, chemistry was a blurred game of snooker that got played with a shot resulting in a new substance and that's that. Biology was well dull and physics – need I say any more?

The one thing about school I remember was a Miss Babister refusing to believe that a story I'd written was my own work. She insisted that I'd copied it out of a book. At the time, I couldn't quite believe it and didn't realise it was a compliment, and probably a better one than passing my English 'O' Level, which I failed at the first attempt and only just passed at the second. I've only got a thousand words, so let's skip school.

A sense of adventure rather than a masterplan got me to North East London Polytechnic, where I failed to excel in applied biology. There are two formative experiences I remember about that period. The first is leaving without my degree and the words of the head of the department ringing in my ears telling me how people who dropped out of the course ended up sweeping up at Victoria Coach Station. I had already tried sweeping the roads, being a dustbin man and sometime roadie for a gang that worked for Harvey Goldsmith. But that's another thousand words.

The fact is I got bitten by a bug. Not a biological one – an ideas one. At the time of leaving North East London Polytechnic, I was living in short-life housing, which was just that – short life. It was housing below standard, usually empty, that some people living in Newham felt should be and could be used. Mainly because we needed somewhere to live, and secondly so did hundreds, and eventually about a thousand or so, other people. During that period I met Richard Stubbs, a man much, much cleverer than me. I also met Ruth Waring, a woman to this day I refer to as 'Strewth', as in God's own truth. Both of them basically turned me into someone who was interested (well, actually obsessed) with housing. The academics of it, the practicalities of it, the management of it. I read everything I could get my hands on, on the matter. I learned about how meetings worked, how local authorities worked, how housing associations worked – everything. And I learned about what people outside the system could do in using the system's rule in the interests of those in need.

I think in the early 80s I must have been one of the most boring people on the planet. If you asked me how I was, I would have told you and then gone on to fascinate you with the theory of decentralised housing management, housing association grants, mini-housing association grants, Black housing association grants (for Black people), housing co-ops, local authority housing grants,

Gilbert strips, Newham and Haringey Councils' racial harassment policies. I was, and still am, a passionate believer in housing, the right to decent housing for all, and to a large degree, it's all down to Richard Stubbs and Strewth Waring. But then, that's another thousand words.

I got into work because I got a job as a clerk in the Housing Department. I photocopied reports written by people who actually had finished their degrees and I read all the reports and took all the information in. When I got a chance to indicate that I knew something about housing, I took the opportunity. I was lucky to meet people who were interested in what I had to say and recognised that I might be able to do something other than photocopying. So I was encouraged by a giant of a man called Dick Shepherd to apply for jobs in the Estate Department of Newham Council. And that's where the next phase started.

A thousand words later, I'm standing in front of a hostile tenants group, trying to explain the need to decant (move a lot of people out) of a block of flats in order that the flats can be refurbished. I also had to explain why the council was evicting people because they had racially terrorised their neighbours. I was having a hard time. Dick Shepherd walked into the meeting, took it over and spoke to people who he'd grown up with in such a way that they ended up giving me a round of applause. He taught me a lesson about leadership and about backing up what you say with what you do and about supporting people on the front line, no matter who they are.

After Newham, I spent some time at Patchwork Housing Association, working with young people with special needs, before joining Ujima Housing Association and then moving on to become Director of the Alcohol Recovery Project, before running Centrepoint and here I am – Chief Executive of Turning Point, the leading social care organisation.

It's hard to know how to conclude, but I think you may have gathered that key people have inspired me throughout. I choose to mention a few in this meagre one thousand words, while missing out so many, save to say thank you to anyone who's reading this who's taken an interest in helping me get on, and I'm sorry I don't have a few thousand words more.

* * *

Graeme Alexander
Trustee, Big Brothers & Sisters (UK)

I was fortunate to spend most of my teenage years training as a ski racer. Not only did it teach me the value of dedication and focus, it also gave me the opportunity to be surrounded by an extraordinary group of people. Among them were Olympic athletes, university students, entrepreneurs and explorers. A remarkable group of people who were grabbing every opportunity life offered them. As a group, they inspired me to view the world with the same energy, commitment and enthusiasm.

I went on to study and work all over the world including London, Auckland, Bangkok, Riyadh and Chicago. Having seen Big Brothers & Sisters operate in the USA it was clear to me the charity needed to be introduced in the UK so that young people have the opportunity to be inspired, just as I was.

MY ADVICE: *Surround yourself with people whom you aspire to be like. Interesting, energetic, good-hearted people. These characteristics will rub off.*

Camila Batmanghelidjh
Director, Kids Company

I have founded The Place 2 Be and Kids Company, both charities supporting vulnerable children based in Peckham, London. The charities provide a place for local children to come and know that they are safe and able to spend time creatively in developing their own activities in an inspiring environment. I have known since I was nine that I would do this.

My inspiration was a combination of humanity and aesthetics. My grandfather was physically like a straight line; a paediatrician, he reached the children of the poor and rich. I grew up seeing people queue up in the street to have their children seen by him. I discovered a sense of vocation through him.

The need to strive for excellence was kindled because of the perfect lines creating the design in Islamic Architecture. Clear and uncluttered they interlink to create a beautiful whole.

I try and plan my projects using the same principles.

MY ADVICE: *Find your own straight line and follow it.*

Dorit Braun OBE
Chief Executive, Parentline Plus

My initial interest was in global/development education as a result of studying and living in Colombia. I had an economics degree from Manchester University, and based my PhD thesis on Colombia's political economy. When I was pregnant for the first time, I felt, very strongly, that people could not empathise with others unless they felt good about themselves – and so my passion about family and parenting education and support was born. It is no coincidence that it was born at the time of giving birth!

I have a long experience of parenting education and training professionals in family support. I have worked in adult and community education and as a Locality Commissioner in a health authority. I then went on to become Chief Executive of the National Stepfamily Association, successfully guiding the organisation through merger with Parent Network and Parentline UK to form Parentline Plus. In 2000, I was awarded an OBE in the Queen's birthday honours list for services to parenting.

Apart from my grandfather, who adored me, and believed I could do anything I set my sights on, and my three sons, who have been my biggest single source of inspiration (as well as of joy and pain) there were two key people who inspired me.

Diana Harrap, who was Inspector for Home Economics in Birmingham at the start of my career, was brilliant at giving feedback. She told me what I was good at and stressed how she observed that I could inspire and lead people, could work with people from their starting points, and could help them see a bigger picture as well as being able to help them to construct that picture. She made sure I was included in lots of initiatives with schools in Birmingham, and then joined the Advisory Group for the project I led when working at the Open University. In this role she continued to offer support, feedback, and most of all to value the work I was doing in demonstrable ways, for instance by brokering introductions to other Schools Inspectors in other LEAs, and by brokering work with schools in Birmingham.

Scott Sinclair is the Director of the Development Education Centre, Birmingham and was my first boss. Scott is a real visionary. When I joined the Development Education Centre I was the first paid member of staff, and the centre was a couple of years old. Scott had a vision of how it could influence locally, nationally and internationally – which he has now achieved. Twenty-something years ago, it could have seemed preposterous, but his combination of vision, strategic leadership and practical thinking showed me that it was worth believing in achieving a goal that you could take small steps towards, and that over time it would work. He also showed me that if you have a clear enough idea, you can be very flexible about adapting to changing circumstances, and therefore can be very opportunistic, without in any sense selling out on the vision.

MY ADVICE: *To succeed in the charitable sector, you really need to believe in what you are doing, and in the benefits it can bring to people. You need to be motivated by a desire to contribute to improving or changing something. And you need to be very willing to learn. Keep an open mind, think laterally, allow yourself to be creative, and look out for other creative people to guide and inspire you.*

Stephen Burke
Director, Daycare Trust

I became the Director of the national childcare charity Daycare Trust in 2000. I have more than 20 years' experience in public relations, journalism and fundraising. From 1996–2000, I was a public relations consultant to national organisations including Daycare Trust, Family Policy Studies Centre, Better Government for Older People, British Society of Gerontology and Development Trusts Assocation. Previously I was head of external relations for Community Service Volunteers and head of public relations for Crime Concern after spells with the Association of Metropolitan

Authorities, National Union of Teachers and NALGO. I am also currently a non-executive Director of Hammersmith & Fulham Primary Care Trust, and since 1994 I have been a councillor in the London Borough of Hammersmith and Fulham. I am Chair of the Association of London Government's health and social services panel and chaired its recent Commission on Race, Health and Social Exclusion.

My life changed when I turned to crime prevention in 1993. After ten years in public relations and journalism, I became head of PR at Crime Concern and worked with its founder Nigel Whiskin. Nigel is a pioneer. He set up the first Victim Support scheme in the 1970s. At Crime Concern he has been changing the way we look at the causes of crime, focusing on the importance of the family, school and community, and working with young people. Nigel's passion and persistence encouraged me to think big and not be afraid of challenging policies and practice. Nothing is too difficult; every problem can be solved. His life is full of firsts and I'm proud of sharing a couple of them with him. He works well with everyone – from young people on disadvantaged estates to the Home Secretary and Royalty. But above all he taught me the importance of every child having a sure start in life – which is why I'm now working for better childcare and early years services at Daycare Trust.

MY ADVICE: *Do something you believe in – and enjoy it.*

Beverly Cohen
Chief Executive, Big Brothers & Sisters UK

I was born in Nova Scotia, Canada and came to the UK in 1974. I have a BA from McGill University, a Masters in Social Work from the University of Toronto, and an MBA from the University of Sussex.

I have one daughter, now 25 years old (a veterinary surgeon), whom I brought up as a single parent and of whom I am immeasurably proud.

My very first volunteer job after going to university was as a 'Big Sister' to 11-year-old Janie. After a while she persuaded me to help out at the homework club in her local community centre, and then in a youth group to which she belonged. These experiences influenced my decision to study social work.

Almost the whole of my professional life has been devoted to children and their families, for eight years in East Sussex Social Services Department, and for the last 18 years in charities (Norwood Child Care 1983–86; NSPCC 1986–2001; and since January 2002 Big Brothers & Sisters UK). It has been an enormous privilege to join Big Brothers & Sisters so early in its life here in the UK.

Other professional and voluntary experience includes: being Chair of two branches of the British Association of Social Workers; being a Housing Association trustee; being a member of Women-in-Action Forum, set up to help women on low incomes to improve their employment and income prospects; lecturing on Child Care Law at the University of Sussex; and teaching Hebrew and religion to young children at my synagogue.

I owe a great deal to so many people with whom I have been privileged to work over the course of my career. From them I have learned both technical skills and to understand the environment in which I strive to make a difference. Whilst I have found much to *admire* in very many of my colleagues past and present, what *inspires* me has often come from elsewhere. One of the people who have helped me most in my career has been Gwen Tucker. Over most of the last 22 years, Gwen has taken care of my daughter, our pets, our home – and me. As a single parent, I couldn't have worked without her, let alone have held senior (often stressful) positions. This, along with her formidable competence in caring for children and animals, and her utter trustworthiness, explain why I have been able confidently to rely on her. But it is her loyalty, her generosity of spirit, her unconditional acceptance of and respect for others, and most of all her wisdom which inspire me.

Gwen's own life hasn't always been easy. But she has climbed her mountains and faced tragedy with courage and dignity – and with a quiet but fierce determination to do the best for those she loves. She is one of the few people I have known who can be truly selfless.

I have always worked in organisations whose ultimate goal is to protect the vulnerable and to improve their lives. However, my day-to-day work has been about money (raising it, making it stretch, accounting for it), market positioning, target-setting, staff performance, legal matters, management information, risk and crisis management, etc. Gwen's example reminds me to focus on what is most important – the people I care about. And in my work that means the children I serve and have served.

MY ADVICE: *'Keep your eye on the ball' at all times. Remember your mission, and don't allow yourself to be sidetracked by day-to-day distractions. Learn to respect and to demonstrate respect for those you aim to help and for all those who share that aim.*

Dorothy Dalton
Charities Consultant and Charities Expedition Leader

I am currently Charities Consultant to Bircham Dyson Bell and Director of Voluntary Sector Development at Horwath Consulting. I am also a non-executive Director of the Inland Revenue. I have been Chief Executive of ACENVO, the Association of Chief Executives of National Voluntary Organisations (now renamed ACEVO), Chief Executive of a national charity and Head Mistress of a girls' independent school. I have a 'first' in Mathematics. I am trustee of several charities including Marie Curie Cancer Care and Institute for Global Ethics UK Trust. I am Vice Chair of the Child Poverty Action Group. I am a governor of and chair the Nominations Committee of International Students House as well as being Chair of Orley Farm School. In 1983 I founded the JoLt Trust which I continue to chair. During my spare time, I organise and lead challenging expeditions for disabled and disadvantaged teenagers to remote corners of the world as well as organising and participating in fundraising expeditions such as canoeing, kayaking and white-water rafting down the Zambezi.

When I first met Samantha (Sam to her friends) she was 16 and I was 42. Sam had applied to join one of the challenging month-long expeditions for disabled and disadvantaged teenagers that I was leading. Sam was born severely disabled. The doctors told her mother, a single parent, that Sam would never walk or talk. Her mother refused to accept the diagnoses. Years of intensive physiotherapy and practice resulted in Sam eventually learning to talk and finally to walk with the aid of crutches.

On the expedition Sam walked everywhere and tried everything. She made up for the many years of not talking by driving everyone mad by her constant chatter. She also disclosed that she had been raped. A few years after the expedition, her mother died suddenly and for the first time Sam found herself on her own. Severe depression and several extremely difficult years went by. However, she survived and with renewed determination set out to achieve her dream of getting a degree in drama and producing plays with able-bodied and disabled actors.

Last year Sam phoned to say that she had made her dream come true. She had successfully completed her drama degree and as part of the course had produced a play with young able-bodied and disabled actors. She now plans to set up and manage a drama company for people with and without disabilities.

Since I met her I have canoed, kayaked and white-water-rafted the Zambezi between Zimbabwe and Zambia; I have cycled the length of Cuba; I have crossed the Jordan Desert on a camel and trekked across the Andes with the support of horses and donkeys. When I am 56 my ultimate challenge will be to ski to the South Pole with seven other women all over the age of 50. I hope I have the determination and courage of my role model.

MY ADVICE: *Sam taught me that however challenging one's dreams are, they are achievable if you want them desperately enough.*

Susan Daniels
Chief Executive, National Deaf Children's Society

I studied at Keele University and received a degree in politics and history. I then worked as a personnel officer, a project manager for telecommunications software systems and as a teacher of the deaf. I then joined RNID (Royal National Institute for the Deaf) initially as Higher Education Development Officer, subsequently as Head of Education, Training and Employment, and then finally Head of

Policy and Development. I moved from RNID to take up the appointment as Chief Executive of the National Deaf Children's Society.

It was while training to become a teacher of the deaf that I met the person who has had the most impact on my professional life. She was an experienced teacher of the deaf and a lecturer at the City Lit Centre for Deaf People in London. She was a very forthright northerner, deaf herself, and showed me that deaf people with the right support and attitude can do anything they put their minds to. The fact that she was deaf herself, a little older, and had achieved success at a time when it was very hard for deaf people to break into the field of education, was extremely inspirational.

She taught me that barriers were there to be overcome and opportunities to be grabbed as and when they arose.

When the National Deaf Children's Society job came up it was she who coached me through the process. I was the only deaf person applying and the only one who was not already a Chief Executive. I would not be where I am today if it were not for her mentoring, support and encouragement.

MY ADVICE: *Young people who want to reach the top in the charity world should get the widest range of experience possible. There is no substitute for qualifications and a lot of hard work. When trying to break into a new field, talk to those who are at the top, ask lots of questions and make sure you listen to the answers. Always assume you have more to learn, no matter how good you think you are at what you do!*

Stuart Etherington
Chief Executive, National Council for Voluntary Organisations

I studied politics at university, and worked as a social worker in a London borough. I have worked in a number of charities starting as a Senior Research Officer at the Joseph Rowntree Trust/Circle 33 Housing Trust and ending up as the Chief Executive of the Royal National Institute for Deaf People (RNID). During my career, I have also continued my studies, gaining an MA in Social Service Planning, an MBA and more recently an MA in International

Relations and Planning. I was appointed Chief Executive of the National Council for Voluntary Organisations in 1994. NCVO is the umbrella organisation for voluntary organisations and charities to represent their interests to Government and other external groups, and to provide services to improve their effectiveness. In 2000, I took a short break to attend the Leadership in the 21st Century programme at Harvard University.

The most inspirational person that I ever met in my career was the President of NCVO, Sir Campbell Adamson. Campbell died two years ago, but during the period when I was Chief Executive of NCVO and he was President, he inspired me in a number of ways.

Firstly he taught me that the direct route is not always the most effective. Secondly, that carrying people with you as far as possible in partnership is a hallmark of modern leadership. Finally, he taught me the value of style, not dress sense, but the way in which the leadership style you adopt has a profound effect on others. He was perhaps the best exponent of the statesmanship style, one that I have tried, albeit imperfectly, to adopt since knowing him. Convincing others and inspiring by example, not assuming that they are merely waiting to be led in a particular direction.

The principal thing that Campbell taught me was that individual engagement with people is crucial. He had the ability, which I have observed in others, that every time you had a conversation with him you felt that he thought that you were the most important person in the world. He could achieve this on a one-to-one basis but I have observed him at a formal dinner of eight where all present felt that they had had a personal conversation, almost a one-to-one exchange with him during the evening. Basically he taught me how to engage with and value individuals, and that nobody's ideas should be dismissed lightly.

MY ADVICE: *First and foremost, be committed to the cause that the organisation represents. There are some in the charitable sector who see this essentially as a technical, managerial job, with a slightly different focus from the public or private sector. In my view you have to be committed to the cause.*

Secondly, you must learn to work with a quite complex governance structure. Unlike the private sector, the voluntary sector has a wide variety of stakeholders and more diffuse performance measurement. Your relationship with your Chair and your Board is going to be crucial to your success.

Finally, recognise that working in the voluntary sector demands a lot of you. You have to go the extra mile but it is a mile worth travelling because of the good that your organisation can do.

Pat Foxton
Director of Communications, Rainbow Trust Children's Charity

After 'A' Levels I started work as a PA in a publishing company and then travelled in Europe. After four years, I got a job as a PA in a recording studio and worked my way up in the music business to Senior Press Office at EMI Records, and eventually Head of Press at Epic (now part of Sony) promoting Liza Minnelli, Don Henley, The Jacksons, Michael Jackson, George Michael, Sade, Luther Vandross and the Pet Shop Boys.

Jonathan Morrish, Vice President of Sony Music, first interviewed me for my job at Epic (where he was then Head of Press) in a pub called the Nellie Dean. I felt privileged to work with him: a gentleman in a sea of sharks, yet he didn't get eaten. He was very organised and taught me to be honourable with people and to trust them. I'd already had a few hard knocks in PR and this advice really changed my work life around. He is a great networker and I tried to follow his example and have been doing so ever since.

When I was diagnosed with terminal colon cancer (at age 35) he was the first person I rang outside my family. We stayed in touch as I convalesced and when I returned to work he protected me from overwork and tiredness. When I recovered I decided to run the London Marathon for Cancer Research and Jonathan helped me raise thousands of pounds from the recording artists.

The taste of charity work was addictive and I decided to change my job. I joined Rainbow Trust who provide respite breaks and support at home for children with life-threatening or terminal illness and their families. Jonathan still helps me at Sony Music with good contacts for our annual fundraising Rainbow Ball.

MY ADVICE: *Contacts, contacts, contacts keep the world going round. I keep in touch with all the journalists, agents, PRs, celebrities, promoters and business contacts regularly and personally. It is a great discipline and a good way of organising one's work life.*

Be enthusiastic when meeting or dealing with people. Don't waste people's time by attending a meeting unbriefed. Read the newspapers and keep up to date with what is going on in the world. Make sure you thank people and return favours.

Be a friend to people. They will value you like gold. Try and cultivate listening skills and remember always to help those who are just starting to get a foot on the ladder. Life is short. Make the most of it. Some people don't get the chance.

Fiona Halton
Director, Pilotlight

Pilotlight is a charity which is a catalyst for social change. We help disadvantaged people by developing new approaches to tackle old and deep-rooted problems. We do this by uniting leaders and innovators from different business sectors to those at the front line.

Throughout my career I have started and grown new initiatives. I began by initiating and running British Film Year which the trade paper *Screen International* described as achieving 'little short of a revolution'. As a Co-Director of Charity Projects I set up The Holborn Great Investment Race where City teams used their skills to raise £750,000. Charity Projects went on to found Comic Relief and I was part of the management team that worked to set up the first day that raised over £13m. Following this I joined Pilotlight and helped set up TimeBank, becoming its Acting Director and took it to national launch.

My dream was to spark change. The person whose friendship inspired me to start to see how this could be done was Marc Samuelson. Marc was incredibly practical and at the same time believed he could move mountains through involving others. He showed me the power of connecting people to make things happen and he did it all with a great twinkle in his eye. He rolled up his sleeves when things got rough and could always find a way through. He never gave up. He inspired me to do the work I do today at Pilotlight which is all about connecting people from different worlds to share their skills to achieve extraordinary outcomes.

MY ADVICE: *Everyone has a spark and it is all about liberating it.*

Avila Kilmurray
Director, Community Foundation of Northern Ireland

I am the Director of a grant-making foundation for community and voluntary action across Northern Ireland. Since 1979, the Foundation has worked with groups of people, on both sides of the sectarian divide, who are committed to building peace and achieving social progress. We mainly support the most disadvantaged communities and marginalised individuals. I have worked for many years in community action and social development across Northern Ireland, and been actively involved with the Women's Movement, Women's Aid, Single Parent organisations and trade union issues.

When I first came to work in community action and peacebuilding in Derry in 1976, I met Cathy Harkin to get her advice on the city which was, at that time, torn apart by violence. Cathy was a community and trade union activist, and was to be the first ever woman President of Derry Trades Council, an extraordinary achievement for a woman who started her working life in a shirt factory at the age of 16. Cathy believed that deprivation was a challenge rather than an insurmountable obstacle.

When Cathy took me under her wing she was acting true to form. She always gave people the benefit of the doubt, estimating that they had something positive to give. She encouraged me to take risks. The trick was not always to be right, but to identify and try out a range of options, and then to analyse what have been effective and what hadn't − and why. This approach was always grounded in a good sense of humour, as well as a certain self-confidence that did not require the fuel of constant success.

The best advice Cathy gave me was that if you want to change the world, it's important to mark out the milestones of progress by the impact on the local, i.e. start in your own neighbourhood. She taught me not to take myself too seriously, and when things are bad I still hear the echo of her voice – 'Sure they could be worse!'

MY ADVICE: *If you want to reach the top of the ladder then, at the very least, remember to leave the ladder in place for others to clamber up. If your ambitions are more general in nature, then be prepared to spend some time changing jobs. Learn how different types of communities and groups work, and try to delve into the issues that impact on social need and change. Reality is a kaleidoscope and you need the imagination to piece it together. Develop an approach that can relate theory to practice – you need both. Be prepared to fail as well as to succeed – but fail with panache and learn from it.*

Lucy Lake
Programme Director of international charity CAMFED

I joined CAMFED in 1994, a charity dedicated to supporting the education of girls and young women in Africa. As Programme Director, I work with governments and local communities to secure education for thousands of girls who would otherwise be denied the chance because of poverty. I assist young women who complete school to use their new-found skills to support themselves, their families and communities.

Before joining CAMFED, I completed a degree in Human Sciences at Oxford University and spent a year teaching science and maths at a rural secondary school in Zimbabwe.

Ann Cotton, founder of CAMFED, believes in the potential of young people to influence change and has given me the opportunity and inspiration to take up this challenge. She has encouraged me to take on responsibility with confidence. When a decision needs to be made, Ann is inclusive. If there's a problem, she will listen and talk it through. Perhaps most importantly, she has shown me how to put these principles into practice. The real tribute to this approach is the fact that the network of young women we work with in Africa are themselves now confidently advising policymakers and community leaders on ways to support young people.

MY ADVICE: *My advice to anyone joining the field of international development is to respect and be guided by the people whose lives you seek to improve, and always be ready to challenge injustice.*

Anne Longfield
Chief Executive, Kids' Clubs Network

Kids' Clubs Network is the national organisation for out-of-school childcare. Established 20 years ago, the organisation has raised the profile of out-of-school childcare at local, regional and national level and has helped develop a network of over 8,000 clubs. The organisation offers advice and support to out of school clubs, parents, children, childcare providers, Government, local authorities, employers and Early Years Development and Childcare Partnerships.

Whilst always being aware that I wanted to spend my time doing a job that was useful, my real inspiration to try to make a difference in childcare came from a lone parent in South London.

I was working in a children's project at the time – enjoying all the fun and rewards that that can bring, but I was taken aback by Hilary's hard work, energy and determination to study, get a job and get the financial stability needed for her and her child.

The project I ran helped her do this. But it was seeing this in action that made me realise how much could be gained if others had the same kind of support. Almost 20 years later this is what still inspires me as Chief Executive of Kids' Club Network.

I know now that the work I do can make a difference for lots of mothers like Hilary and it is her energy and determination that I try and live up to every day.

Richard McCarthy
Chief Executive, Peabody Trust

I joined Peabody Trust as Chief Executive in 1999. Prior to this, I was Chief Executive of the Horizon Housing Group and before, I was at Hyde Housing Association for 15 years, rising from Trainee Housing Officer to Operations Director. Peabody is a large London-based housing association and regeneration agency. It is also a registered charity.

Len Bishop was Chief Executive at Hyde Housing Association for my first 15 years of employment. He gave me the freedom to innovate and take risks, and the support, resources and recognition to deliver real change. His determination and commitment to meeting housing needs and provide high standards of customer service were a constant source of inspiration, along with his outstanding intellectual ability and creativity. He made me believe I could achieve and was always interested in what I did. He was a sounding board for my ideas and suggestions and a source of helpful challenges and criticisms.

MY ADVICE: *Don't be afraid to contribute your ideas and suggestions. You will find a warm response and often the opportunity to turn these ideas into reality. You can shape your own future so make the most of it!*

Mary Marsh
Chief Executive, NSPCC

For the last two years I have been the Director and Chief Executive of the NSPCC which is one of the big UK charities. All my previous jobs have been in education. In the 90s I was a Headteacher of two comprehensive schools, Holland Park School in London and Queens' School in Watford. While I was Deputy Head at St Christopher School in Letchworth in the 80s I took up opportunities for personal development including my interest in ICT. Doing an MBA at London Business School part-time opened up new opportunities in my career. In the 70s I enjoyed eight years as a full-time mother when my four sons were young. My first qualification after school was a degree in Geography at Nottingham University.

Stuart was a family friend whom I knew throughout my childhood and as I grew up and had my own children. He was a very senior civil servant in the Scottish Office. I enjoyed his stimulating company and his complete belief in me and my potential. He inspired me to aim high. I know that he helped me to believe in myself so that I have felt able to make some flying leaps in my career progression. I am only sorry he is no longer alive to share this.

MY ADVICE: *Be ready to take advantage of opportunities; in building your life you do make some of your own luck. When things go wrong face up to it, feel (and share) pain, anger and frustration. Work through it and learn from this. Every experience is an opportunity to get stronger and ready for the next challenge.*

Daleep Mukarji
Director, Christian Aid

Over 25 years ago I started my working life as a doctor in a rural Christian hospital in South India. I came across poverty, disparity and injustice that I had never really seen or understood. Soon I realised you could not improve health by health care and hospitals alone, and that I needed to be involved in social and economic development. After the necessary training I was able to start a community health and rural development programme for a population of over 100,000 people supported partly by Christian Aid. After eight years I felt I needed to leave and hand over to someone else. I then worked for nine years as the Secretary of the Council of Churches in India's Christian Medical Association. In 1994 we moved to the World Council of Churches in Geneva where I was invited to be Secretary for Health, Community and Justice.

In 1998 I took over as Director of Christian Aid, the official relief and development agency of 40 sponsoring churches in the UK and the Republic of Ireland. Christian Aid works with about 600 partners and in 60 countries where its essential purpose is 'to expose the scandal of poverty, contribute to its eradication and to challenge structures and systems which keep people poor and marginalised'. As Director my role is to give this organisation strategic focus and build an organisation which is professional and committed so it really makes a difference in the problems of poverty and exclusion.

My medical college chaplain and friend Reverend A. C. Oommen inspired me to link my training to my faith and be relevant in the context of the needs and problems of rural India. Over the years he has advised, encouraged, challenged and supported me and my family in my professional and personal decisions. Our friendship began in 1964 and we have worked together on many issues related to the role of the churches in health and social development in India.

Reverend Oommen helped me to understand what I really wanted to do and supported me as I gave up medicine to live and work in a rural community with the very poor and marginalised. He helped me to see this was both my calling and also that I had the necessary talent and leadership quality to make a difference to those in poverty. As I changed jobs, took new courses and moved on in life, he was available to advise and encourage me.

MY ADVICE: *Have dreams and visions of what you can be and do, and then pursue them. You can make a difference. But you cannot change the world if you are not willing to sometimes change yourself!*

Anne-Marie Piper
Charity Partner, Farrer & Co Law Firm

I graduated from University College, London in 1979 and was called to the Bar in 1980. I then joined the private client department of City firm Richards Butler in 1983 and, after requalifying as a solicitor, became a partner there in 1989. In 1994 I joined Paisner & Co where I headed the firm's Charities Group until 2001, when I moved to Farrer & Co as a partner.

I specialise in charity law and act for sponsors of new charities; directors, trustees and officers of existing charities and other not-for-profit bodies, individuals and companies wishing to make charitable gifts or do business with charities. I am the Founder and former Secretary of the Charity Law Association, and also lecture and write regularly on charity law subjects.

Professor Chris Arnold, an academic lawyer working at the City law firm of which I was a partner, was for me an inspiration and a guide.

Starting a trend that was to be followed by many similar firms, mine decided that the specialist area of law that I practised was not one that it wished to offer. As a very junior partner just about to give birth to my first child, my self-esteem plummeted in tandem with my assessment of my future employability.

Chris patiently helped me to understand that no one need be a one-hit-wonder. With quiet encouragement and very practical help, in pretty much equal measures, Chris gave me the confidence and the will to start again and the belief that I could succeed again and, for that, I shall always be extremely grateful.

David Robinson OBE
Senior Adviser at Community Links

I am the founder of Community Links – a network of projects run by local people and tackling practically and creatively the problems of our inner city community in East London. Within this network we have pioneered new ideas and new ways of working. We share this good practice nationally through publications and training programmes. Last year more than 30,000 people benefited directly from Community Links projects in 60 key sites, and 80 per cent of our front-line services were delivered by people who first became involved as users of that service.

When I was shaping my ideas and trying to build support for Community Links I wrote to the directors of the national charities that I most admired – all the big names, many still around. Most never answered. Some replied but were too busy to see me. Several did make the time and then used it to criticise our ideas and to undermine my confidence! I was young, probably naïve, but well meaning and deeply dispirited. Then Alec Dickson rang, personally. He was the founder of CSV and VSO – two of the biggest volunteering agencies in the field. He made the time to see me, once, then again, and intermittently thereafter for the rest of his life. He rang on Christmas Eve, at the end of the first slow, difficult year, to wish Community Links, with characteristic brevity, a 'successful New Year'. I asked him at our second meeting if he thought I should give up on Community Links for now, perhaps try again when I was a little older as so many had advised. He asked me if I still believed that the ideas were 'worthwhile'. I said 'I do'. He said 'Then you go on'. It was not advice. It was an order.

MY ADVICE: *Alec taught me two things. The first I understood* *immediately, the second I have grown to appreciate in more recent years.*

Never give up on any idea you believe in. Your day will come.

Understand that on your own your achievements will always be limited, no matter what position you may attain. It is through encouraging, supporting and inspiring others that our dreams take flight and that we break free from the constraints of personal capacity. Never stop sharing your vision, and the visions of others.

Stephen Shields
Director, SHINE

I manage the charity SHINE (Support and Help In Education) which is a grant-making trust. SHINE supports educational initiatives which encourage disadvantaged children and young people to raise their (educational) achievement levels. As well as managing the financial, administrative and day-to-day running of the charity, I feel the main part of my job is to help SHINE trustees and staff remain focused on the needs of the children and young people we serve. What led me here? Over 20 years of working with children and young people in both a social work/voluntary sector and an educational setting, and the very real pathos and understanding this has brought me.

My first job when I left university in 1982 was with The Richmond Fellowship which works to promote the mental welfare of young people and support their rehabilitation in cases where they have been institutionalised in psychiatric hospitals or young offenders' units. In 1985 I moved to The Blue Triangle Housing Association, an organisation supporting young, single homeless people move into independent living. I returned to university for three years in 1988 after which, among other things, for several years I formed part of the pastoral care and guidance team at Europe's largest secondary school. In 1996 I began working for The National Lottery Charities Board, since renamed The Community Fund, distributing grants for the charitable sector side of the 'good causes' proceeds from the National Lottery. I was appointed Director of SHINE in July 2000, and I have been here since.

My greatest influence? A combination of people really: first boss

– who shouted a lot, my voluntary sector colleagues – really 'nice', people I've helped – maybe those I couldn't .

But I guess I learned most from the young people I've worked with in education and the voluntary sector over many years. Complex, and at times difficult, they were all real. I learned that people are not always what they seem: mostly they are better. Refreshingly – sometimes brutally – honest, young people have been my first, and are my constant mentors.

MY ADVICE: *What I learned from the Y.P. themselves: be real.*

Jane Tewson CBE
Director, Pilotlight Australia

Leaving school with few qualifications and still unsure whether dyslexia was a term used for 'middle class failures', I became passionate about giving people a voice who would not normally have one. I began with the idea that charities should 'work with' not 'give to' the people they were there to help, and have founded five charities on this principle, starting with Charity Projects (1984), Comic Relief (co-founded 1986), Pilotlight UK (1998), TimeBank (1999) and Pilotlight Australia (2000). *The Times* referred to me as one of the top ten innovators of the 1990s, and Charles Handy included me in his book *The Alchemists*, but I still believe that the basic principle behind what I do works because it is based on common sense and something everyone can relate to.

My inspiration has always come from people doing extraordinary things against the odds. Early on in my working life I became aware that I didn't have what was needed to work directly with disadvantaged people, but that I wanted to support those people who were doing this work. Joel Joffe is my inspiration on many levels – his moral position led him to take up often – unpopular causes. Originally from South Africa, he defended Nelson Mandela in his treason trial. On his move to the UK he was one of the founders of Allied Dunbar (now trading within Zurich Financial Services) and until recently he was Chair of Oxfam and is a Trustee of many cutting-edge charities.

I didn't know Joel, but had heard much about his range of skills and passions. In my mid-twenties I helped to create Comic Relief, a charity which grew very quickly. I approached Joel for help and he mentored me through managing its growth – he inspired me with his strategic thinking, supported me as a brilliant manager with developing Comic Relief, and spent probably at least a couple of days a month mentoring me personally and supporting Comic Relief's other Directors.

Joel really helped build my confidence and confirmed the value of trusting 'my gut' – he taught me to listen more and have faith in myself. The combination of his strength and moral fibre, matched by complete humility and huge range of skills, showed me what is possible on many different fronts. Here I feel I also need to mention his beautiful garden and the many trees he and his wife Vanetta planted – this special man also recognising the need to find a place of peace and to feed his own soul.

MY ADVICE: *Dream dreams – ask for help and go to the very best in their fields to get it. Listen hard and maintain close connections with where it really matters – the coal face. Focus on issues and avoid being distracted by process.*

Eileen Ware
Charity PR Consultant and Campaigner (End Child Poverty Coalition, and Family Service Units)

I worked as a shorthand secretary/typist on leaving school at 16, then a journalist on the local paper at 19 for three years. After that I joined Shelter, the national campaign for the homeless just after it was set up. I began as a public relations officer, and later set up the youth fundraising department and then the youth education department. Since then I have worked in charities in public and I now work closely with the Family Welfare Association, and for the Campaign to End Child Poverty, a coalition of the leading children's Charities which is growing steadily in its support.

Growing up I always had my parents' support and my first boss – a very strict senior secretary – taught me to check everything and leave nothing to chance. This has helped me organise myself and organise events. When I joined Shelter, I worked for Des Wilson who had launched the charity and become Director of the Campaign. This was a new-style, hard-hitting charity headed by young people in their early 20s, which was young in those days for the responsibilities we were undertaking. We worked hard together as a team and had a lot of fun, too. Des taught me to use my organisational skills to interest the media in our work. Through him I learned many skills: how to attract an audience through the media, advertising or speeches, and how to turn that interest into support for the campaign to help the homeless.

Like everyone else I made mistakes, but I did learn to try things again, to be persistent, to ask for help or support when I needed it and to be a perfectionist. If something is worth doing, it is really worth doing properly.

MY ADVICE: *Do your very best – you can do no more. Even if you do not succeed in the task, you will as least know that you have tried honestly.*

religion and faith

Rt Rev and Rt Hon George Carey (Lord Carey of Clifton)
former Archbishop of Canterbury

'*It is perhaps significant that, though state education has existed in England since 1870, no Archbishop so far has passed through it. The first Prime Minister to do so was Lloyd George. Nor has anyone sat in St. Augustine's Chair, since the Reformation, who was not a student at Oxford or Cambridge . . . It is inconceivable that either talent or suitability can be so narrowly confined.*'

Such is the conclusion of the last but one edition of '*Cantuar: The Archbishops in their Office*' (1988) by Edward Carpenter, written thirteen years before I became the 103rd Archbishop of Canterbury.

Frankly, when I was growing up such an ambition to sit in the Chair of St.Augustine in Canterbury Cathedral would not have entered my head in a million years. For a start, I never went to church and neither did my family. Socially, archbishops and bishops were associated in my mind with the higher echelons of society, whereas I was born into a very poor East London family.

How I ended up as Archbishop is due not only to the unfathomable grace of Almighty God, but also to a number of very special friends who believed in me, who saw potential in me, and who goaded and encouraged me over many years.

I was the eldest of five children born to George and Ruby Carey, a struggling yet happy working-class couple who lived in the London district of Bow. Mum and dad gave us the best gift of all – a very happy home where laughter rang out every day and where love ruled. It was, as I have observed, a very poor home. We lived from hand to mouth. I can still recall those times, especially during the war, when we didn't know where our next meal would come from. I remember one occasion when we found mother sobbing in the kitchen when she discovered that the money in her purse wasn't even enough to buy a loaf of bread for her hungry brood. I suppose it was that kind of experience that determined that the form of Christianity I would eventually espouse would be practical and have as its aim to change society as well as the individual.

By the time war ended my family had been evacuated three times for long periods which had led to an unsettled education resulting in my failing the dreaded 11+ exam. This led to me languishing in a secondary school with no hope of matriculating at the age of 16 and thus going on to university. But however unsatisfactory my secondary education was, I encountered two brilliant and dedicated teachers: Mr Bass and Mr Kennedy. Mr Bass was the Headmaster and what he gave to me was the gift of self-belief; that there was no such thing as 'it can't be done'. Such was his respect and belief in each of his pupils that he never gave up expecting the best from any of us. He made me a prefect and I was so proud of that honour but, to this day, I recall the time when I did something that disappointed him greatly. 'Carey,' he said when I was summoned to his book-lined office, 'I expect great things from you. Please don't disappoint me. You can do far better than that, you know.' I left his office with those words ringing in my ears: 'You can do better than that, you know.' From that moment on I knew that someone believed in me. He lived to see me become Archbishop – I knew it gave him enormous pleasure.

Mr Kennedy was a Scot who had served as a naval officer who spiced his English lessons with tales of naval combat and seagoing adventures that enlarged our imaginations and coloured our understanding of life. What I received from Mr Kennedy was a love of English literature. I remember the time I was chosen to read out an essay in class. Having a fondness for long words I used the word 'nonchalantly'. He stopped me: 'What do you mean by "nonchalantly"?' I said feebly: 'Well, sir. I think it means "casually" or "calmly". He replied: 'You are right, but never use words to show off. Language is meant to communicate effectively. Say what you mean!'

What Mr Kennedy started, my first boss, Mr Vincent, continued. At the age of 15, I left school to become an office boy in the London Electricity Board in London. Mr Vincent was the rather austere and forbidding Manager of the branch; a man of few words, preferring disapproving grunts to communicate his moods. One day he saw me with my head in a book as usual and ordered me into his office. 'Have you ever read the works of Charles Dickens?' he demanded. 'No sir,' I replied. 'Then I am going to make sure you do!' he remarked, handing me a well-thumbed copy of *David Copperfield*. Over the next two years I must have read every one of Dickens's classics and benefited from his magisterial prose and stories. In spite of Mr Vincent's unbending and disapproving style I sensed that he took some pride in my development and by constant grunts I was able to surmise that I was pleasing him. And such affirmation encouraged me to show him that I was able to digest great works of literature and engage with the ideas of great writers.

At the age of about 16 I discovered the local Anglican Church of Dagenham, whose squat and defiant tower could be seen from our council house across the allotments and the railway line. For 800 years the small church had served the people of Dagenham and had a good and lively congregation of all ages – as it does today. What drew me to the church was the lively youth fellowship. I met a group of young people slightly older than myself – the Harris twins, Edna Millings, Ron Rushmer, Norman Sidebottom and many others. Also in the Church at the time was a young girl three years my junior, Eileen Hood, of Scottish parents – perhaps the prettiest girl on the block. How fortunate I was to marry her a few years later.

The Harris boys took me under their wing. They must have sensed my hunger for knowledge and in addition to their intelligent Christian faith they introduced me to music. To be sure I was already a fan of music but it was the big band sound and jazz that I loved. At the age of 16 I was a devotee of Stan Kenton, Louis Armstrong, Duke Ellington, Tommy Dorsey, Ted Heath, Dizzy Gillespie and many others. John and David Harris introduced me to classical music. Most Saturday afternoons were spent in their home listening to music and discussing the respective merits of great composers and musicians. To this day I cannot hear, say, Elgar's *Dream of Gerontius* without going in my imagination to that small living room in Dagenham where the three of us would listen to such glorious music.

And there was Jack Titterton who I met at Dagenham Parish Church. To be sure, there was nothing special about Jack. He was a toolmaker at the Ford Motor Company – a specialist at his trade, an ordinary man – but a Christian man. Like many teenagers I was rather embarrassed about becoming too religious. 'Christianity – yes,' my heart said, 'religion – no.' But there was nothing sissy about Jack – he was a tough man's man. What Jack contributed to my development was an awareness that to be a Christian meant putting oneself on the frontline of concerns for this world and its future. Far from being a sissy thing, espousing the Christian faith meant following a leader – Jesus Christ – into areas of suffering and conflict where many are afraid to go. Jack taught me to be unafraid about my beliefs but reminded me by his very natural behaviour that Christianity was a way of life and far more than a religion.

If then Carpenter's statement was fulfilled so unexpectedly in me, I have no doubt that I owe so much to the legacy of Mr Bass, Mr Kennedy, Mr Vincent, the Harris twins, Jack Titterton and of course my parents and Eileen Hood. Whoever we are, whatever our social and educational background, my story is that with God's help nothing is impossible. Never give up trying – and never give up hoping, believing and expecting.

* * *

His Grace Bishop Angaelos
General Bishop of the Coptic Orthodox Church, United Kingdom

Being a bishop in the Coptic Orthodox Church I started my ecclesiastical life as a monk, and in the ancient tradition of monasticism, the concept of discipleship and mentoring, both divine and human, is one of the foundations of growth and success. Since becoming a bishop, I have built on my experience of youth ministry in the UK and have established a Joint UK Youth Committee (JYC), a national youth association (COYA), the Fellowship of Coptic University Students (FOCUS) and travel extensively, lecturing to Coptic youth around the world. I am based at the Coptic Centre in Stevenage, but also oversee various other matters.

Before serving in the United Kingdom, I was secretary to His Holiness Pope Shenouda III, Supreme head of the Coptic Church. During this time, I had the opportunity to be mentored directly by His Holiness in monastic, spiritual and administrative aspects of life, an experience that continues to affect my everyday leadership, decision-making and daily living. Now, as a spiritual father and guide myself, I realise the need to hand down what I have received, and from here comes continuity and authenticity of teaching and practice.

MY ADVICE: *The presence of God and strong faith in any life is in itself a form of mentoring, and leads to success, but at the same time, there is a need for human guidance.*

Sister Rita Dawson
Chief Executive, St Margaret's Hospice, Clydebank

I am an only daughter and have six brothers, all older than me. I come from a sporting family and my brothers were all pretty competitive, which made me very independent. I also learned at an early age that if you want something you have to work hard for it.

There was a Curate in our parish who was always striving to bring out the best in young people. He never missed football matches or tennis games which were very much part of our village life. He was very caring and compassionate, a man of great faith and wisdom. He held the belief that every child has the ability to achieve their full potential.

I started my training in paediatric nursing, and all through the first year I found it extremely difficult because of the very nature of the work and the stress of seeing children suffer from painful illnesses at such a young age.

From early on, one person who had a huge influence on my life was Sister Carmel, who is a Sister of Charity, the organisation that owns and runs St Margaret's Hospice. Sister Carmel inspired, directed and guided me to achieve all that I have and helped me to be the kind of person I am today. I am now a highly trained and qualified professional. I work as the Chief Executive of a large hospice in Clydebank in Scotland, where my early training and perseverance have led me into a very full life. I deal with patients diagnosed with cancer. I see them every day which allows me the privilege of journeying with them and their relatives, experiencing the highs and lows of what is left of their life. I also help families to restructure their lives after they have lost their loved ones.

MY ADVICE: *You need to work, train for something and believe in yourself. No matter what you want to do, as long as you have the belief and confidence in yourself, you can achieve anything, with encouragement from others.*

Very Rev Andrew McLellan
Her Majesty's Chief Inspector of Prisons for Scotland and Minister of Religion

I am a minister of the Church of Scotland, and before taking up my present full-time appointment as Her Majesty's Chief Inspector of Prisons for Scotland, I was for 32 years a parish minister. I was minister of St Andrew's and St George's in Edinburgh from 1986–2002. I have been Convenor of the Church and Nation Committee of the Church of Scotland, and I was Moderator of the General Assembly in 2000. Throughout my year as Moderator I paid particular attention to poverty, prisons and preaching. I was also until recently the chairman of the Scottish Religious Advisory Committee of the BBC.

Jean Vanier is the founder of L'Arche, communities of people with learning difficulties and their assistants. He turned away from an academic career to share his life with those whom most people exclude. To his surprise, he found that his life was transformed, deepened and enriched by those who appeared to have little to give. In his books and in his personal life he has helped me, and many others, to make Christian faith loving and helpful. I have learned from him to cherish those who appear to be on the sidelines, for they have gifts that all of us need.

MY ADVICE: *In any profession, it is a vital lesson to learn to understand the gifts that those most in need can bring.*

Very Rev John Miller
Former Moderator of the General Assembly of the Church of Scotland and Minister of Religion

I was minister of a church in a large council housing estate in Glasgow. I saw young people facing great hardships, and many died young. I was at a loss as to how to cope. Then I read a book called *Night* written by a survivor of the Holocaust, Elie Wiesel. It told of his experience in Auschwitz. He had faced the death of his family, his hope and his faith, but he had gone on living. I wrote to him and he replied. His courage, and his readiness to respond to my letter, have been an inspiration to me.

MY ADVICE: *Never be afraid to make contact, even by letter, with people whose words or actions have made an impact on you – even if they're famous. You may get help and encouragement you never expected.*

Rabbi Julia Neuberger
Rabbi and Chief Executive, King's Fund

I work as the Chief Executive of the King's Fund, an independent health care charity which works to improve the health of Londoners by making change happen in health and social care. I was educated at Newnham College, Cambridge and Leo Baeck College, London. I became a Rabbi in 1977, and served the South London Liberal Synagogue for 12 years before going to the King's Fund Institute as a Visiting Fellow, to work on research ethics committees in the UK. I then spent eight months as a fellow at Harvard Medical School in the US, and returned to London to work as Chairman of Camden & Islington Community Health Services NHS Trust until I moved to the King's Fund in 1997. I was a Civil Service Commissioner and am a member of the Committee on Standards in Public Life, a Trustee of the Imperial War Museum, and have written several books on Judaism, women, healthcare ethics and on caring for dying people.

My main inspiration to become a Rabbi came from one of my teachers at Cambridge, who has since become a Rabbi himself. He is Professor Nicholas de Lange. He arrived in my third year, and suddenly illuminated Jewish history, and Jewish–Christian relationships, for me. He suggested I thought about becoming a Rabbi, and he supported me in my application and interviews for rabbinic college. He also showed me that you didn't have to be fully certain before you tried something, which has stayed with me ever since.

MY ADVICE: *You can go for something even if you are not completely sure it is what you want to do.*

Archbishop Keith Patrick O'Brien
Archbishop of St Andrews and Edinburgh

I had always wanted to be a priest and when my family moved from Ireland to Scotland, I thought the 'time had come' when I was in Primary Seven and there was an opportunity to apply for one of the junior training colleges of the Catholic Church. However, after application, I was turned down, because of a heart murmur.

I continued at secondary school, but was 'turned down' again because of this heart murmur when I had completed my studies. In the meantime, my mother had died and I found increased consolation in the Church and in my desire to help others.

My parish priest in Edinburgh, Father Willie McLaughlin, helped me at the time of my mother's death and indeed as I continued my studies at university and then at seminary when I was eventually accepted. His home became a second home for me and his help and advice were incalculable in my years as a priest. I was only sorry that his death occurred in March of 1985, just some three months before my appointment as Archbishop of St Andrews and Edinburgh was announced.

MY ADVICE: *Have a specific goal in life; work towards that goal whatever obstacles arise; and have the help and advice of a mature person, who has already achieved his or her goal, and who can act as an ongoing guide.*

Major John Thompson
Free Churches Chaplain (Salvation Army) at London Heathrow Airport

After school, in the City of Birmingham, I worked in retail and then the motor industry. I entered training, at the age of 20, as a Salvation Army Officer, and was ordained and commissioned as a Lieutenant, to South Wales, two years later. I married a year later, and together with my wife who is also a Salvation Army Officer, we served jointly, leading congregations and work in South Wales (where I was promoted to the rank of Captain), South London, East Anglia and Teesside.

In 1982 I was appointed to the Yorkshire Divisional HQ as a Youth Officer and County Chaplain to the Scout Association in West Yorkshire. After five years, I moved to undertake a similar role for the North London Division and during this time received promotion to the rank of Major. In 1992 I resumed 'parish' work with my wife at Staines, Middlesex, and in 1997 we transferred to a similar joint ministry at Southport, Merseyside. In 2000 we were appointed to London Heathrow as Airport Chaplains where we divide our work across different terminals. In the course of our 'walking the terminals', contact is made with thousands of passengers and their relatives thoughout the year. As well as providing Worship Services for Christmas, Thanksgiving, Holy Week and Pentecost, we also observe September 11th at Heathrow, which filled the chapel to capacity, and we provide support and counsel where it is needed. Our work can range from comforting families at a time of bereavement, to providing ministry to asylum-seekers.

Apart from my parents, the example of other Christians, especially my Sunday School Teacher, Edith Ball, encouraged me into faith as a child. Later, as a teenager, the ministries of Salvation Army Officers, such as John Tomlinson, Doris Denham and Gordon Bailey, influenced my response to God's call into the same vocation. They were people who showed enthusiasm, care and love for ordinary people. They took time to listen to and encourage me. I studied and took time to understand their work in preaching and pastoral work. They gave me opportunities to practise the art of public speaking and caring for the needy in various locations around the West Midlands.

MY ADVICE: *Listen, observe and learn. Be obedient to the voice of your conscience, testing it alongside God's Word (the Bible) and the spiritual guidance of your church leaders.*

human rights and environment

Geoffrey Robertson QC
Human Rights Lawyer

I t would have been anachronistic, when I was at University in the early 1970s, to envisage a 'career' in human rights. Then, the very phrase smacked of amateur idealism. In Britain, human rights were something you wished, in an altruistic way, for the rest of the world, but talk of 'civil liberties' – especially with reference to Northern Ireland – and you risked being branded as subversive. So human rights was not an interest which careers advisers would recommend pursuing, other than as a part-time, *pro bono* charitable service for the oppressed, preferably in foreign lands.

I joined Amnesty International, and well remember my disappointment at the first meeting. Our task, we were instructed, was to write grovelling letters to brutal heads of state. 'Dear General Pinochet,' I would begin, 'the Oxford University branch of Amnesty is very concerned at reports of torture chambers in Santiago . . .' Or, to 'His Excellency Idi Amin Dada VC, we respectfully request that you might graciously be pleased to order an inquest to be held into the deaths of the three judges of your Court of Appeal, whose bodies (headless) were found floating in the river outside Kampala.'

It struck me that the human rights movement would never get very far by begging tyrants to be less tyrannical, so I retreated to the study of law – criminal law and international law – which were then entirely separate subjects. It was only when these twain met, many years later, that the phrase 'human rights' came to have real meaning. That is because any talk of 'rights' is merely rhetoric, unless those rights are capable of enforcement.

The story of how, at the turn into the twenty-first century, human rights began its transformation from a pious hope into a doctrine of international law, with its own courts and enforcement agencies, is astonishing. Just ten years ago it would have been fantastical to predict the arrest of Pinochet or the trial of Milosevic, or the advent of an International Criminal Court. For centuries, the world had worked on the assumption that nation states possessed 'sovereignty' - i.e. an immunity which permitted their political and military leaders to oppress their own peoples with impunity, because this was an internal affair in which other countries could not intervene. But today, we recognise that this immunity can be overridden if domestic oppression takes the form of a 'crime against humanity' - a crime so heinous that the very fact that fellow humans can conceive and commit it demeans us all as members of the human race. Crimes like genocide (e.g. 'ethnic cleansing'), widespread and systematic torture, or the mass murder of innocent civilians, can never be forgotten or forgiven: the perpetrators must be stopped, by force if necessary, then tried and punished.

This sea-change in attitudes to human rights has necessarily created a good deal of employment: there are careers not only for lawyers, but for administrators (e.g. in UN operations in Kosovo, East Timor, and Afghanistan), investigators, translators, forensic anthropologists, peace-keepers, election monitors, fund-raisers, journalists, doctors, teachers, refugee workers and the like. Governmental and non-governmental organisations offer positions that can intersect and interchange. Although there will always be a place for the well-intentioned amateur, the future will depend upon workers with full-time commitment and professional expertise. That is why I hesitate to offer my own experience as any model for a successful career trajectory: my generation had no role models, and I sometimes attribute such success as I am credited with to the uninspiring truth that I did not have much competition. When I read the outstanding qualifications of the numerous candidates for the few places in my chambers, or for the vacant positions at the

War Crimes Court over which I preside, I realise how difficult it must seem to gain a firm foothold on the first rung of a career ladder that is extending all the time.

There is one experience, however, which I believe all who have made a difference in human rights have in common: they have drawn their inspiration – in fact, their passion – from involvement with victims of human rights abuses. No book, however uplifting, and no television picture, however powerful, can substitute for the emotional impact of sharing their grief or injustice or humiliation, or feeling the sharp end of state oppression. It is through empathy with the victim, recognising the nobility of their will to survive and their determination to overcome suffering, that the dedicated idealism for effective human rights work will be forged.

That dedication will put in perspective the 'success' of wealthier contemporaries (who will justify their own insouciance about the wrongs of the world with jibes about 'liberal consciences' and 'do-gooders'). It will, more importantly, get you through the times when missions fail or colleagues get maimed by tropical diseases or land mines or snipers, or when the whole humanitarian cause is derided as offering no more than 'a bed for the night' in a world which – at least since September 11 2001 – seems more savage and polarised than ever.

I have been privileged to defend countless victims of state oppression, in many countries, and I unhesitatingly attribute to them the stimulus for my own human rights involvements. Some had been persecuted because they were good – like the Catholic Youth workers locked up for years in Singapore because of their work for the poor. Some were persecuted because they were bad – like Michael X, the murderer I met on death row in Trinidad, who persuaded me to devote a lot of my legal life to stopping executions in the Caribbean. Let me tell you about two prisoners of conscience I met on Amnesty missions in the mid-1980s who became my particular human rights heroes: the one unknown and now untraceable, the other celebrated throughout the civilised world.

Robert Ratshitanga was a prisoner in a country of which I had never heard until Amnesty asked me to go there. The state of Venda no longer exists – if indeed it ever really did. It was a 'native homeland' carved out of South Africa by the apartheid government, which pretended that it was independent, although its laws and their enforcement were dictated from Pretoria. Venda's 'statehood' was a sham, and went unrecognised by any other country: it was condemned by the UN and resented by the majority of black South Africans who were struggling for true independence. Robert Ratshitanga's crime had been to assist that struggle in the most innocuous way: he was a local shopkeeper, and when three starving ANC fighters turned up at his door one morning, he provided them with a plate of porridge before they went back to the bush. This meant he was guilty of 'harbouring' terrorists, a crime which under the Terrorism Act carried a minimum penalty of five years in prison.

The obvious injustice of this mandatory minimum sentence had attracted Amnesty's concern, and it was a measure of the South African government's effort to improve its human rights image that prisoners in Robert's position were (at least while the Amnesty mission was in town) offered a merciful alternative. If they pleaded guilty to a different offence – 'treason to the state of Venda' – their sentence would be in the discretion of the judge, who was prepared to order their immediate release. Since the five years mandated by the Terrorism Act at Venda's typhoid-ridden prisons was often a death sentence, the prisoners all accepted the deal – all except Robert Ratshitanga.

I met him in the cells: he was forty-five, a man of extraordinary presence and dignity. For the six months since his arrest, he had been held in solitary confinement in a stifling corrugated-iron cell in a disease infested bush prison. He had nonetheless managed to acquire a Biro and toilet paper: from the sole of his shoe he produced for me his prison diary, an Andrex scroll in minute but copperplate handwriting which detailed his brutal treatment. As a consequence he was in poor health and believed he would die in prison if he had to serve the full term of five years, but to secure his release he would have to accept a plea of treason 'with an intention to impair the sovereignty of the state of Venda'. As Robert explained to me, 'there is no way, absolutely no way, that I can bring myself to acknowledge the existence of the state of Venda'.

There was no moving him. His lawyer tried, and so did I. But this man, for all the suffering and probable death that a five-year sentence would entail, could not acknowledge the existence of Venda as an independent sovereign state. He was right, of course, as a matter of principle: the 'state' of Venda was a sick joke perpetrated by the Afrikaaner government as a cover for apartheid. But would it really matter to anyone if, to save his life, he accepted in court that he had impaired its non-existent sovereignty? It mattered to Robert Ratshitanga. With all the integrity which must have attended Sir Thomas More's refusal to take an oath in full knowledge of the deadly consequences, he unswervingly declined to receive mercy by entering a fraudulent plea. So he was instead committed under the South African Terrorism Act, and was marched off into captivity and obscurity, where subsequent inquiries have failed to locate him. He lives on vividly in my mind as a true prisoner of conscience. Much as I respect the iron will that stayed in the soul of Nelson Mandela, and enjoyed at first hand the feisty righteousness of Bishop Tutu, it was the meeting with Robert Ratshitanga which convinced me of the moral imperative of overthrowing apartheid.

Human rights heroes, of course, often turn out to have feet of clay – which is why I found it easiest to admire one whose witty self-deprecation and genuine humility commended him to all except the humourless and incompetent Stalinists whose tyranny he overthrew. I met Vaclev Havel in Prague in the years before the 'velvet revolution', when I was engaged on missions to support the Czech Jazz Society which had, improbably, become a target for state persecution. I stood with him on the steps of the city's central court in 1986 after the society's president, Kavel Srp, had been sentenced to prison on a trumped-up fraud charge. We looked down at several hundred of his youngish supporters who spilled into the adjacent square, and they began to sing – a ragged, half-crooned chorus of 'We Shall Overcome'. Havel smiled tightly, and whispered 'You can tell which are the secret police – they are the ones who know all the words.'

The secret police were everywhere in those years, playing a cat-and-mouse game with this famous dissident, who had served three years in prison for launching 'Charter 77', a human rights manifesto which challenged the communist government's denials of free speech and civil liberties. We would meet in cafés overlooking the Vlatava river, where he would provide crucial information about political prisoners, the families who needed financial support, and the lawyers who could be trusted, alternating this necessary gossip with philosophical observations about the need to revise the map of middle Europe so disastrously drawn at Yalta. He was always nervous – the authorities could return him to prison at any time; always apologetic for his English (which was fine), and always ironic. Once, when I found I did not have enough devalued Czech currency to pay for the meal, I offered US dollars – a currency accepted with alacrity everywhere in the city, notwithstanding an official embargo. Havel was horrified, and explained (I kicked myself for not realising) that he would be immediately arrested by the secret police watching us from the far table, as an accomplice in black-marketeering. 'This is the first rule of being a dissident – you must scrupulously obey the law.'

I have never much liked jazz – you keep thinking it will turn into a tune, and it doesn't. I could not at first understand why it was suppressed by the Nazis, and by Stalin, and why the Jazz Society was so feared by the Czech government. The answer became clear when I attended a late night concert one evening at the Lucerna – a cavernous theatre in the heart of Prague owned by Havel's family. Totalitarians distrust jazz because it's music you can talk under. The talk under the music that morning was indeed subversive, but only three years later the audience in the Lucerna dispensed with this musical camouflage and, led by Havel, turned the theatre into a people's convention on how to restore democracy.

Robert Ratshitanga and Vaclev Havel are examples of all the men and women who have suffered by refusing to compromise their principles under the pressure of state tyranny; from such sacrifices human rights workers can summon the spirit to make a full-time career commitment to a cause to which they might otherwise have just sent a donation. But remember, whether you wish to work for refugees or victims of torture, or on the prosecution of war criminals, that these causes now cry out for well-developed professional skills, so idealism may not be a sufficient condition for employment. It will always, I think, be a necessary one.

Bob Alexander QC (Lord Alexander of Weedon)

Barrister, Conservative Member of the House of Lords

As a barrister, I have specialised in commercial, business and financial arbitration and mediation. I also give legal advice and provide some advocacy services principally in constitutional issues. I am joint head of 3–4 South Square Chambers with Michael Crystal QC.

I was the Chairman of the House of Lords Delegated Powers and Deregulation Committee for seven years until Spring 2002, and was a member of the Independent Commission on Voting Reform (the Jenkins Commission), which reported in 1998. I am also an Honorary Visiting Professor in the Law Department at University College London and have chaired continuing education seminars on human rights for the Faculty, and I am a member of the Council of the Constitution Unit.

I am also the Chairman of the Royal Shakespeare Company, Chancellor of Exeter University, and was Chairman of the MCC for a year recently, which all reflect my outside interests.

Far and away the most influential figure was Ken Polack, the first fellow of Law at King's College, Cambridge, my college.

I read English for two years, then I suddenly realised that I lacked the talent to be an actor, the will to be a teacher and the intrusiveness to be a journalist.

So I changed to law because a friend said his father was a solicitor in Crawley New Town and would take me in articles. Hardly exciting, but I had no high opinion of my own talents. Enter Ken Polack. He enthused me for the law as a discipline, and fresh from his own pupilage in the Temple, told me to drop the idea of being a solicitor and give the Bar a chance. The Bar then seemed frightening and élitist but he was determined and so I gave it a go and it proved right for me. What an inspiration, and my gratitude will be life-long. He sparked my enthusiasm, the most precious recipe for success.

MY ADVICE: *The only moral I can think of is that to be touched by even one good teacher is a prize beyond telling.*

Vicky Garner
Campaigns Director, Surfers Against Sewage (SAS)

It is my job to decide what issues Surfers Against Sewage are going to campaign on and to devise the best approach, whether lobbying politicians, staging a peaceful demonstration or working with the media. Since I was little I have always had a sense of indignation at injustice. I grew up in Cornwall and my love of the sea drove me to study Marine Geology at Cardiff University. While I was there I watched SAS's antics on the news and after I graduated returned to Cornwall and joined SAS as a volunteer, working at nights in a pub. After completing a MSc degree in Marine Science, I joined SAS as the personal assistant to the then director, Chris Hines, and have worked my way up to my current position.

Chris Hines drove me to see the potential in myself and to become one of the changemakers. He always earned people's respect by being honest, armed with the facts and being prepared to talk, and always looking for solutions. The best advice he ever gave me was to keep it fun.

MY ADVICE: *Find an issue you feel passionate about – the kind of thing that you can talk about for hours. Do not be disrespectful – in the world of campaigning you will only make headway if you have respect for others. Keep your feet on the ground.*

Read and talk, be open to conversations and meetings. Lead by example: you can't expect others to do what you won't do yourself. If you want to make a difference to the world, you've got to seize the day and enjoy doing it.

Anthony Hudson
Architect

I studied engineering, and then architecture, qualifying as an architect in three stages, first at Churchill College, Cambridge, then University of Westminster, London and finally for Professional Practice as a RIBA Registered Architect in 1983. I worked for eight years with a number of architectural practices in Norwich, Chardigargh, India, and London. In 1985 I formed my own practice Anthony Hudson Architects and worked on the restoration of listed buildings, new-build houses, renovations and remodelling of existing houses and recording studios. As the practice grew and after ten years, I went into partnership with another architect, Sarah Featherstone, for another seven years. Now as Hudson Architects our work includes one-off houses, housing, mixed-use urban and rural regeneration initiatives, art galleries and museums, education and research buildings, cafés and restaurants. We work in the UK, elsewhere in Europe and in India. Hudson Architects also endeavour to raise public awareness and involvement in architecture and have participated and initiated events and exhibitions to that end, including the *How did they do that?* exhibition at the RIBA.

I didn't think of being an architect until I was 20. In fact previously I had no notion of what it was about. In a way it was a culmination of lots of interests and inspirations – like my history teacher who took us on trips round Norfolk to see wonderful old buildings or my mathematics teacher who made maths seem like a wonderful puzzle. But it was my uncle who was one of my biggest sources of inspiration, encouragement and support. He was a Local Authority Quantity Surveyor after being a bomber navigator in the Second World War, shot down over Germany, imprisoned and losing his toes to frostbite. From these experiences and his own delving into history he has developed an amazing understanding of the way things work at all levels of life. In particular he worked on controversial buildings and through talking about these made me realise that there was much more to architecture than just pretty façades. He had the time, and still has, to discuss the pros and cons of all kinds of buildings and illustrate them with anecdotes. This has been an inspiration.

MY ADVICE: *Be inquisitive about your surroundings and always try to record and understand in whatever way you feel appropriate whether it be by drawing, painting, filming, writing or just chatting with somebody else what makes you so excited about being in a particular place.*

Professor Mike Hulme
Executive Director, Tyndall Centre for Climate Change Research

I am currently the Executive Director for the Tyndall Centre for Climate Change Research, the national UK centre for research into solutions to climate change. We look at all kinds of aspects of climate change, from global warming to the recent flooding in the UK.

I obtained a degree in geography from the University of Durham in 1981 and a PhD from the University of Wales. I then lectured in geography for four years at the University of Salford, before moving to the University of East Anglia in 1988 to work as a researcher into global climate change. I secured my current position after successfully leading a consortium of universities to bid to host the Tyndall Centre.

I have published over 120 scientific journal articles and book chapters on these and other topics together with over 220 reports and popular articles. I was a Co-ordinating Lead Author for the chapter on 'Climate Scenario Development' for the Third Assessment Report of the United Nations Panel on Climate Change, as well as a contributing author for several other chapters. I have prepared climate scenarios for the UK government, including the UKCIP98 and UKCIP02 scenarios, the European Commission, UNEP, WWF-International and the IPCC. I have advised numerous companies and non-governmental organisations about climate change and its implications.

The person who was most influential for me as a late teenager was the late Reverend Jim 'Boss' Meiklejohn MBE, who was a family friend in the town in which I grew up, St Andrews in Fife, Scotland. Aged 72 when I met him, the Reverend Meiklejohn was

55 years older then me, yet he was perhaps the first person to fully treat *me* as an independent adult. He took a genuine interest in my studies, in my hobbies and in my personal development. He gave me confidence to change from a timid, introverted teenager into a more confident young adult able to communicate with, and help, others. Although not offering me any specific or long-lasting career advice, he did show me that it was more important to be true to myself than simply to mimic others, and that showing care and consideration for others usually brought rewards exceeding those secured by stepping on other people.

MY ADVICE: *Question everything and work it out for yourself. If you have an idea, pursue it. Recognise that your life experience is unique and therefore your contribution to society is also unique. Be inspired by others, but never try to copy them. When travelling abroad take time to explore and appreciate other people, places and cultures. Treat others how you would wish to be treated. Easy really!*

Joel Joffe CBE (Lord Joffe)
Human Rights Lawyer

I was born and educated in South Africa, and worked as a commercial and then a human rights lawyer in Johannesburg appearing for the defence in a number of major trials including that of Nelson Mandela.

Through my working life I have also worked in the financial services industry, in health (running hospitals and health trusts in the UK) and as the Chairman and/or Trustee of a number of charities. I was the Chair of Oxfam until last year.

I was inspired by Bram Fischer QC a leading barrister in South Africa and the then leader of the banned South African Communist Party. Bram was an exceptionally able lawyer totally committed to the human rights of his clients and all South Africans. He was a person of immense courage but gentle and kind and loved and respected by all who knew him. I met him while practising law and we worked closely together on a number of political trials.

Bram taught me by example. He was meticulous in his work as a barrister, was courteous but firm in court and cared for his clients as human beings. He treated me as an equal even though I was 25 years younger and he made me feel valued.

MY ADVICE: *Remember always that human rights law is primarily about justice and that the financial rewards are secondary.*

Marilyn Mornington
District Judge

I work as a District Judge in Birkenhead and Liverpool, and am the Chair of the Northern Circuit Domestic Violence Group. I also chair the Inter-Governmental Initiative on Domestic Violence, Raising the Standards, and am a Member of the Lord Chancellor's Advisory Group on Domestic Violence. More locally, I am the Chair of the Wirral Domestic Violence Forum. I am also an Adviser to ACPO, Chair of Kids in Need and Distress, Honorary Patron of the Community District Nurses Association and Member of the Metropolitan Police Project, Adhikar International, all of which connect to my work against domestic violence.

As a working-class girl from Liverpool I was lucky enough to win a scholarship to a warm, caring school, Notre Dame in Woolton. The mother of one of my closest school friends, Dr Peggy Norris, became my inspiration. When she was in her 20s, Peggy was one of the first doctors into the Nazi death camps after the Second World War. This experience and her deep faith led her to campaign tirelessly for human rights and dignity. She was equally a loving wife, mother to five remarkable children, full time GP and a marvellous homemaker, all whilst retaining her beauty and feminity. I have striven for a life like hers, one she inspired me to believe a woman could achieve with hard work. My path for helping people was firstly through being a barrister and judge, and latterly, finding my niche, in joining the struggle to save the lives of the victims of domestic violence and their children.

MY ADVICE: *Whilst it is important to be able to provide your family with a comfortable standard of living, money should never be a goal in itself. Lifelong satisfaction will be achieved through hard work, discipline, belief in what you are doing and the highest professional standards. Always try to achieve a balance between your professional, family and social life.*

Leonor Stjepic
Director, The Galapagos Conservation Trust

I started out working in the commercial sector for 14 years, working in an antique packing and shipping company, a Mexican merchant bank, a publishing company, a recording studio and as a self-employed consultant, all of which taught me a lot about setting up and managing projects. I then settled for nearly five years as the Head of Administrative Services and Fundraising Executive for the National Playing Fields Association. During this time I also studied for a professional diploma in Management, and in 2001 gained my MBA with the Open University Business School. I also worked voluntarily as a founder member of the Amnesty Working Group for Children, and visited Croatia to volunteer in a refugee camp during the war there. During 2000, I worked as the Development Manager for Index on Censorship, and in 2001 became the Director of the Galapagos Conservation Trust.

My uncle, Agustin Roa, was the person who most inspired me. Having fled Spain at the end of the Spanish Civil War, he came to England and fought in the British Army against Hitler. After the war he had to start again – exiled from his country, with little money and far from friends and family.

He taught me four valuable things: firstly, that often fear – of failure, of ridicule, of the new – stops us from reaching our potential. I learnt from him not to fear failure or what others may think. Secondly, you are never too old to learn – at the age of 82 my uncle learnt how to use a PC. I had been unable to go to university but he encouraged me to keep learning and I now have an MBA. Thirdly, fight injustice – this inspired me to join Amnesty International. From then on I knew that I wanted to work in the voluntary sector. It took me 13 years to achieve that ambition and now I am the Director of the Galapagos Conservation Trust. And finally, nobody is better than you or worse than you. This gave me the self-confidence to deal with people at all levels.

MY ADVICE: *Learn from all experiences, however negative they may seem at the time. They will help you cope with whatever happens in the future. Be prepared to be flexible – working in the charity world means that you will* *often be called upon to do a variety of things. One day you may be stuffing envelopes and the next attending a Royal event. Don't be put off by people saying no to you. Get on with trying to get a yes from the next person. Don't be afraid to ask for help. Be open to new experiences and new people, you never know who may give you your next good idea. Only work in this sector if you really believe in what the charity is doing — it will be hard work, challenging, emotionally wearing at times, but ultimately very enriching and fulfilling.*

farming and countryside

Michael Eavis
Proprietor of Worthy Farm, Somerset
and Founder and Organiser of the Glastonbury Festival

I was raised on Worthy Farm during the onset of World War II. Although my family of Methodists were basically unwar-like, my earliest memory of my father was him wearing his badly fitting Home Guard uniform. One night while he was milking the cows I remember another home guard person coming in the cow stall with a gun telling him that he was late for practice. I thought he was going to shoot my father!

We had a lot of religion in the household and when we had the preacher down for Sunday dinner we gave him a hard time. There were four boys at that time and we weren't prepared to take what was offered verbatim. Politics, religion and social issues were reasons for a good argument – and we did! No doubt changing sides and ideas as we were trying to formulate principles for our life ahead.

Mother was quite stern. She came from London and my father fancied her, I think, because she was better educated and much brighter than the local girls that he had promised to marry! She taught in all the local schools, usually as a headmistress. I remember her cycling to school with me on the back of her bike; I must have been four or five at the time. That was after dishing out porridge and fried eggs to us early in the morning. She had drive, ambition and serious amounts of energy – and she was still having more babies. She instilled in us that success was all that really mattered and there was no mention of failure. We see survival television programmes showing bears and other large animals pushing their young around aggressively in order for them to cope with their potential predators. This was an attitude adopted by my mother to prepare us for the storms of life ahead. Love fitted into it somehow, I'm sure.

I went to the village school to start with, which I don't remember much about apart from lying on a coconut mat after school dinner for half an hour every day, a habit I never recovered from. I wasn't a clever type and I was rather eclipsed by my younger brother who showed signs of brilliance. He finished up being a top-flight headmaster of a school in Newcastle and I finished up on the farm.

I went to Wells Cathedral School as a boarder when I was ten, which I found difficult to start with. Mother was quite sure that whatever happened I would finish up better at Wells than I would have done at the local secondary modern. I had some good friends there who helped me develop my personality and particularly my humour. Some of the teachers were so weird that most of the lessons were spent trying to work out ways of understanding what they were up to, so I didn't learn much really. I saw myself as a bit of a bystander, watching and laughing and enjoying my friends' company – and now it's the festival that keeps me laughing!

To cut a long story short, I then went into the Merchant Navy at 16 and went off to sea into the real world. I had never seen my father cry before, but when I left the farm to go to sea he said goodbye and broke down in tears. I couldn't really work out why.

The harsh reality of life at sea struck me once we sailed from Hull into the North Sea. A frozen rope came up over the capstan and hit a fellow next to me out cold. We had to put him off the ship and I never knew whether he survived or not. Around the world we went, hauling anything from railway carriages to Africa and bringing back elephants to London Zoo. The casualties I saw from alcohol and venereal diseases made me feel that Methodist basic principles seemed to make sense. The same applies of course to the drug culture of today. The irony is that here I am now running one of the biggest shows in the world, and I constantly have to reconcile the merits of the festival against the down side of the drug culture.

My beloved father died when I was only 19, so I had to leave the life on the ocean waves and return to the call of the farm. I was very excited and got stuck into it. The bank manager gave me a grim account of the money side of things but gave me a stack of loans to have a go – and I did. As a family we were strong on politics and various crusades, but we weren't really the best of farmers. When the Isle of Wight and Bath Blues festivals came into my sights in the late '60s, I saw a vision of a future for me. I went at it like a bull at a gate. My political background, a flair for pop music that I was punished for at Wells Cathedral School, and my huge affection for the farm made everything fall into place.

The moral of the story is, I suppose, to find a purpose in life, use what ability you can muster and stay firm with your principles. Just remember: there are always more people out there saying it can't be done than people who say that it can. Don't take no for an answer. Fight your corner and believe in yourself.

Helen Browning OBE
Organic Farmer

I farm Eastbrook Farm, a 1,350-acre organic livestock and arable farm in Wiltshire. Our enterprises include pigs, two dairy herds, beef cattle, veal calves, sheep, 600 acres of cereal and 50 acres of vegetables. I am also the founder of Eastbrook Farms Organic Meat which I established in the late 1980s. This business incorporates a nationwide home delivery service. It has also formed a network of top-quality organic pig farmers, the pork from which is marketed as branded organic pork products into the multiple retailers. I was a member of the Government's Policy Commission on the Future of Farming and Food, which issued its report in 2002. I am a Meat and Livestock Commissioner and member of the Red Meat Industry Forum, a member of the Soil Association, Agriculture and Environment Biotechnology Commission, and chairman of the Food Ethics Council. I was awarded an OBE in 1998 for services to organic farming.

Much of my inspiration, passion and desire to change the way we grow our food, care for our countryside and our farm animals comes not from any human source, but from the natural world. I grew up at Eastbrook on the farm I now run, a rather sickly child, a dunce academically, but with the freedom to roam the countryside on foot, horse and bike, and my personal philosophy was honed by that intimate knowledge of the land, the elements and the seasons.

If I had to choose just one person who has made a huge difference to my life, it would have to be Patrick Holden, Director of the Soil Association. Having worked closely with him for 14 years, through a time which has seen the organic movement grow from a core of deeply committed individuals into the mainsteam consciousness, I have always been astonished, and often infuriated, by his energy, conviction and overwhelming optimism. Most important to me, however, is Patrick's dedication to the search for a more profound understanding of life, and his preparedness to share some of that exploration in an undogmatic, generous and supportive spirit.

MY ADVICE: *I would go down to the woods, or face the blustery sea, or climb that hill or mountain if you can cope with that sort of thing. Respect and empathise with the elements, the seasons and the world that gives not a jot for us humans. Nature is still the best mentor of all.*

Ewen Cameron
Chairman, Countryside Agency

I am currently Chairman of the Countryside Agency and the Government's Rural Advocate. I am also a farmer and Chairman of Lets Go Travel Limited, which won Travel Agent of the Year 2001–02. In the past I have been National President of the Country Land & Business Association. I was also founder Chairman of Orchard FM Radio in 1988–89, our local radio station.

Apart from my father who inspired me to follow him into a life of public service, I have met many people whose approach I have admired and sought to emulate, but none more so than the late Sir Charles Troughton, Chairman of the British Council and an old friend of my family. He let it be known to me, and I am sure many other youngsters, that he had total confidence in our ability to excel at whatever we turned our hand to, providing we never accepted less than 100 per cent effort from ourselves. He drove the message home whenever I was starting something new, whether going on a course, taking an exam or even starting a job. He informed me that I was not just going to get by, but I was going to approach this new challenge with a view to excelling or shining, and what's more you felt he knew you could do it.

MY ADVICE: *Only accept the highest standards, above all from yourself. Learn to focus and listen well to others.*

Don't forget to dream. Nurture your dreams, hone your skills and remain focused, and sooner or later the pieces will fall into place for your dreams to come true.

Temper the enthusiasms I hope you have with the ability to stand back. Try to see the immediate priority within the broader and longer-term patterns of life. That way comes maturity and wisdom.

Ben Gill
President of the National Farmers' Union (NFU) E & W

I was educated at Barnard Castle School, Co. Durham and St John's College, Cambridge University, and then went to work at Secondary School, Namasagali, Uganda, from 1972–75, as a teacher and starting a school farm. I took over the family farm in North Yorkshire in 1978 and still run this today.

I became involved in the NFU in 1980 starting with local branch meetings, moving on to county meetings, then to National committees by 1985. I have served in several positions within the NFU starting as National Livestock Chairman 1987–91, then Vice President in 1991 and Deputy President 1992–97, and finally President in 1998. I have also held various Research Council posts between 1991 until 1997 and have been President of the Confederation of European Agriculture since 2000.

Fellow North Yorkshire farmer, Ronnie Foster, was already a long-standing member of the NFU when I became involved. I have never met anyone who has been so devoted to the betterment of his fellow farmers and his industry while still having to maintain his direct day-to-day involvement with his own business.

He has always been the fulfilment of the phrase, 'If you want a job doing, go to a busy man'. Nothing has ever been too much for Ronnie to do and at all times he has demonstrated a degree of patience and understanding based on a level of common sense that was hard to match anywhere else.

The best way to have effect is by example and there is no doubt in my mind that the, at times, selfless example that Ronnie set could not have been a better one to follow. It made me feel even more determined to address the representational needs of all the farming community, but particularly the smaller farmer.

MY ADVICE: *It is very easy to become demoralised by the constant criticism of minorities who often create a level of noise way above their relevance or importance. Dialogue at all times is important with all sectors to listen and explain; to take the necessary expert advice where it is needed and then to come to conclusions that you are personally happy with. If you do not know the answer then never be afraid to say so.*

Jeannette Orrey
Catering Manager, St Peter's Primary School

I am the only Catering Manager within the Nottinghamshire Education Authority to independently cater school meals and this is since deregulation in April 2000. For ten years I have worked as the Catering Manager for St Peter's School, East Bridgford. Currently I cater for 170 children per day. When I first started at the school the uptake in school meals was 90 per day. My job involves the general management of the school kitchen, including cooking, cleaning and the serving of meals. I am also responsible for the day-to-day running of all the kitchen-based equipment and making sure everything runs smoothly.

St Peter's School kitchen has gone from strength to strength in recent years. All of the meat and vegetables used in the kitchen is locally produced and fully traceable. This has meant going out and meeting local farmers and visiting farm shops to get the best possible prices.

In 2001 I entered a British meat competition, coming second and also gaining a five-star award. Since then I have written articles for the local newspapers and industry magazines. In 2001, and again in 2002, I was awarded the Clean Food Award Certificate of Excellence and I am in the process of gaining my Advanced Food Hygiene Certificate.

In October 2002 I was joint winner of the Local Food Initiative of the Year which is run by the Soil Association in conjunction with the *Mail on Sunday*'s *You* magazine. This was a very proud day for me and all the staff at St Peter's. Going to London to receive our award at the Dorchester Hotel was a very memorable day.

The person who has inspired me is David Maddison, the Headteacher of St Peter's Primary School. David is great at giving ideas and suggestions and encouraging you to think about them, turn them around and make them your own. His one statement that particularly sticks in my mind is, 'Know what is possible, do what's realistic!'

He has guided my career so far and has enabled me to achieve things I never thought possible. This has given me the confidence to take on new challenges, knowing that if I need any advice he is there. Our favourite phrase is 'Let's just see where the future takes us.'

MY ADVICE: *Anything is possible if you believe in yourself.*

Fiona Reynolds CBE
Director-General, The National Trust

After finishing school, I went to university to study geography and land economy. I started my career as Secretary to the Council for National Parks and went on to become Assistant Director (Policy) then Director of the Council for the Protection of Rural England. After six years in this exciting role, I worked for three years as Director of the Women's Unit at the Cabinet Office before becoming Director-General of the National Trust in 2001. I hold several non-executive positions on environmental bodies and was most recently a Member of the Commission on the Future of Food and Farming.

Going back to my time at university, I arrived at Cambridge full of trepidation about how I would measure up to the bright and articulate students around me. My tutor, Lucy Adrian, saw at once that I needed a confidence boost. But she didn't take pity on me – far from it! Her approach was – slowly and without me noticing – to build up my self-assurance. She did this by introducing me to ideas and authors that really inspired and enthused me. She encouraged my efforts but always sought more from me, helping me to fulfil my potential. I shall always be grateful to her.

food, restaurants and hotels

Perween Warsi
Founder and Managing Director, S & A Foods

I moved to the UK with my husband Talib in 1975, having been born and raised in India. Talib is a GP and we moved to this country when he was presented with an excellent job opportunity here.

I have always had a passion and flair for cooking and creating recipes, in the traditional way. After some time in the UK, I began trying numerous 'Indian' dishes from British supermarkets and was very disappointed with the quality. They were bland and boring – not the vibrant, fresh taste of traditional Indian food.

Consequently, I decided to enter the market with quality, authentic Indian dishes prepared in the traditional way. I started very small, and in 1986 began making finger foods for a local takeaway. My products proved very popular and orders began to increase. To cope with the increasing demand, I took on a couple of ladies to support me and we soon grew to five product lines making hundreds of items a week. I named the business S & A Foods after my two sons, Sadiq and Abid.

My vision, from day one, was to see consumers throughout the nation enjoying my products. I saw the natural route to growth was through the supermarkets with national distribution channels, so I began presenting my products to supermarkets to set up trials. After much persistence and legwork, I managed to persuade ASDA and Safeway to use my products in blind tastings. This resulted in me winning my first ever contract with ASDA.

Needing extra backing for the business we joined with the Hughes Food Group plc in 1987, which allowed us to invest in a new purpose-built factory on a Greenfield site in Derby.

By 1989 we had diversified beyond finger foods into the Indian ready-meals market to meet the growing demand of our customers. We had a slight setback in 1990 when the Hughes Food Group plc went into receivership despite our success. But my husband and I managed to win back control of the company in a management buy-out in November 1991.

We now produce complete meals and accompaniments from across the globe, including India, China, Malaysia and Thailand. We have also pioneered numerous award-winning concepts including the Curry Pot at ASDA, Waitrose Noodle Bar, Balti Meals and the Meal for One.

It would be difficult to pinpoint any one person that has provided me with inspiration. There have been a number of 'influences' and 'influencers' on my life in the past and I continue to find inspiration from others even now.

My family has been incredibly supportive and inspirational for me in both a personal and business sense, particularly my mother and father. My mother has always encouraged me in everything I do and we are still very close. She inspired me to break the mould, despite being an Asian woman. She encouraged me to be myself and show my true character and strengths, proving that Asian women can succeed in whatever they do. She taught me to be self-sufficient and confident in my approach to life.

My father was also a huge inspiration to me. A phrase he used, which I continually refer to throughout my life, is 'Keep your eyes on the stars and your feet on the ground.' He taught me not to create barriers, but to think beyond the norm, whilst remembering my roots and keeping a sensible outlook on life.

My father taught me to rely upon my intuition and be a good listener, learning from the experience of others.

My husband was also incredibly supportive of my business initiative and I would not be where I am now without his patience and encouragement. In the early days when the business was in its infancy and the children were young, life was particularly hard. I would regularly pick the children up from school and return home, working until the early hours.

In modern-day terms, I would say Archie Norman and Allan Leighton are my 'business heroes' – their ability to create a culture of creativity within an organisation, and turn companies around, fascinates me.

I also have great admiration for Anita Roddick – her passion for her cause and desire to assist the environment, a huge driving force in her life, has led to tremendous success. An ambitious and focused woman who sets an example to all women wanting to achieve in business.

Similarly, Ellen MacArthur, the yachtswoman, simply for her sheer determination and what I call 'get up and go'. A woman who lives for her dreams and continually pushes her mental and physical boundaries, setting herself new and hard challenges to maintain her passion for sailing.

I also admire Nelson Mandela's determination and passion, his ability to motivate people and lead them forward on issues, which matter to him, both in the past and particularly in the present – succeeding beyond adversity. I'd love to find out where he draws his strength, what drives him to keep going and achieve what he does.

All of the people I have gained my inspiration from are passionate about their subject, determined to succeed and have tremendous tenacity. Succeeding in life is about setting goals and thinking creatively about how to meet those goals. I try to bring this into my organisation through my enthusiasm for food and innovative ideas.

People in this country are encouraged to 'think outside the box'. I say, why have a box at all? Why restrict yourself? It is much better to brainstorm ideas and 'aim for the stars' and then find a way to achieve them. I truly believe anything is possible if you have the will to make things happen.

I am naturally therefore a very positive person. I cannot stand negativity in any form – there is always a better way of doing things and I refuse to linger on problems or mistakes. You must always look forward in this business, identifying the next opportunity, product or service. I believe that positivity in a leader encourages people in an organisation to be positive about the business and feel like a part of it. A negative outlook is self-perpetuating.

I believe in gaining inspiration from all kinds of different people in all walks of life. You can learn so much, simply from speaking to people – at all levels and in all sectors. Being a good listener is important for people in leadership positions. I encourage my people to feedback their opinions and ideas about the S & A Foods business from senior management positions to the shop floor – everyone has a voice.

We have a business innovation scheme for our people at S & A Foods called 'My Bright Idea'. It rewards our employees for original ideas that help challenge and change any aspect of the company's operations. It is an integral part of our on-going commitment to improve every aspect of our business and continually evolve to meet market demands.

You cannot run your own business unless you are passionate about it, because you will live and breathe the business for the rest of your working life. I am passionate about S & A Foods – as passionate now as I was when I started the business, but this stage of the business is even more exciting – continually searching for new initiatives and dishes across the globe. Innovation is the lifeblood of the company and our ability to anticipate future trends to meet the demands of our customers, positions us at the forefront of the market.

I have been held up as an inspiration for women in business over recent years. Although extremely flattering, I do not take these surveys very seriously. But I do believe that women are natural leaders – they are innately multi-tasking and compassionate. They have to work especially hard to achieve success – whatever their chosen profession – and gain respect, particularly in male-dominated sectors. Women should be afforded support and encouragement from their male counterparts, the same level of support and encouragement that a working husband readily receives from his wife.

If I can in some way provide inspiration for women to succeed in whatever work they are involved in – not just running their own business – then that is very rewarding for me personally.

I had no experience and no marketing spend when I started S & A Foods. I simply had an 'idea' and an ambition to succeed, and was able to achieve success with authentic, quality products, hard work and word of mouth.

I would encourage all people to follow their dreams, in a business or personal capacity. With hard work and determination you can succeed in whatever you do. Simply maintain a focus and develop a goal to aim for. It is important though to continually move the goalposts and break through your personal barriers, to challenge your thinking and maintain an enthusiasm for whatever you do.

★ ★ ★

Loulla Astin
TV Chef and Restaurateur, Kosmos Taverna, Manchester

As a Cypriot living in the UK I love to sample all the different cuisines that are on offer in this country. As a person from the Mediterranean I live to eat rather than eating to live. My passions are for fresh ingredients, herbs, olive oil, garlic and all things seasonal in the tradition of my grandparents and parents.

My grandmother inspired me to prepare and cook dishes which had been handed down through the generations. She was self-sufficient when she grew her own vegetables at the farm, had her own citrus trees and olive orchards, reared chickens and rabbits and also had a few goats for the meat and milk. My grandmother only had a little Primus stove to cook with and often cooked outside on an open fire. It was very simple food, but very tasty.

When I first came to England, I studied as a fashion designer, and not a chef. After I married, my husband worked with my father in his pioneering catering business providing Greek food for the first time in Manchester – my mum was the head chef. In 1981, we opened our own restaurant, the now-famous Kosmos Taverna in Manchester, and I had to learn the trade very quickly. I'm still learning as every good chef should, and am experimenting with new Greek vegetarian dishes. Success has also brought media attention and since 1991 I have regularly appeared on television leading up to my own series, *Simply Greek*. My next goal is to publish my own cookery book.

MY ADVICE: *If you have a dream, cherish your dream. Make it come true and do it now.*

Alan Bell
Dining Room Manager, Chatham Wayside Inn, USA

After leaving Boroughmuir High School in Edinburgh, I joined Standard Life Assurance Company. From there I moved to the USA to become a High School Coach. Currently I run a semi-fine dining restaurant on Cape Cod in the USA.

I became interested in playing basketball while I was in High School. I joined Boroughmuir Basketball Club under the watchful eye of Bill McInnes (now Centre Manager for Westerhailes Education Centre in Edinburgh). The 14 years that I was with Boroughmuir taught me not only to play basketball (improving my own personal skills), but gave me a sense of belonging. It gave me the means to be competitive in life without being mean. It taught me to stick with something even when I believed my skill level was not that great. My unsung hero doesn't even know how he influenced my life, because it was over a long period of time, and now a long distance geographically too.

MY ADVICE: *Don't wait for things to happen; go out and make them happen. Take in everything that everyone has to offer. Give back to others your lessons in life. Don't wait, like I did, to recognise those who have helped you in life. There is no 'I' in 'TEAM'.*

Matthew Hooberman
Catering Consultant

I help set up bars, restaurants, hotels and, mainly, member's clubs. My background is in US and British politics which taught me about hospitality and charm, and my break came when I helped set up the member's club Soho House (in London and Somerset at Babington House).

My early inspiration was from Paul Jacobs, who was a freelance investigative journalist and writer in the United States. His campaign slogan when he unsuccessfully ran for the US Senate in California was 'Get Out from Under'. He uncovered government scandals and I remember his campaign on the government cover-up of medical information following nuclear tests in the 1950s carried out in Nevada. This showed cancer clusters developing in villages in Utah. The people were not informed but were monitored after wind blew radioactive material their way. Paul was a friend of my parents and he would shock them in front of me, which is probably why I loved him so much. Sadly he died in 1976 from cancer. I was 15 when he died. From then on I wanted to influence decisions and speak up.

MY ADVICE: *Always be sure you are telling the truth and maintain your integrity at all times. And Get Out from Under.*

Fiona Leishman
Restaurateur and Businesswoman

I studied French and marketing at university in Scotland, and spent a year living and working in France. When I returned to Scotland, I met my future husband and business partner. We dreamt of running our own restaurant and spent two years drumming up the necessary support and capital to convert a derelict old mill in central Scotland into our own small, but stylish venue. The restaurant was called Braeval and opened in 1986. My husband was the chef, and I was responsible for service, looking after our guests and the administration of the business. We were very young, determined and hardworking, and even holidays were spent exploring the cooking of other chefs and restaurateurs. We received many awards culminating in a much-treasured Michelin Star in 1991, and made successful cookery series for BBC Scotland. The business partnership was dissolved in 1997, but I continued to operate Braeval until 1999 when I sold it.

In 2001 I was invited by Gordon Ramsay to be General Manager of his first Scottish restaurant, Amaryllis, located in Glasgow within the prestigious One Devonshire Gardens hotel. Amaryllis received its Michelin star just one year after it opened.

I will never forget my first meeting with two people who immediately inspired me and who went on to become mentors and good friends. Eric and Betty Allen, who own Airds hotel at Port Appin on the west coast of Scotland, had embarked, like me, on the hotel/restaurant scene with no formal training. They have invested all their energies in transforming a simple highland inn into an unpretentious, comfortable and well-appointed hotel. Betty's menus specialise in using the wealth of fresh local produce, and the Allens were also rewarded in 1991 with a Michelin star which they have retained ever since. Eric and Betty were always generous with their advice and encouragement. It was clear to me from the outset that their example of commitment, hard work and a determination to avoid compromise lies at the heart of successful business. I also learnt that word of mouth recommendation is everything in the restaurant business and you are only as good as your last meal.

Other iconic figures in the restaurant world are Marco Pierre White who, when I first met him in the late 1980s, was cooking some of the most exciting and creative food in Britain; Paul and Kay Henderson who own the jewel in Devon's crown, Gidleigh Park, and whose example shows how to take comfort, style and excellence to a supreme level; and, of course, Gordon Ramsay, whose meteoric rise has blazed a trail for all aspiring young cooks and whose skills as a chef are second to none.

MY ADVICE: *Restaurant life can involve working long hours and you have to ask yourself if you really want to commit to the degree of physical and mental energy required. Try to get work experience with someone well rated in the food/hotel guides to see what life in the business is like. Start reading a trade journal like* Caterer *to get all the inside information. Always look clean and tidy when you present yourself for an interview as presentation is important in this business. Work hard, don't be put off by small hurdles and enjoy yourself.*

Paul Matteucci
Co-Proprietor, Vasco & Piero's Pavilion Restaurant, London

I studied economics at university in London, then went on to study for an MA in Business Information Technology & e-Commerce at Middlesex University. I joined Price Waterhouse as a trainee chartered accountant in 1990.

That year, I was sent to work for Bank Handlowy in Warsaw, Poland, where I met and fell in love with a girl called Ewa Luniewska. As a child she used to study in the bathroom as there were two brothers, her parents and herself living in a tiny two-bedroom flat on the border of Siberia. Her parents did not want her to study, as in those days before the Berlin Wall came down, the greater the education the less one earned. Ewa ignored their advice. She is now Head of a Department of ING Bank Warsaw. She showed me that one should follow one's dreams whatever the obstacles. This story reminds me every day that one should follow one's own path in life. Hence I ignored all conventional wisdom and went into the restaurant business because I enjoy it.

MY ADVICE: *Get a good education, no learning is wasted. Choose the role that you enjoy and get lots of experience even for no or low pay, the rewards will come later. Always think long-term and have long-term goals.*

retail and fashion

Linda Bennett
Founder and Managing Director, L K Bennett

I left university at the age of 22 having completed a business-related degree but not knowing exactly what I wanted to do with it. I knew I wanted to do something creative and felt that I should identify a product I was passionate about and build a career around it.

I have always been interested in fashion and particularly shoes – I had been collecting vintage shoes from an early age. I decided to enrol myself on a footwear design course at Cordwainers College in Hackney, having discovered that it was the only place in London with a course in shoe design. A year later I found myself gaining work experience in the design studio of the well-known French shoe designer Robert Clergerie. I spent a lot of time learning the processes that took place in the factory, which gave me an invaluable insight into the construction of footwear.

A few months later I took myself off to an international footwear fair in Germany. As I entered a huge pavilion packed full of colourful shoes I felt a frisson of excitement – I knew I had found my metier. Here I came into contact with the factories that could turn my design ideas into reality.

My first shop opened in Wimbledon Village in 1990 with the help of a bank loan of £15,000. Despite the recession of the early 1990s the business expanded cautiously and organically, and by 1994 we had our first store in central London. This proved to be extremely successful as we had a much wider audience than we had in Wimbledon. My sister Tania joined the business around this time and together we opened an average of two shops per year. In 1997 we launched a range of womenswear, which has strengthened the brand by extending the product base.

We now have 30 stores including outlets in Paris, Dublin, Manchester and Glasgow as well as a number of shops in and around London. We are planning to open more stores in the UK and would like to become a global brand with stores in the Far East and the United States.

A couple of months ago I won the Ernst & Young 2002 Entrepreneur of the Year Award for Consumer Products and have also recently won the *Drapers Record* Award for best small multiple retailer. I believe the key to the success of the business is the simple, elegant yet quirky styling of the clothing and footwear.

Probably the person who played the most significant part in my life as a mentor figure was my mother. I remember her being very interested in fashion, I particularly recall a pair of dusty pink suede shoes from the 1970s, which were especially beautiful. She spent a number of years in Denmark in the late 50s and early 60s when it was a mecca for furniture design and homeware. My mother instilled in us as children the importance of good design. She is a very tenacious woman and doesn't give up easily – qualities you need when starting up a business. She always encouraged us to believe that anything was achievable if you put your mind to it and worked hard enough at it. She also encouraged her children to think in a lateral way: the best solution to a tricky problem is not always the most obvious one. A large part of running a business involves problem solving skills.

Building the company from one shop to an international company involves an enormous learning curve. It is important to be flexible and to be able to think on many levels because you find yourself facing different challenges at every stage in the growth of the business. I also think it is very important to be open to learning about different aspects of the business at each step. It is also vital to surround yourself with a strong team and if possible to hire people who are better than you in the various areas of retail, leaving you the time to plan the strategy for the next phase of expansion. It is key never to become complacent, to keep an eye on the competition and never to underestimate the importance of continually coming up with new and exciting design – product is everything.

Retailing is a great career path for any young person as it combines business with design. There are great opportunities for those who prove themselves; the best way to achieve this is to understand what the customer wants and the best way to understand the needs of the customer is to work on the shop floor. I would advise any young person considering a career in retail to spend some time selling a product that they are genuinely interested in.

***

Simon Burke
Chairman, Hamley's plc

I was educated in Dublin and qualified as a chartered accountant before working at two accountancy firms. I joined the Virgin Group on the accounting side, learning about new deals, and then became the Managing Director of Virgin Retail, moving on to merge together and run Virgin Our Price records as Chief Executive. I was then Chief Executive of the Virgin Entertainment Group running all the consumer entertainment businesses. In 1999, I became the Chairman and Chief Executive of Hamley's plc to lead the turnaround of the famous toy retailer and make the business grow. All through my career I have worked with companies at critical times to make new deals and realise new opportunity for businesses in the retail sector.

For a year back in 1985 I worked with David James, the well-known company doctor. Although employed in only a junior capacity, I was given all kinds of responsibility by David, including the writing of a rescue proposal for the company, dealing with a major fraud, and helping to sell various businesses. David encouraged me to do all this, telling me how good I was and not to worry that I was still young and very junior.

Three years later, when I had a chance to become Managing Director of Virgin Retail, the loss-making Megastores business, I wasn't sure if I could tackle it, never having had any experience of running or turning around a business. But I remembered my time with David James and how he had helped me see that I could do all kinds of things even without experience. So I went for it and it changed my life: since then I have been turning around businesses and enjoying it hugely.

MY ADVICE: *Choose very carefully where you go to work, aim to be noticed and let one of the respected retail leaders bring you on. This will give you enormous advantage later on.*

Timothy Everest
Tailor

As one of the leading practitioners of the New Bespoke Movement, I have spent the past decade introducing a new generation of men and women to the joys of handmade clothing. I have also had a creative involvement in films such as *Mission Impossible* and *Eyes Wide Shut*, and have designed for the British Olympic teams and worked for the Oscars. My capsule collections are now available in some 30 stores worldwide including New York, Paris, Milan and Tokyo.

In 1999, I also joined Daks as Creative Director and have worked there to put the classic British label back on the fashion front pages. I continue to work as Creative consultant to both Daks and Marks & Spencer's for whom I developed designs for the Autograph & Sartorial ranges. Everything is underpinned by meticulous attention to quality and detail in my atelier.

Tommy Nutter was a very successful Savile Row tailor who had made suits for The Beatles and The Rolling Stones. He employed me when I first came to London. He was my boss and a friend.

Tommy Nutter introduced me to the wonderful traditions of Savile Row as well as his unique understanding as to how it was to be modern. His approach was almost 'Back to the Future', firmly rooted in the heritage of tailoring but designing and articulating this to a contemporary audience.

I was taught to be myself, an individual, and to trust my instincts with the best advice of 'be patient with your impatience'. He gave me the opportunity to learn the trade and develop personally, which later inspired me to start my own company.

MY ADVICE: *Be patient with your impatience. It is very important to listen and learn if you want to achieve your dream.*

Johnny Grey
Interior Architect and Kitchen Designer

I work as an interior architect designing sociable kitchens as well as whole houses. I have a design studio in Hampshire and a showroom in San Francisco. My work takes me all over the world. I also write books on design. I currently have three in print and one in production. I act as a consultant to the kitchen industry here and in the USA.

With the invention of the unfitted kitchen, I put into words what many people felt; that fitted kitchens were a cold, flawed and commercial way of designing kitchens. It changed the course of kitchen and interior design in the early 1980s, from harsh wall-to-wall laminate-coated units into furnished rooms with freestanding furniture and the serious use of applied design through such ideas as soft geometry and democratic planning.

I passed my degree in architecture at the Architectural Association School of Architecture in 1977. I set up my own workshop making furniture and designing interiors. Kitchens became my focal point after I received publicity for my first project for Sam Chesterton – a crazy, small Gothic kitchen in Tooting – made mostly of freestanding furniture. I always knew I wanted to be a designer and loved the process of making things. My head works so much faster than my hands. The frustration made me realise that design was my vocation.

I have always found it easy to ask for advice and had been blessed with supportive parents. They kept my vision to be involved in design and architecture going through an unimaginative schooling. My greatest need for mentoring was during my twenties, after I had achieved my architectural degree. I needed help to focus my career and my aunt Elizabeth David, the food writer, provided it for a period. She was pragmatic and fiercely individual in her thinking. She had achieved much through this combination of self-belief and clear thinking.

After I had my first publicity in the *Sunday Times* in 1980 I became overwhelmed and fell ill with glandular fever and other complications. For many months I was unable to do much and looked around desperately for help. I met an extraordinary man, Dr Raja Srivastava. He was more than a doctor. A multi-skilled man with a background as an eminent research pathologist, he also had degrees in acupuncture, pharmacology and homeopathy as well as skills in ayurvedic medicine and knowledge of Sanskrit and Veydic languages. He combined the mentality of East and West. To recover my health, he explained, in addition to treatment, I would need to change my way of living, simplify my goals and deepen my spiritual values. Our relationship transcended conventional boundaries. He was my spiritual adviser, doctor, honorary father and mentor. Without his help I don't believe I would be alive today.

MY ADVICE: *Learn the value of good health and how to maintain it.*

Imtaz Khaliq
Couture Tailor and Visiting Lecturer at The London Institute

From starting out making clothes for my family in Bradford at the age of ten, I am now in my eleventh year of running a successful business in Bond Street and have been named by *Cosmopolitan* as one of the top four tailors in London. I have designed clothes for Michelle Pfeiffer and was shortlisted for the Asian Woman of Achievement awards 2002.

I was brought up as a Muslim girl. I was in a minority at school, with only a couple of Asian faces in my class. My father came to Bradford from Pakistan in the 1950s with nothing. He found a job and home. Once he had established himself my mother came to join him and then started a family. I was born in Bradford, one of five children. All the people who have had any impact on my life have seen my trait of steely determination that I have inherited from my father. My dad's struggle and hard work, in setting up his own businesses, has always been an inspiration to me. I also had to work hard but in my case to overcome the low expectations of a girl from my culture in the 1970s.

I studied at Jacob Kramer College in Leeds, and the London College of Fashion, for four years. I then studied for a degree at Westminster University, whilst in the early years of running my business. I realized that the lecturers' enthusiasm for their subject came from continual learning and that I would also have to immerse myself fully in my subject. This led me to read extensively and to search out knowledge from film, theatre, museums and popular culture. This thirst for knowledge encouraged me to become a lecturer of Fashion Marketing at Westminster University. My first taste of success came at the age of 18 while I was showing my final collection at Jacob Kramer College. My work was singled out for praise by local and national press and celebrities, including Pat Phoenix from *Coronation Street*.

In different areas of my life, I have had different role models, in both my business career and my personal development. The people that have helped me develop my skill are my needlework teacher Mrs Ross; my dad's friend's mum, who encouraged me to use the sewing machine; my mum's best friend Ahktar, who taught me everything she knew about sewing; and Josey who worked for Dad, who I covered for in the summer holidays. My sister Nahid was a big inspiration because she also had to overcome low expectations. We were both in it together and she is now a successful criminal lawyer. Shirley Tate, an influential black woman doing a PhD in Linguistics, and Liz De Vrees, also an academic, taught me the importance of education. Terry Burke at Westminster University and Bob Manke at Philadelphia College of Textiles and Science taught me Retail Marketing, and influenced my decision to become a teacher. My work mates at Harrods, Harvey Nichols and Sacs Fifth Avenue introduced me to the working life, and my student apprentice Birthe Baerkgaard gave me the freedom to be a more rounded person. Cynthia Dawn Lewis, my best friend at college, taught me to dare to be different. Her motto was, 'Go for Gold'.

MY ADVICE: *Believe in yourself, and don't let anybody limit you.*

Julia Ogilvy
Deputy Chairman, Hamilton & Inches

Like many friends I left university with little certainty about my future. My skills seemed limited. I was a well-organised, motivated person who loved the arts, fashion and retail, and could type! Following advice from friends, I decided to look for a secretarial job in marketing and ended up as a public relations assistant and then Marketing Manager for Garrards, the Crown Jewellers in London. It was the perfect job and for five years I was happy with my lot. However, I was lucky enough to have a remarkable boss, Naim Attallah, the Chief Executive of the Asprey Group at the time, who saw the potential in me. He offered me, at the age of 27, the role of Managing Director for one of the Asprey Group's companies, the Scottish jewellers Hamilton & Inches. It seemed a tough challenge but he refused to take no for an answer although I certainly tried. In general, his advice was rarely practical, but was more about building self-belief and confidence. He saw I had potential as a businesswoman and allowed me to fulfil dreams I never knew I had. I have since been lucky enough to become a part-owner of Hamilton & Inches when I was part of the team that led the company in a Management buy out in 1998. I have also been fortunate to win some marvellous business awards on behalf of my team including Scottish Businesswoman of the Year in 2001.

Aware of the value of my own mentor to my career, I am now a Patron of the charity Big Brothers & Sisters and a member of the Edinburgh advisory board where we are building up mentoring partnerships here in Scotland for young people who need a Big Brother or Sister.

MY ADVICE: *Try to find a mentor, particularly in an area of interest to you. Never give up on the dreams you have and believe in your own potential.*

Victoria Richards
Textile Designer

I design fabrics mainly as fashion sold through the Conran Shop, the Crafts Council Shop at the V&A Museum, and Leeds City Art

Gallery shop. I have also designed specially commissioned fabrics for private houses and for the festal vestments for Coventry Cathedral. One of my designs is held in the V&A Museum Collection. I also get a lot of interest in my designs for Channel 4 newscaster Jon Snow's ties.

I studied textile design at art college and started work on my own with a 'Setting Up' grant from the Crafts Council, and later on a 'Go and See' Grant from the Prince's Youth Business Trust. I now work from my own studio space in South London, and often exhibit at the Chelsea Crafts Fair.

Textile designer Sally Greaves-Lord taught me and was the inspiration behind my decision to set up my own fabric design company in 1986. Sally is a pioneer in the world of textiles. She graduated from my own degree course a few years before I did, and during my final year at college Sally was a visiting lecturer and my personal tutor. It was a combination of her experience, her enthusiasm and the freshness of her many design ideas that gave me the confidence to establish my own business. Since being taught by Sally she has become my friend and we have also shared a studio. Our work is very different, but we have a common passion for good design. Her love for what she does is infectious. Both of us are committed to improving what we do, and to make sure that we can thrive by doing so.

MY ADVICE: *Before you decide to set up a textile design studio make sure that you have the time, energy and, above all, commitment to get it off the ground. It is a competitive world and the work can often be physically exhausting. A sympathetic bank manager helps too, as the financial rewards can be pretty slim at the outset.*

Where possible, gain direct experience, perhaps by working in an established studio. This way you can find out where your strengths (and of course weaknesses) are and where to improve. Never be shy to ask others for advice. Look for inspiration everywhere.

Julian Richer
Retail Entrepreneur and Founder, Richer Sounds

I have stakes in around a dozen mostly small businesses including Richer Sounds, the UK's biggest hi-fi retailer, having opened my first shop at the age of 19. My first shop still holds the record for both the highest sales per square foot of any retail outlet in the world and, more importantly, for giving the biggest percentage of its profits to charity of any of the 1.3 million companies in the UK. In March 2002, Richer Sounds was judged the best British company to work for by the *Sunday Times*.

I now spend more time on my philanthropic interests, which include free consulting work for the heads of some of the UK's largest charities, including the RSPCA's Freedom Foods and the Soil Association, and a Foundation which helped 250 good causes last year. I am also a director of Duchy Originals (the Prince of Wales's charitable trading company) and one of only eight official 'Ambassadors for Youth'.

I am the youngest Governor of Clifton College, my old school, and this is despite my poor performance there. I have advised some of the country's largest organisations at Chief Executive level on staff motivation, customer service, cultural change, communication and suggestion schemes. I have written two business books, *The Richer Way* and *Richer on Leadership*.

Vic Odden is the person who inspired my career. Sadly he has now passed away, but he was a very successful discount photographic retailer. He was a friend, partner and inspirational figure. At the age of 19 I discovered he was trying to dispose of one of his two units on London Bridge Walk. I was very green and asked him if he would sell it to me on the basis that 70,000 wealthy City commuters passed the shop every day. The only problem was that I didn't have any money, so I asked him to dinner over which he let me take over the lease of the shop and very kindly lent me £20,000, a huge sum in those days. I repaid him within nine months and I was off! In the 17 years that I knew him, we never had a cross word between us. He was a truly wonderful man who gave me a very important break.

I guess the thing I remember most about him is that he was a really nice guy, who everybody loved. He was very calm and patient; completely the opposite to me, and that is probably the reason we got on so well. He actually had a majority share in my business for some years until I was able to buy him out. He saw me make so many mistakes over the years, but took it all in his stride.

Vic was a great retailer, a great marketeer and a great salesman, and the lessons I learnt from him were invaluable.

MY ADVICE: *Be determined. Take advantage of opportunities that arise. Work 'smart' rather than long hours. Be sure to balance your life: a healthy diet, regular gentle exercise and plenty of fun will improve your work capacity and make your life enjoyable and last longer!*

Roger Saul
President of Mulberry, Owner of Charlton House Hotel and Restaurant

I started Mulberry aged 19 whilst studying business at college in London. When I reached London I knew I wanted to be in fashion. In the early 70s, the job to have, like a DJ today, was that of a Boutique Manager.

So I looked at who was the best around and went to see John Michael Ingram who ran a retail group called 'JM' which included The Westerner, Guys & Dolls and John Michael Shops. I asked him if he needed a management trainee and I think initially he was bemused as this was a new way of getting a job in fashion retailing. No one had ever approached him like that before.

He took me on and I made the coffee, sorted out his stationery system, worked in the shops and finally bought accessories for his Guys & Dolls Shops. The all-round experience was invaluable. He put me on the bottom of the ladder whilst inspiring me with his approach and charismatic leadership. In both his roles as designer and entrepreneur he made me realise it was possible to achieve what then seemed like great heights.

In those early days I learnt many things. Firstly, although John Michael had taken me under his wing and given me this opportunity, his other managers either perceived me as a threat or an unnecessary expenditure. So patronage from 'The Boss', whilst often opening the door, can sometimes make it doubly hard to succeed within an organisation.

I have since experienced the same at Mulberry time and again from the boss's viewpoint. I have always kept an eye out for talented young people and brought them into the company wherever possible. The tendency is that if they don't have some management experience and 'slot' into a position, their colleagues will view them as a threat as they are seen to have the boss's ear.

Another lesson I learnt was that if you wish to get that all important interview or meeting you have to have done something exceptional or entrepreneurial to gain the attention of your potential mentor. There is never a lack of talent around and for every good job there are hundreds of willing applicants.

You must always be humble and be prepared to slum it. The press office (PR) in any fashion company must be one of the most demanding and backbreaking departments. Its success can and does make or break any company, therefore a good boss will keep a tight eye on how it performs. We have had endless young people who come in on work experience and work their hearts out for little or no reward, hoping that they can survive the maelstrom, make a mark and go forward.

I have seen three such people go on to become senior managers or marketing directors, equally I have seen many who've come in and said 'This work is beneath me, I came to get work experience and I ended up making the coffee!' It's your choice!

Good people will always find a way to make their mark. If you are one of these, you probably know it, have a fierce pride in your ability and will come back time and gain until you created your opportunity.

John Michael's mercurial character must have rubbed off on me in more ways than one as he was never content with just one business. He owned elegant menswear shops, Oxford Street boutiques and specialist gift retail shops as well as a design consultancy.

My progress with Mulberry went from designing, manufacturing and wholesaling accessories in the 70s to opening retail shops in the 80s as well as designing and marketing men's and ladies' clothing. In the 90s I started the Mulberry Home collection which really encompasses all forms of interior product design. Then, six years ago I took the ultimate challenge for a designer and opened my own hotel and restaurant. This means creating an environment that people visit for an experience which is both real and yet intangible. I suppose you could say it is also the ultimate risk as you are dependent 100% on your team providing a product and service which is going to touch all your customers' senses. Very often it is a young team and, rather like the theatre, that team is constantly performing to and for the public.

I have always tried to link charity with any of our endeavours as I believe we must give back to those who either haven't had the opportunity to succeed or will never get it. Our latest campaign started literally from nothing. The Bottletop Campaign has become the leading fashion HIV/AIDS charity this year. We have set out to raise money and awareness to provide funds for HIV/AIDS education in Third World countries. We have done it by taking locally made products and turning them into fashion items, capturing the imagination of the press, celebrities and public alike. Our mentor has been Jerry Rawlings, the ex-president of Ghana, who has unlocked doors for us with Kofi Annan, Bill Clinton and Nelson Mandela.

MY ADVICE: *Always believe that it is possible to achieve the impossible. Believe in yourself. Fashion is a fickle and whimsical industry. When things are going against you, ride with it and catch the key moment to go forward again.*

cookery and gardening

Delia Smith
Chef and Author

Looking back over my life I can't single out one particular mentor, or one particular piece of advice, that helped me achieve my goals. But what I certainly can do is identify three people who played pivotal roles in shaping my life and career.

It all started rather badly, with my failing the 11+ and leaving school with no academic achievements or qualifications at all. My despairing parents – in the belief that something creative with my hands might suit – sent me to a hairdressing salon in Mayfair. I had a gloriously happy time there, but didn't seem to have much talent for that particular craft either.

After doing lots of interesting – but uncompelling – jobs, I was taken at the age of 22 to a little French restaurant which specialised in regional French cooking. I began to quiz the chef who always served the main course himself directly from the kitchen: how could I learn to cook such delicious food?

He suggested I come along on Saturday evening to wash dishes and learn first-hand. And so I did. I became enthralled, fascinated, and the more I learnt the more I wanted to learn. The chef's name was Leo Evans, and when I told him I was going to work very hard at any job I could lay my hands on and save up to go to a smart cookery school, his wise counsel was 'They'll teach you how to make smart dinner-party food, but they won't teach you about real cooking.'

He then gave me three paperback books: Elizabeth David's *French*

Provincial Cooking, Philip Harben the TV chef's *The ABC of Cookery* and *The Penguin Book of Wine*. He also recommended that if I really wanted to learn to cook, then just get into the kitchen and start cooking. I've often looked back at that advice with deep gratitude. Not having had any professional training put me in very good stead later on when I began to teach home cooks. I was, as it were, one of them. Instead of learning all the 'rules' I was able to create my own, always with the specific needs of the home cook in mind.

My second mentor is my literary agent and best friend of 34 years, Deborah Owen. When we met in 1969 home cooking was epitomised by two extremes in the world of communications: glossy colour supplements at one end of the spectrum way beyond the capabilities of most people, and at the other end the women's weekly magazines doing endlessly boring midweek dishes with mince. There was no real teaching coming from anywhere.

My (very ambitious) ambition was to fill the gap, and at the same time to focus not solely on the classic French tradition but to rediscover the roots of British cooking, which had begun to decline along with rural life in the wake of the industrial revolution and the enclosure acts which robbed the country people of their land. Two World Wars accelerated the process with their food shortages and 'utility' cooking. The simple art of cookery, which had traditionally been handed down from mother to daughter, had been for the most part lost.

Debbie Owen caught my dream. I was a nothing, a no one with no qualifications with, as I said earlier, an extremely ambitious ambition. But I had discovered in Debbie what every single human being needs to succeed in life, and that is someone to believe in them. Since then we have worked very closely, and all the way through I have needed that support and belief – and can honestly say I could never have achieved what I have achieved without it.

My third mentor is my husband Michael – and I don't *just* mean because I'm married to him, which is an obvious support to anyone, but because he has been a wise counsellor on a professional level too. There have been some tough decisions and some hairy moments in my career when both Debbie and I have needed his help and guidance. His being an editor, too, has meant a great deal, so my inability either to spell or punctuate has never been a handicap in a long and prolific writing career.

Both Debbie and Michael have also helped me cope with the most difficult part of my career – and that is fame. Fame can inflict heavy burdens on people and can easily corrupt an ego which is not firmly kept in check. This brings me to what I would consider the best advice I can give to a young person.

MY ADVICE: *Don't be a slave to your ego, be humble, be willing to fail. Because the ego is afraid to fail or to lose face, it prevents someone reaching out to their full potential. Everyone has specific gifts and everyone should be ambitious but at the same time be able to make mistakes. Getting it wrong without worrying what others say or think is, I believe, one of the great secrets of success.*

* * *

Rocky Coles
Horticulturist

From an early age, I have always been interested in plants and watching them grow. During my life at school, I had other interests which included drama and music, which I still enjoy today, but my love of plants prompted me to study a horticultural course at Moulton College, Northamptonshire. Before gaining my National Diploma in Horticulture I worked at Glenn's Florist. I am currently working at the Wyevale Garden Centre in Wellingborough where I have gained my forklift licence.

At college, I gained confidence and with help and guidance from my subject manager, Nick Brown, I entered and represented the college in regional competitions and went on to win the title of *Young Horticulturist of the Year 2002* which is organised by the Institute of Horticulture. Through winning the competition, I was interviewed by various newspapers and television stations. The prize for winning the competition was a travel bursary of £1,500. I am planning to use the winnings on a horticultural project in New Zealand.

MY ADVICE: *My advice for anyone interested in a career in horticulture is to apply for a course at a college, to work hard and to enjoy and take advantage of all the opportunities that come your way.*

Mary Contini
Director, Valvona & Crolla

I am a Director of my family's prize-winning delicatessen and wine merchant, Valvona & Crolla Limited in Edinburgh, and an author of three cookery books. In addition to television, I write for newspapers and magazines. After studying biological science at university I started my career in management with a large chain store before marrying and having my first child. Later I joined my husband in Valvona & Crolla. I campaign through writing to improve children's diet and have written two cookery books focusing on children and one for my daughter Francesca.

My father and husband's father were Italian immigrants in the 1930s and had to work extremely hard to look after themselves and their families. From an early age I was encouraged to work hard and to achieve to the best of my ability.

Victor Crolla, the original founder of Valvona & Crolla, remains an inspiration to me. He was always happy and cheerful in his work and always prepared to help others who needed support. 'Excellent' was the word he used every day and strove to make every day better than the last. He was a hard taskmaster and trained me to work hard in everything I set out to do. He believed that anything is possible if you want to do it. I believe that is true.

He supported my husband Philip and myself when we were establishing ourselves and was always available to offer advice when needed. Still at 85 years old he remains as canny and insightful as ever.

MY ADVICE: *Work hard and be honest in everything you do. Try to find out what you love to do and make every effort to be enthusiastic about doing it. Also it pays to be flexible and have more than one skill in the competitive workplace these days.*

Rachel de Thame
Television presenter, author and gardener

Although I currently enjoy success as a television gardener, my path to the screen has been varied and interesting. I studied ballet to a professional standard at the Royal Ballet School, but after a prolonged bout of glandular fever I was forced to give up my dream of a dancing career. Staying within the artistic sphere, I channelled my efforts into history of art – with a course at City Lit in London – and spent a short period of time working for a respected firm of international art dealers. I was subsequently spotted by model agency Laraine Ashton, beginning a long and productive modelling career with them before moving on to Models One and IMG. By this time I had become a mother, and was able to tailor my work to fit around the needs of small children. A major part of my career at this time included appearances in television commercials and I began to be recommended by casting agents for acting roles. By 1998 I had appeared in the mini series *Merlin* and the British feature film *Bodywork*.

However, acting was not my ideal choice of long-term career, and after much thought I decided to make gardening – a passion inherited from my father who is an exceptional gardener the focus of my future working life. Despite coming late to professional horticulture, I was determined to turn my life-long love of plants and gardens into a career. Having opted for a change of direction in my mid-thirties, I embarked on two years of study at The English Gardening School, where I was lucky enough to have among my tutors the truly inspirational Roy Lancaster, who is justly renowned for his work as a plantsman, planthunter, author and television and radio broadcaster.

Roy has a rare talent for conveying his subject with totally infectious enthusiasm. He is passionate about plants, and it is impossible to hear him talk or read his books and articles without being inspired. His readiness to share his knowledge, his personal advice to me on taking my first tentative steps into the work of television gardening, and his ongoing support, have all been enormously important to me. Roy picked up on my genuine interest and encouraged me from the start. He opened my eyes to a world filled with wondrous plants and showed me that there is also extraordinary beauty in the most familiar native flower in the hedgerow.

The focus that mature students often bring to their work paid dividends; I graduated with distinction from The English Gardening School, auditioned successfully for BBC2's *Gardeners' World* and the rest, as they say is history. I became part of the regular presenting team, and have gone on to film my own series *Small Town Gardens*, as well as covering all the major RHS events, including The Chelsea Flower Show. Widening my horizons still further, I now write a regular column for the *Daily Telegraph*, contribute to numerous gardening publications and am currently working on my third book. Though I keep my hand in the world of art and antiques – as one of the presenters on BBC1's *Going for a Song* – I count myself extremely lucky to be surrounded by beautiful plants on a daily basis.

MY ADVICE: *In my experience, perseverance usually pays off in the end. Never assume that there is only one route to achieving your goals, or that those goals remain fixed throughout your working life. There is nothing to stop you altering your career track and starting afresh with something completely different.*

Loyd Grossman
Presenter, *Masterchef*

I was inspired and encouraged by Abbott Lowell Cummings, an American architectural historian who taught me as an under-graduate. Abbott's rather recherché area of expertise was early New England timber-framed buildings, a subject on which he was both passionate and articulate. Whilst I didn't go on to be an architectural historian (much as I would have liked to at one stage) Abbott reinforced the only career advice my father ever gave me: don't do anything you're not in love with. The joy of study, the thrill of discovery, how to not just look but see, were all things Abbott helped instil in me. Abbott will be 80 in 2003 and is working on a new book.

MY ADVICE: *Don't do anything you're not in love with.*

Janice Reilly
Head of Development, Royal Botanic Garden Edinburgh

I have responsibility for driving forward the fundraising efforts at the Royal Botanic Garden Edinburgh, helping the organisation sustain and develop important projects with a target of £20 million. I have been a fundraiser for over eight years and, like a lot of people, I have 'fallen' into the profession which is one of the fastest-growing and dynamic sectors in the UK.

Over the years I have read a lot of great books on lateral and positive thinking and have been fortunate to meet a number of motivating people early in my career. However, two individuals shine through as key mentors: Jim Best, a Canadian financier, who having lived around the world now resides in London. Jim has the amazing ability to communicate with people at all levels, making them feel part of things and involved in outcomes. I have learnt a lot from his refreshing and direct approach to assessing situations – he can be tough but is generally always correct in his assessment; Andrew Cubie, a leading Scottish lawyer, is truly 'clever' and has a talent in juggling many competing demands and priorities. He is an excellent motivator who can turn problems on their head and make solutions seem simple. He can also be very challenging, which is good.

I met Jim and Andrew at social occasions that were work-related. What I noticed instantly is that they spent some time asking about 'me' and my goals, whereas generally I do the quizzing as all good fundraisers are trained to do. They have both advised me against taking unsuitable jobs and have stopped me throwing in the towel at times. They remind me of what I have achieved and how much more I have yet to contribute. I am indeed lucky to know them.

MY ADVICE: *Learn to accept constructive criticism of your work and recognise that it is not a criticism of you personally. Also every day is a new day – so start with the most positive approach you can, even if yesterday was a nightmare.*

Gary Rhodes
Chef

I have a real passion and enthusiasm for British foods. Their flavours are so enjoyable to eat, whether created in my restaurants or cooked by others who have found inspiration in my books or from my television work.

I first experimented with cookery as a teenager, preparing family meals whilst my mother was at work. I went on to train at Thanet Technical College in Broadstairs, Kent and was awarded both Student and Chef of the year. After I graduated, I realised that if I was really to develop my career and technique, I would need to travel to Europe, which at that time had the best hotel chefs and cuisine. My first job was as Commis Chef at the Amsterdam Hilton where I began to experiment for the first time with nouvelle cuisine and to challenge the preconceptions of how food should be prepared. After that, success was swift and my cookery CV includes Sous Chef at the Reform Club, Pall Mall and the Capital Hotel in Knightsbridge; Head Chef, at age 26, at the Castle Hotel, Somerset; then Head Chef at the Greenhouse restaurant, London, reviving great British classics culminating in a Michelin Star for the restaurant in 1996.

In 1997, I opened my first restaurant, with Sodexho in support, in the city of London, 'city rhodes', achieving Michelin Star status. More restaurants were to follow, with the second London plot – Rhodes in the Square – also finding the same Michelin Guide recognition. I have recorded ten BBC TV series, the most recent, *Gary Rhodes Cookery Year – Autumn into Winter* broadcast 2002, with books to accompany and surpass the television average. My work takes me all over the world, including trips to Australia, South Africa, Japan and the Caribbean, becoming the Ambassador for food and drink in Grenada. Cars and motor racing are my second passion after cooking, having the pleasure to cook for the Jordan Formula One team at La Monza!

A great lady of inspiration, tutor to us all, who now is viewed as a culinary institution in her own right, shared thoughts and encouragement with me through reading words rather than hearing them. At the age of 13, and cooking at home on a fairly regular basis, I decided to take on the full family Sunday roast.

My first experience of such a full meal with a dessert to follow, the steamed lemon sponge with lemon sauce, was taken from Puddings and Desserts by Marguerite Patten. With no modern blenders and food processors to help, it was read and followed within the passion of its sentences stage by stage.

After the two hours of lemon steam filling the room, each brother and sister showing signs of inspiration from the powerful nest these pillows of warm puffs were carrying, it was time to reveal. Anxiety met with anticipation as the ceramic bowl was lifted and the thick lemon syrupy sauce poured. Inspiration within me was born, not purely from the success that sat in front of us, but with the glee that appeared on all faces, and soon with the lemon plate spooned clean. I had realised what pleasure could be shared with others.

Marguerite has since become a good friend. Today in 2003, and in her eighties, she continues to inspire others, not once losing her personal feelings for this industry, in many ways simply growing stronger. Thank you Marguerite – my feelings, too, live on.

MY ADVICE: *Be honest and believe in yourself and your own abilities. Realise the commitment that's required to succeed, as with any chosen career. When the hours and days become longer and harder maintain a positive mind, never allowing negatives to get the better of you. Absorb what you can from people ahead, ready to share with others behind.*

Joe Swift
Garden Designer and TV Presenter

After school in North London, I went to art school for a year, played in a rock band in London pubs and clubs for another year, worked on a kibbutz in Israel for six months and travelled around Europe. In 1985 I started work as a gardener and landscaper for a gardening company for two years, then took another year out to travel in Australia, where I worked as a landscaper in Sydney and Melbourne, before crewing on a yacht through Papua New Guinea and Indonesia. In 1998, back in London, I set up my own landscaping company designing and building gardens in the London area, while I studied garden design at The English Garden School, Chelsea Physic Gardens. In 1997, I set up the Plant Room garden retail and design shop in Islington which acts as my base for design work. Since the start of the Plant Room, I now increasingly do more television presenting including regular appearances on *BBC Gardener's World* TV, and as co-presenter of *Chelsea Flower Show, Hampton Court Flower Show* and *Gardener's World Live* as well as a range of other TV projects from *Comic Relief* to UK style programme, *Take 3 Guys*. I published my book *The Plant Room* in 2001.

A gardener called Antonia Sturgess is the person who most inspired me in my career. As a young man of 18, I didn't have a clue what I wanted to do with my life, but managed to get a job working for a local gardening company and fortunately was put under her guidance. Although to start I was given all the mundane jobs such as sweeping, weeding and mowing she would teach me something new every day whether it was how to prune, how to plant or simply how to appreciate the colour or the scent of a particular bloom of the season.

On top of the gardening she was a real guide in my life in that she showed me how important it was to be reliable, conscientious, patient and thorough. She recognised my enthusiasm for my job and encouraged me positively in everything I did. In the long run I found that designing gardens brought together all my skills, and still try to learn something new every day.

I am lucky to love what I do, and I am also extremely lucky to have worked with Antonia at a crucial stage in my life.

MY ADVICE: *Try to find the work that you love and learn something new every day.*

Alan Titchmarsh MBE
Gardener and Writer

I was born and brought up on the edge of Ilkley Moor and started growing things at the age of 10 in my parents' back garden. Rashly I left school at 15 and became an apprentice gardener in the local nursery, following this with full-time training at horticultural college and the Royal Botanic Gardens, Kew.

Television and radio came along once I'd side-stepped into horticultural journalism, and I have been until recently the main presenter of *Gardeners' World* and *Ground Force*. My latest series is BBC2's *How to be a Gardener*. I write regularly in *BBC Gardeners' World Magazine*, as well as being gardening correspondent of *The Daily Express* and *Sunday Express*, and have also written more than thirty gardening books and four novels. My memoirs, *Trowel and Error*, were published in 2002. I have received two honorary degrees and am a Freeman of the City of London. I was named Yorkshire Man of the Year in 1997, was appointed MBE in the 2000 New Year Honours List, and became a Deputy Lieutenant of the County of Hampshire in 2001.

Harry Rhodes was six feet tall, with a Roman nose on which perched a pair of rimless glasses. He was a keen gardener, and my favourite teacher of all time from when I was about nine years old. He was well spoken and jolly, and it seemed that he was always smiling, always enthusiastic and – most importantly – always encouraging. Where other teachers would be of the 'Sit down and shut up' school of education, Harry Rhodes was the 'Get up and show me' type. If you showed the slightest aptitude for anything, he fanned the flame. It's down to him, as much as anyone, that I became a gardener.

Harry was an encourager and an enabler. When you thought that you could not do something, he was the one to say you could. He marked himself out as being all the more human because of his friendliness. Not that he was a pushover. He could maintain discipline with practised ease, and could achieve silence by the raising of an eyebrow. I remember him happily and with gratitude, and every pupil that ever there was will have fond memories of those teachers who, like him, made their subjects come alive and who somehow manage to rise above the low pay, the ridiculous demands on their time and those disruptive kids who just don't seem to want to learn.

If it hadn't been for Harry, I might well have settled for less. I'm glad I didn't.

education and
science

Sir John Sulston
Former Director of the Sanger Centre founded by the
Medical Research Council and the Wellcome Trust,
Nobel Prize winner and winner of the Mirror's Pride of
Britain Lifetime Achievement Award for work to
sequence the human genome

When Sarah Brown invited me to write this contribution, I was at first doubtful. My own fortunes have been a matter of chance, not of planning, and my life has been pretty straightforward. But then I thought: there are two things to say. The first is to thank the many mentors to whom I owe so much; indeed the concern is that there is not enough space to include them all. It seems to me that lots of us are like that. We gain different things from different people, and we need different people at different times in our lives. The second is to relate my – our – own experience of mentoring, and to urge you to seize it if you have such an opportunity.

My first mentors were my parents, who stayed together until they died – the usual way in their generation, not so general now. My father, as an Anglican priest, gave me faith in God, which lasted until my teenage years when I found such arbitrary belief increasingly untenable as I learned of other creeds. So then I had to become agnostic, which was a great sadness for us both, but he left me a lasting desire to be of service to others. He was of farming stock, and although his own agricultural efforts were reduced to a small garden he gave me a love of nature and of putting my hands in the soil.

My mother came from a line of teachers allied to Midlands engineers. Perhaps through her I inherited a love of mechanisms, but certainly she was my verbal mentor for years. Our conversations were mostly in the kitchen, answering my questions, never hostile to my comments, always encouraging to my ideas but softly redirecting them as she saw fit. So gentle she was that I didn't realise how strong her Christian faith was, too, until I opened a letter from her after her death. So both my parents were disappointed in my rejection of their belief – but it had to be. Indeed that rejection seems with hindsight to be the one of the few things that I've done entirely on my own. Perhaps the other was wanting to be a scientist of some sort – indeed of all sorts, for I never really wanted to choose any particular branch but was interested in them all.

Mr Smith lived a few doors down the street. He was an electrical engineer, and gave me a kit of parts to make a crystal radio, that worked with no power. Later he gave me an old battery radio to convert, and later still I begged a broken television from a shop and made that work. Mr Smith was sure that I too would go into electrical engineering, and it was disappointing to him when, for some reason I can't now fathom, I chose biology. Another rejection, you see: being a mentor doesn't mean that you succeed in your own aims – what you're doing is to help a new and independent human being to develop.

Oddly, the most inspirational thing I remember from my school days is learning physics with Donald Lloyd. It made me tremble with excitement to calculate the universe, stretching out far beyond what a human, or indeed the whole human race, can personally experience. The power of the mind, to think and to dream. Perhaps I went into biology precisely because it seemed yet more mysterious.

Then came university, which went by in a blur because I'm not a book-learning person, and then Colin Reese my research supervisor. It was tremendous fun being in a laboratory full time and using the equipment to do things that had never been done before. From Colin I learned to make things work, and that playing was not enough, that tasks must be finished, brought to a conclusion that one could publish or use in some way.

From Colin I went on to Leslie Orgel in California. Equally demanding of completions, he also spoiled me, made me want to take myself seriously as a scientist. Too seriously perhaps – it's easier to adopt the style than to make a correspondingly serious contribution – but that didn't matter. We all need people who make us feel good about ourselves. And again there was the sense of rolling out my mind, for biology was beginning its most exciting phase, becoming comprehensible. Leslie wanted to help me become an independent scientist, a group leader at his lab. But it was too early for me.

Instead I joined Sydney Brenner's group at the Medical Research Council's laboratory in Cambridge. He gave me ideas and space to grow in, and I stayed there for many years. Indeed it was Sydney who left, before me, when he retired. And so it seemed I would be independent at last. But of course it was not so at all.

One of my most recent mentors is Aaron Klug, who negotiated the setting up of the Sanger Centre. He teaches me opportunism and reaching out further than seems immediately possible. By reaching, one may attain, and if not then at least one has tried. And speaking of the lab brings us at last to Fred Sanger. I learned of him when I was at school: the quiet Quaker who twice solved the problem of reading out the secret codes of life. For many years I admired him from afar – he was my distant abstract mentor, until by a marvellous stroke of serendipity we were able to name our new centre after him. *The Times* photographed us together for their millennium colour magazine portraying mentors and protégés.

But standing behind them all, and indispensable beyond all, is Daphne. We met in 1964 and married in 1966. It's been a while. Daphne is so many things to me, of course, but in terms of mentoring it's clear. Where others have given me buoyancy, sails, and a keel, she has given me a rudder. Without that I would drift aimlessly.

It was Daphne who led us into serious mentoring of our own. After our two children were born, she decided to stay at home to look after them, but she wanted to do something more. So we became involved with short-term foster care and mentoring for

Cambridgeshire Social Services, and they guided us in our new role. The word mentoring wasn't used then, but it was the same thing. Ours consisted of having a long-term relationship with a large one-parent family, going out together to the park or sometimes to the coast, playing and talking together, supporting and being around. We are now being invited to the weddings of that family. It wasn't always easy, but we had excellent social workers who advised us when we got stuck. The great thing about Social Services is that people come to it as of right, rather than feeling they are having to accept charity. Charities have a role in filling the gaps, but we should also celebrate and support the wonderful and often undervalued work of the state, and show how it's not a one-way service, but thrives on channelling the goodwill of us all.

So I've had many mentors in my life, each giving me something different. Sometimes nowadays people tell me that I've been helpful to them; nice if so, though I wouldn't want to be the sole influence on anyone! But if the flow is indeed two-way, that makes me happier than anything. I think the best advice to the budding scientist is to choose, if you can, to do what you most care about, and then do it with passion.

Maybe I've mistaken the whole idea of mentoring, in spreading it out and dividing it up in this way. But I don't think so. It's true that some mentors are called upon for years, even a lifetime of service. And no mentor can ever feel that they can break the link – it must always be there to be called upon in time of need. But most often, mentoring is for a limited period, serving to fledge a growing human for the next stage of their life. And then, like any other fledgling, they must fly free.

Acknowledgement

To all my mentors, both those mentioned here and all the others.

Footnote

In describing my ancestry, I've spoken as though behaviours in me have come down from specific parts of my family. This shouldn't be taken too literally. It's very likely that we shall discover that behaviours can be inherited to some extent, but at present this is pure speculation. And it's unlikely to be as simple as a gene for this or a gene for that, but rather a matter of many genes working in concert and interacting with external influences. We'll find out one day – an ambition for some of the readers of this book to sort out?

* * *

Sir Neil Chalmers
Director of The Natural History Museum

I am a zoologist and trained at Oxford and Cambridge Universities with a research career in the field of behavioural ecology, studying monkeys in their natural habitats, principally in East Africa and Brazil. After a number of years spent as a lecturer at the University of East Africa, I joined the Open University in Britain, in 1970, soon after its foundation. I spent 18 years teaching there and continuing my research studies. During that time I became heavily involved in the problem of making science accessible to lay people, using a wide variety of media and education techniques. I also became involved in the management issues finishing my time at the Open University as Dean of Science. I became Director of The Natural History Museum in 1988 and have continued to work there to make science more accessible and useful to a wide variety of people. The new Darwin Centre has brought the Museum's science into the public arena in a new way.

My dream was always to become a research biologist and see the world. What could possibly be better than to find out more about the animals and the plants on our planet and to go to beautiful parts of the world to do so? Whilst I was a university student in Britain, I had the good fortune to be taught by Niko Tinbergen, an intense and charismatic Dutch Nobel Prize winner. He had done marvellous research on the behaviour of fish, birds and insects, and I asked him whether anyone had ever studied our own nearest relatives, the monkeys and apes, in their natural surroundings. Rather than dismissing this earnest request of mine, as he might well have done, he told me that no, very little had been done of this sort, and strongly encouraged me to have a go. He made it possible for me to go to Cambridge, which was one of the few universities at the time beginning to study monkeys and apes, and from there I went off to Uganda for five of the most enthralling and formative years of my life. The experience of working in a newly independent African country was profound. The beauty of the country, the quality and character of its people, gave me a perspective that was very different from my own London-centred upbringing, and one that influences me to this day. It was Niko Tinbergen's combination of enthusiastic encouragement and practical help that made this all possible.

MY ADVICE: *If you are an aspiring young biologist, learn all you can about animals and plants at school and university, get a good degree, then be bold. There is so much to be discovered about our natural world if we are to look after it properly. Go out and discover it.*

Des Coffey
Partnership Coordinator, Excellence in Cities

I have spent my lifetime in schools, starting with reception class at St Cuthbert's Infant School in 1948 at the age of four and now beginning a 38th year in providing education in Manchester. Pupil, student, teacher, headteacher, Ofsted inspector, LEA inspector, external examiner, have all been steps along the way to my current position as Partnership Coordinator for Excellence in Cities with responsibility for the very young to those going on to higher education.

For a late reader and one who has some sense of fear, even now, of schools and education in general, I have spent a very happy lifetime in education and I hold one man responsible. Nearly 50 years ago, in 1954, I started Junior 4 at St Cuthbert's Junior School in Withington in Manchester. I had learnt to read only two years earlier and moved into the 'top class' in the school with some anxiety.

R. J. Hoare taught Junior 4 and provided me with lessons which I remember clearly to this day. It wasn't just in the more normal aspects of learning but in all aspects that Bob Hoare gave his class of

48 pupils the benefit of his interests and experience. R. J. Hoare, author of *Wings over the Atlantic,* a bestselling hardback, and *People in History*, Master of the Westland Roll, football coach extraordinaire, inspirational teacher of shoe-cleaning methodologies and a truly encouraging teacher. He knew us all well and gave each and every one of us great support. It was a good year and put me on the track to grammar school. What I didn't realise at the time was that Bob Hoare and his influence was to guide me on a particular career path and into becoming a teacher. He also developed in me a strong interest in sport. Athletics, cricket, football, even crown green bowling became absorbing interests.

Later on in 1962 I became a teacher trainee at Strawberry Hill in London. Within days I was sought out by the librarian, a man who it seemed all the students found a source of comfort and inspiration. After seven years, Bob had recognised my name on college lists and renewed our acquaintance. He really hadn't changed. Still no hair and it seemed that he also had the same dark blue woollen tracksuit for his daily runs around the grounds. He helped me during my time at college and was there to offer congratulation when I qualified. His death was announced several years later in the student newsletter. I remembered Bob then and I remember him now. When I clean my shoes, when I try to write and when I am working with young people I remember his style and his commitment. I owe much to Bob, becoming a headteacher, school inspector, senior officer in education and maintaining an avid interest in sport can all be attributed to him.

Interest in sport has been a constant element of work. Playing until age took its toll and then becoming part of the organisation of sport has led to being a trustee of Manchester City Football Club's Community Scheme, providing a variety of opportunities in sport and education to young people in Manchester. An example of this work is BlueZone, the club's study support centre, and the Learning Through Football initiative provided free to all Manchester schools.

Professor Roderick Floud
Vice-Chancellor, London Metropolitan University and President, Universities UK.

I studied history at Oxford University and then taught economic history at University College London, Cambridge University, Birkbeck College, London and Stanford University (California). I have written books and articles on the British machine-tool industry and on quantitative methods for historians, and for the past 20 years have been conducting and publishing research into the changing height and weight of the British population, as a guide to its changing standard of living. In 1988 I became Provost of City of London Polytechnic, later London Guildhall University, which has recently become London Metropolitan University. I am President of Universities UK, representing all 114 university institutions in the UK, from 2001–03. I am an Academician of the Academy of the Social Sciences and a Fellow of the British Academy.

I did not meet Robert Fogel, later the first economic historian to win a Nobel Prize for economics, until I was well-established in my career, but I had long admired his books and articles. When he invited me to work with him, I was flattered and intrigued, since he had identified – in records of heights and weights – an entirely new source of information about the changing welfare of people in the past. Tackling this source involved using the methods of statistics, history and human biology. Bob taught me the need to worry at a problem like a dog at a bone, approaching it from all angles and trying to see all its implications. He showed me the power of historical imagination and of using ideas from one discipline to illuminate another. I still find the subject, now called 'anthropometric history', endlessly fascinating.

MY ADVICE: *Always seize an opportunity, for it may open out your life.*

Jenny Francis
Headteacher, Cwmfelinfach Primary School, Newport

After I finished my 'A' Levels, I went to Teacher Training College in Bath, specialising in mathematics and environmental studies, and then I started teaching. I have taught in a number of schools in

Wales, becoming a Deputy Head in 1978. In 1988 I was appointed Headteacher of Cwmfelinfach Primary School. As a headteacher, I have continued my studies gaining first a diploma in primary management, and more recently a diploma in computer studies, and certificate in advanced business studies. My school encourages School to Industry Links, and we won a Queen's Silver Jubilee Award in 1992, and Investor in People Standard in 1994 and 1998. Since 1995, we have explored links with construction and engineering industries, starting as part of a school self-help project to develop the school yard. Since 1998, we have arranged construction taster days with local colleges though the CITB Centre: this is particularly relevant to our pupils as many of their parents work in jobs connected to this industry. In 2002, we began a pilot of the CITB Award Scheme with the construction department of Ystradd Mynach College to support disaffected pupils by giving them the opportunity to achieve through practical activities by obtaining a recognised award. At Cwmfelinfach Primary School, we also have multilateral partnerships with five other European Schools where staff and pupils both visit other schools in Europe, and host visits at our school. We have a full and varied programme to promote the Arts including our own artist in residence, Tony Gobel, who in 2002 assisted the children to produce a huge mosaic depicting the 'Legends of Cwmfelinfach'.

The person who guided me most in my life, other than my parents, was probably my godmother Silvia Wilson. She was a civil servant and a wartime friend of my mother's. She shared my personal journey through childhood into adolescence, then on to college and finally marriage. She never judged, always encouraged, helped me keep things in perspective but above all appeared to have absolute confidence in my ability to succeed. Throughout my childhood she wrote to me regularly, and every school holiday I either visited her or she came to stay. Together we would explore the local countryside of which she had extensive knowledge, or visit museums and other places of interest. As she lived in Islington in London, staying with her gave me access to the wonders of London.

She taught me so much, but most of all she made learning interesting, enjoyable and fun. She broadened my horizons and gave me vision. She had a greater influence on my future than all my formal education. Her message to me was always to be 'the best that you can be: in whatever you do'.

MY ADVICE: *Success in any venture requires a clear vision. Never be afraid to grasp new opportunities and responsibilities. Be creative and innovative, take risks and reap the rewards of your vision.*

Susan Greenfield CBE (Baroness Greenfield)
Director & Fullerian Professor of Physiology, The Royal Institution of Great Britain and Professor of Pharmacology, Oxford University

I first studied at St Hilda's College, Oxford and subsequently took a DPhil in the University of Pharmacology, Oxford. I have worked as a research scientist in the Department of Physiology, Oxford, the College de France, Paris and NYU Medical Center, New York. I was then appointed University Lecturer in Synaptic Pharmacology and Fellow and Tutor in Medicine, Lincoln College, Oxford. I also went on a Visiting Research Fellowship to the Institute of Neuroscience in La Jolla, USA and Queen's College, Belfast. I became a Professor of Pharmacology in 1996 and have 21 Honorary Degrees from British universities. I was appointed Director of the Royal Institution of Great Britain in 1998 and share this post jointly in Oxford. In addition, I am a Founding Director of Synaptica Ltd, an Oxford University-based spin-out company specialising in novel approaches to neurodegeneration, and Boxmind-Brainworks, a company developing non-pharmaceutical approaches to Alzheimer's Disease. I also have an interest in science policy and have involved myself in several government initiatives, and was granted a non-party political Life Peerage in 2001.

What inspired me was having mentors at every stage of my career who 'believed in me more than I believed in myself', namely an inspirational school teacher, a marvellous tutor at my college in Oxford who persuaded me that I could be a scientist, even though I had no formal qualifications, and finally, Professor John Stein, with whom I worked as a Post Doctorate and who's now become one of my closest friends, with whom I can talk about everything concerning the brain. It made a huge difference to me because one feels that people have faith in you and also that, when you are going through moments of self-doubt, they tell you that you can achieve what you are trying to do.

MY ADVICE: *Choose whatever you do by whatever you enjoy doing, rather than according to the status or money it might bring. You have to be prepared to be different from other people and carve your own particular niche or area in which you are going to make your contribution and you have to be prepared to work very, very hard.*

Hyacinth Hall
Retired Primary School Headteacher

I was educated in my home country Jamaica from the age of four years and went to a Teacher Training College in my teens to do a three-year teacher training course, a career both expected and encouraged. I left college after one year, having felt among other concerns that I had made the wrong choice of college. I did various teaching jobs in Jamaica, including a short spell at the Salvation Army Institute for the Blind, working in braille with primary-aged children.

In 1958 I visited a friend in London, England, and ended up taking an office job, which was lucrative but unsuitable for me. So I applied to re-enter teacher training college, which I did in 1964 as a mature student. I graduated from Keswick Hall with a Teacher's Certificate in Primary Education in 1967 and did an Open University degree in Educational Studies in 1971–72. From 1967 I worked in the London Borough of Haringey for 19½ years, mainly in the inner city, progressing from being a class teacher and having posts of special responsibility to being a Deputy and then a Headteacher. I was the first black Headteacher to be appointed in Haringey. In 1985, I needed another challenge and moved as Headteacher to a Bristol Inner City Primary School, and again was the first black Headteacher to be appointed in Bristol.

Throughout my education and career, I have so many people

who helped and inspired me: Miss Crosbourne, my class teacher at infant school in Jamaica who taught me to enjoy learning; Gemma Ross, my education lecturer at college who showed me professionalism and advised good planning; Marjory Williams, a vicar's widow who I met at the Chinese Church in London who helped me refocus on the spiritual aspect of my life at a rootless time; Ena Abrahams, my Schools' Adviser in Haringey who guided my professional development and helped me face challenges through her confidence in me and my potential.

During my time as a teacher and Deputy Head in Haringey, I worked closely with two friends, Dilys John Foster and Gulzar Kanji. We shared a unique cooperation, emphasising achievement through hard work and peer professional support. We used to reason amongst ourselves that as Afro-Caribbean, Asian from East Africa and Welsh, if we couldn't produce a relevant curriculum for our multicultural classrooms then no one could!

Two children also played an important part in my life in different ways: Catarina who, at the age of only seven, asked me if she could offer me any help when she saw me looking strained at school. It taught me the wisdom of youth. 'Jesse' was an intelligent five year old who, even in a school with tremendous learning difficulties, social and emotional needs, stood out. 'Jesse' felt that no one understood her needs, and my Deputy and I sought help from all the support services and her mother to no avail. The problem, sexual abuse in the family, hadn't yet been suspected or diagnosed. Later we both would have spotted it. However, what was obvious then and now is that we don't know everything or have all the answers. We needed the expertise of others and their cooperation in the job.

MY ADVICE: *Be professional. Work consistently hard, plan well, pace yourself, know when to stop. As a teacher, listen to your children, give them ownership in their activities. Have confidence in yourself and respond to confidence of others in you. Cooperate with other professionals and with parents. Remember you don't have all the answers — though sometimes even children have them. Seek help, intellectual, emotional and professional.*

Keith Hewson
Director of Music, Egglescliffe School Performing Arts College

I was born in a North East of England coal mining village called Blackhall. My father was a coal miner and my mother cooked and served meals in the local school kitchen. After failing the 11+ exam in 1960 I attended a secondary modern school which had an unimpressive record for raising the academic standards of its pupils. Most boys left this school at the age of 14 without academic qualifications, to start work in the local coal mine. At 14 years of age I was academically limited but I was good at one thing and that was playing the piano. My parents, thankfully, had sent me to lessons from the age of seven and I loved practising and performing.

My uncle, George Davis, was a history teacher in a school in Romford, Essex and whilst on a visit to Blackhall, he asked me if I was sure that I wanted to work in the mines. My answer was, 'No, but without qualifications, what else could I do?' His reply was, 'You could train to become a music teacher.' I laughed out loud and only stopped laughing when I realised he was serious! This was the first time in my life that someone had ever shown genuine faith in me; someone actually believed that I had the ability to succeed at something, other than working in a coal mine. From that day in 1964 my outlook on life changed; suddenly I found a new confidence and I had a real target in life to aim at. Since then I have never looked back.

Uncle George encouraged me to enrol at the Stockton Billingham Technical College to study music and gain the necessary 'O' and 'A' Levels which I would need to gain entry to a music college. I worked very hard for three years, catching up on years of lost ground. In 1967 I gained entry to the Royal Northern College of Music to study piano gaining a degree in music in 1970. After one year at Leeds University and after seven years of real hard work I finally became a fully qualified teacher of music.

In 1979 after gaining teaching experience in two schools I became Director of Music at Egglescliffe School where I am today. In that time the Egglescliffe School Orchestra has made 12 appearances at the Royal Festival Hall/National Festival of Music for Youth Finals winning nine Outstanding Performance Awards; eight appearances at the Albert Hall Schools proms; one performance at the Millennium Dome and one performance on *Blue Peter*. The Egglescliffe School Brass Band has also made 12 appearances at the Royal Festival Hall/National Festival of Music for Youth Finals and was the Runner-up in the National Youth Brass Band Championships of Great Britain in 2002.

In 1999 I gained Advanced Skills Teacher status, and in 2002 I was invited by the government to serve on the Music and Dance Scheme Advisory group. In 2002 I was voted *Classic FM* Music Teacher of the Year. I often think if Uncle George Davis were alive now, he would be so proud!

MY ADVICE: *Working daily with musicians and music is the most wonderful, rewarding experience that you could ever wish for. To achieve success is a bonus but as I have proved, anyone can achieve it as long as you: listen carefully to all the advice that is offered you during your career; plan carefully each stage of your career; work and practise hard at all times; believe in yourself and your ability to improve; never settle for second best when best is always possible; never give up, even when the going gets incredibly tough and don't lose your sense of humour – music is fun, so enjoy it!*

Helen Hyde
Headmistress, Watford Grammar School

I came to this county in 1970 from South Africa where I had achieved a Bachelor of Arts Honours degree specialising in theology and French as well as a teaching diploma. I began teaching French at Acland Burghley, an inner city school, in 1970. I moved up the ladder there to become Head of Modern Languages and a Senior Teacher with responsibility for primary liaison.

In 1984 I became the Deputy Head of Highgate Wood School in Haringey. I remained there for four years before becoming the Headmistress of Watford Grammar School for Girls in 1987. During the four years I took a higher degree – Master of theology at Kings College, London. I have now been the Headmistress of Watford Grammar School for Girls for 15 years; in that time the school has grown from 900 to its current size of 1,230 pupils. It has been a voluntary controlled school, a grant-maintained school, and is now a voluntary-aided school.

Teaching and running a school is a privilege and a pleasure. What can be more rewarding than working with a team of outstanding caring professionals – together we watch young pupils arrive at our large secondary school timid and uncertain. We nurture, stretch, support and challenge them to help them grow, and develop into mature young people ready to face the challenges and opportunities that they will face in the 21st century.

As you enter my multi-faith, multi-cultural school it is like opening a precious jewel box. Each pupil is a jewel, each and every jewel sparkles and is special. We have children of no religion, we have Jews, Christians, Sikhs, Hindus, Muslims, Buddhists and members of the Bahai faith. This is a true microcosm of society at large, of the local community and of the colleges and universities to which these children will go. We celebrate our differences – these differences are a source of wonder to all of us as well as being a marvellous living resource.

We are a caring community, an extended family where we share academic and creative learning. We work together to build self-esteem and confidence. We learn how to share what we have and to understand the needs of others. Life gains in meaning if you do your best and if you help and support others. My school inspires me.

Watching my pupils learn and have fun together has taught me that if there is a God or a superior force there are many routes to reaching that force, many paths to the top of the mountain – each as true and meaningful as another. The girls are tolerant and understanding – they are eager to learn from one another.

My multi-cultural, multi-faith school has taught me, a practising Jewess, the meaning of tolerance, mutual respect and love. We celebrate differences in the context of knowledge and under-standing. The girls take many assemblies and they write the prayer to be read – it is always appropriate to all the girls in the hall. The pupils, their religions, their traditions, are the true 'spice of life'.

My pupils and staff continue to inspire me – I am astounded by their enthusiasm, their thirst for knowledge and their excitement. I learn so much from them each day. What a privilege to work with these girls and staff. I love every minute of it.

MY ADVICE: *Live each day to the fullest. Make each day special whether you are a teacher or a student. You never have the same day again so if you have made mistakes, think about them and then move on and start your new day with determination and drive always to do better and to help those around you.*

Joe Kusner MBE
Former Head of Art, Acland Burghley School, North West London

A snapshop of the life of an art teacher: I was born in Lithuania. Surviving the severe hardships of the war years and the monstrous horrors of the holocaust (though my mother did not) I escaped at the age of eight with my father and two sisters in 1946. We trudged across countries and then continents, often in hiding, depending on the kindness of strangers and our own fortitude to stay alive.

At last in 1948 I arrived in South Africa with little education and without a word of English or Afrikaans. My instinctive love of art was soon recognised by my primary school teacher, Paddy Lyons, who praised my watercolours. I was encouraged to enter (and won) a national art competition for students. Ten years later I found myself at Witwatersrand Technical College. There I was stimulated not only by Joyce Leonard, an inspiring teacher, but by my fellow student, Barry Feinberg, whose vision of art, philosophy and politics had (and continues to have) a profound effect on my life.

In 1960, like many South Africans of my generation, I saw my next destination as London where I hoped to develop my work and life. I was lucky enough to get a teaching job at Acland Burghley secondary school in north London and stayed for some 40 years. At the start teaching was tough in a school which at the time had many disadvantaged (and disruptive) students. Gradually, in part through a shared interest in sport, I developed a rapport with many of them and was further rewarded when some developed a passion for art. I discovered that young people can blossom virtually overnight if sufficiently motivated and I was encouraged to even greater efforts. By the 1970s and 1980s the local school authority was strongly supporting the philosophy and approach of our art department: personal tutorials, sketchbooks, action plans which included frequent visits to galleries and museums were its hallmark. Nowadays I am proud to meet former students and discover how many of them remember their art lessons with pleasure and appreciation. It is satisfying to find that my own enthusiasm for art and life seems to have been infectious.

On reflection, it would be difficult to name only one person who influenced me since so many people, students as well as teachers, have done so. Perhaps, too, my early adversities strengthened me, aroused an understanding and zest for life as well as interest and concern for other human beings – especially young people – and nurtured my deep and abiding love of teaching.

MY ADVICE: *Inspiration is not a one-way process.*

Sir Paul Nurse
Biological Scientist, Nobel Prize Winner and Chief Executive, Cancer Research UK

I studied biology at the University of Birmingham and have been a scientist ever since. I continue to run my own laboratory, which is focused on understanding the processes that occur when a cell divides. These processes are central to understanding how cancer develops and led me to work for Cancer Research UK, as it is called now. Over the years, I took on more management responsibilities and I am now Chief Executive of the organisation – the largest of its kind outside of the United States.

I have had curiosity about the natural world since my early childhood and this was encouraged by my primary school teachers who made the world seem such an interesting place. I attended an academic state secondary school where I was fortunate to have an excellent biology teacher, Keith Neal, who encouraged his pupils to do real experiments, which were great fun.

I was never particularly fond of exams, but I found experiments really rewarding and a much more effective way for me to satisfy my curiosity about things. Perhaps most importantly, I found doing experiments to be really enjoyable. And this is one of the best pieces of advice handed down to me – do what you enjoy!

MY ADVICE: *I think there are three important things I would say in relation to biology and to being a scientist. Firstly, seek out and ask the important questions. We have come a long way in biology and we know a great deal, but there are many more important questions about the natural word which remain unanswered – pursuing these will help keep your interest when things get tough. Secondly, think differently. Try to view problems in different ways and don't be afraid to go against the flow. Thirdly, and perhaps most importantly, don't forget to laugh. Humour is a great asset; it is important when you are asking all those important questions not to take yourself too seriously!*

Wendy Parmley
Principal, Archbishop Michael Ramsey Technology College (AMR.TC)

AMR.TC is a 1,000-strong mixed comprehensive voluntary-aided school with specialist status for 11-19 year olds. We serve the estates of Camberwell, Peckham and Brixton in South London. I was the Headteacher of the school from 1992 to 2001, and have worked with the staff and students in raising our performance and leading school improvement. My main task now is to find ways of delivering the strategic vision of creating the AMR.TC 'Communiversity' – a multi-faceted learning environment to meet the needs of the whole person in a safe place, whilst at the same time continuing to work in close 'partnership in leadership' with the new Headteacher, my former Deputy, so that the rate of improvement can be sustained.

In 2001, I was made Principal of the school by the Governors which has enabled me to go on secondment to the Design Council. This means that I am also currently a co-opted member of the Learning & Public Services Team at the Design Council.

Two people have inspired and guided me in my career, Pat Roberts and John Stevenson OBE, and both in similar ways in the first two stages of the journey to the top of my chosen profession. I am still in regular contact with both mentors.

Pat Roberts was Deputy Head and interviewed me for my first job at a school in East London. Although distant in the structure, she was my ultimate boss. Pat made a difference to me in a number of ways both personally and professionally. Being from the North of England, I was a long way from home and she empathised, having moved south herself. She also has daughters a similar age to me. Pat advised me on accommodation and safety issues for a young woman living alone in London. Professionally, Pat spotted the potential in me to reach the top and, by guiding me into continuing my professional development by attending relevant courses, enabled me to gain the self-confidence required to go for promotion at an early age. In my second year of teaching, I worked with Pat on a chapter for a book on language across the curriculum and I quickly learnt the art of active research and collaboration by modelling myself on her behaviour.

Pat's advice to me was to build up a track record of evidence and experience which would speak for itself . . . and she also taught me how to dress properly in readiness for the next job. Credibility of one's potential capability counts for 90 per cent of one's appearance on first meeting and first impressions do count.

John Stevenson was Headmaster at my next school. I first joined as Head of Sixth Form but five terms later became Consortium Co-ordinator across four schools and afterwards returned to John's school as Deputy Head. John inspired me by his sheer professionalism and his style. In particular, the way in which he made me sensitive to the effect of the environment upon people's behaviour has become increasingly relevant to me. I watched and listened to him teach, prepare for meetings and conduct himself in a way that was almost actor-like, in role as Head taking on the duty and responsibility with the accountability for one's actions uppermost. He also taught me how to switch off and to find the time to 'sharpen one's own saw' and so be refreshed and ready to face each new day and its special challenge with renewed vigour.

MY ADVICE: *Be fair and frank in your dealings with people at all levels, deal with issues as swiftly as they arise, and remember, the children in our* *care only have one chance and we as adults are responsible for making it their best chance.*

Sir Martin Rees FRS
Astronomer Royal, King's College, Cambridge

I've spent most of my career as a university teacher and research scientist. I am now a Royal Society Research Professor at the University of Cambridge, and also Visiting Professor at Imperial College London and at Leicester University. I held research jobs in the UK and the US, before becoming a professor at Sussex University, and then for 10 years, Director of Cambridge's Institute of Astronomy.

I have served on many bodies connected with education, space research, arms control and international collaboration in science, and have always tried to communicate my work to a wide public.

As well as scientific papers I've written six books (the most recent being *Just Six Numbers*, *Our Cosmic Habitat* and *Our Final Century?*), and numerous magazine and newspaper articles on scientific and general subjects.

I was very fortunate in many of my teachers, who taught me enough to gain entry to university. But it's those who I encountered early on who've left the deepest impression. If I had to single out one formative influence, it would be my first geography teacher.

Don Bayliss, a Mancunian, was a fine geographer. In his spare time he gained a PhD and wrote on local history. For more than 30 years, he worked at the same school, Bedstone in Shropshire. He taught geography brilliantly, but what was even more marvellous was the way he taught everything else. G.K. Chesterton averred that, 'if something is worth doing, it is worth doing badly'. This seemed to be Don Bayliss's maxim. The most unmusical among us had violins put in our hands; we were all encouraged to draw, paint and make models; to go on small-scale expeditions and gather wildlife; to sing, act and play games. Some pupils had untapped talent, but Don Bayliss tapped the untalent of the rest of us. I still can't draw well, but I enjoy trying. I learnt, early on, to appreciate natural history. I'm not musical, but I still like to bash out slow movements on the piano when nobody's listening.

I turned out to be good at maths, and that led me towards a career in science. But Don Bayliss inspired me to do and enjoy many things I was bad at. For that, and for much else, I'm eternally grateful to him.

MY ADVICE: *One of the wisest remarks I know, from C. S. Lewis, is really a warning: 'Most people spend most of their lives doing neither what they want to be doing nor what they ought to be doing.'*

Julie Reilly
Headteacher, Comberton Middle School

I am the Headteacher of Comberton Middle School in Kidderminster, Worcestershire where we have 640 pupils aged 9-13 years. I am also Chairperson of Gateway Refuge Bromsgrove, a place for women and children who seek refuge from domestic violence.

Children have been and continue to be my inspiration. From student, to teacher, to headteacher, I have been guided by those I have had the privilege to teach. The hands I've held, the smiles I've received and the tears I've wiped away have taught me to respect and learn from the children of the day, our tomorrow, our future.

So many children in our society look disadvantage and adversity in the eye and, with someone who values them at their side, rise above it.

MY ADVICE: *To student teachers I would say, value every child, teach them to value others and always remember that you have the capacity to touch souls and shape lives.*

Clare Nkweto Simmonds
Technical Consultant, Oracle Corporation and
Big Brothers & Sisters mentor

I was at school in Tanzania, and then studied Film and Literature at the University of Warwick, graduating in 1994. Since then I have had various jobs including PA to the Commercial Director at Birmingham City Football Club, and Project Administrator to launch two housing projects. In 1997, I returned to study at Aston University for a year to get a Masters degree. I then joined Oracle Corporation where I have worked as a Technical Consultant since 1998.

In 1996, I joined a black graduates' mentoring scheme (Imani). It was a year-long project incorporating professional development courses, personal development courses and being placed with a professional mentor working in your chosen career. I had just finished a degree in film and literature and was interested in working in the media, so I was placed with news presenter Ronke Phillips.

Ronke and I hit it off straight away, and it was similar to having a new friend in my life. As we had interests in common we often met for social events or just for a chat. However, unlike an ordinary friend, Ronke was also committed to helping me develop to my full potential. Throughout the year she put in many hours talking me through career options, helping me with my CV, interview technique and arranging work shadow opportunities for me. When I hit any personal or career setbacks during the year, Ronke would be straight round with moral support. When I finally decided that I would not pursue a media career and moved towards working in the IT industry, Ronke was fully supportive and helped out. She was uncritical and always there for me, and for that I will always be grateful.

The next year I completed my MSc Information Technology (conversion course) and before I had finished the course, I had already secured a job as Technical Consultant with Oracle. I am now pursuing a career I love, surrounded by supportive people like Ronke.

It was an honour to be mentored. Ronke and I are still good friends and it was because of this positive experience that I decided to become a mentor with Big Brothers & Sisters.

MY ADVICE: *If at first you don't succeed, keep trying and stay positive! Although there are lots of shorter IT courses out there, they are difficult to get real work with. Aspire to go to university, as a degree will enable you to gain graduate entry into the IT industry. If you do not initially gain the 'A' Levels required, attend access courses or start with HSC/HND qualifications and then progress to the full university degree course.*

Remember a journey of a thousand miles begins with one step.

the NHS and medicine

Sir Magdi Yacoub
Heart Surgeon and Founder, Chain of Hope charity

I feel it is a great privilege to have the opportunity to do a job, which I am totally committed to, love so much and therefore enjoy most, if not all, aspects of it. How did that come about?

I grew up in Egypt, having been born in a small village in the north of the country, in the Nile Delta. My father was a surgeon who worked for the government and therefore was posted in different parts of Egypt. These places varied from small villages like the one where I was born, to different-sized towns and cities and eventually to the capital, Cairo. As a young boy, I had to change school every few years, which meant losing touch with most of my friends and trying to adapt to a new environment. Initially, I thought this was very stressful but as time went on, I began to enjoy the 'challenge' and discovered that meeting different people was both enjoyable and educational. That lesson has stayed with me to the present day. As I admired and identified with my father and his profession from a very young age, I declared (around the age five to seven years) that I wanted to be a heart surgeon for a variety of reasons including the tragic death of a young aunt from narrowing of a heart valve which I was told by my father was correctable only in very few centres around the world at that time. That type of gross inequality in health care delivery around the world is only slightly better today, an issue which needs to be addressed. My father said that I was not well suited for this venture and that seemed to make me try harder. When I finished medical school at Cairo University, I came to the UK to pursue higher education and training in cardiac surgery.

Several people were a source of great inspiration to me. Space will allow me to mention only three. The late Sir Peter Medawar impressed me by his contribution to mankind in more than one field. His work in transplantation biology, for which he was awarded the Nobel Prize, was the first to show that the immune system can be modulated, and this was one of the main reasons why organ transplantation became a reality. Interestingly, his pursuit of inducing specific immune tolerance, allowing the transplanted organ to be accepted without the need for giving drugs for life, is still the Holy Grail of all transplant surgeons and physicians. He was also a philosopher and a humanist who contributed significantly to our thinking both through his lectures and many books on the subject. I had the privilege to attend one of his lectures while I was a junior faculty at the University of Chicago in the late 60s, then I got to know him better after returning to the UK.

Another person who had an important influence on me was the late Lord Brock who was a cardiac surgeon with an incisive mind which he used to great advantage in simplifying problems which looked complex. The third person is Mr O.S. Tubbs, another cardiothoracic surgeon, who was a perfectionist and a real gentleman, who practised what he preached and was an absolute model for all of his trainees, including myself.

After my year in Chicago, I returned to Harefield Hospital which is a regional cardiothoracic centre surrounded by beautiful countryside. This place acted as an inspiration to me as, apart from the natural beauty of the surrounding environment, it is unique in having special spirit and work ethics devoted to patient care within the NHS. The hospital later joined the Royal Brompton Hospital, another institution with a long, distinguished history in the field of heart and chest medicine and surgery.

One of the important influences on my career has been the British Heart Foundation (BHF), a charity funded by the community and devoted to heart research. The BHF supported my work and research over many years. This makes me proud but I also feel the tremendous responsibility because I know that this support comes from the community at large who elected to help. Supporting research is such a noble cause, as it has the potential of saving many lives and enhancing our knowledge. A lot of it will happen in the future and therefore requires foresight and determination. My life has been and continues to be shaped by many people and events. I hope to pay back at least some of the debt I owe to the people and the wonderful world we all live in.

One way of doing that is to help the global community, particularly the developing world where there is a great deal of preventable suffering and disease. In an attempt to contribute to that, I helped in the establishment and running of a charity called Chain of Hope. It is dedicated to help children with heart disease through going on missions to several countries in Africa, the Middle East, Jamaica and other places to operate on these children and help in establishing sustainable units in the country to continue the work. In addition, the charity brings children to the UK for 'corrective' operations. During their stay in the UK, the children are looked after by local and other host families who act as an important link in the chain.

I believe that an important principle which has worked for me is to pursue a career in something (whatever it is) which the individual concerned feels very strongly about, loves, is totally committed to and therefore will find it enjoyable, to pursue over long periods of time.

* * *

Professor Michael Adler CBE
Professor of Genito-Urinary Medicine, Royal Free and University College Medical School

I studied medicine at Middlesex Hospital Medical School in London and qualified in 1965. I specialised in sexually transmitted diseases and HIV/AIDS, and was appointed to the first chair in the UK in this subject in 1979. I have served on various government and research committees and was seconded to the Department of Health to develop a national sexual health and HIV strategy. I am particularly interested in sexual health and HIV/AIDS in the developing world.

Two people made a difference for me in my career, one of whom said, 'you can do it' and the other who said, 'you had better do it'. I was studying arts at 'A' Levels with a place at Cambridge to read English when I decided that I wanted to do medicine. I was not very academic (whatever that really means) and had not enjoyed science. The school were not supportive except for my personal tutor, Harold Greenleaves. He was a rather traditional, quiet and conservative man feared by most of us. I knew he had reservations, but supported me, 'you can do it'. I have never forgotten him and still keep in touch with him now in his 90s.

The Dean at the Middlesex Hospital Medical School, Sir Brian Windeyer, an All Black rugby international, was not impressed by my scraped 'A' Level results. Unusual for a London medical school at that time, he told me to give up rugger which, unlike 'A' Levels, I enjoyed and was rather good at. He gave me one year to prove myself, 'you had better do it or you are out'. I can still feel his boot on my behind, but of course it was what I needed. Someone who supported me but realised that I needed to learn how to apply myself. I never failed another exam or looked back. The rest is history, and yes, I did play rugby again.

Andrew Calder
Professor of Obstetrics and Gynaecology

I was educated at Glasgow Academy and the Glasgow University Medical School, followed by postgraduate training in obstetrics and gynaecology in Glasgow teaching hospitals. I have since worked as a Clinical Research Fellow in the Nuffield Department of Obstetrics and Gynaecology, University of Oxford and as a Lecturer, then Senior Lecturer in Obstetrics and Gynaecology in the University of Glasgow. Since 1986, I have been Professor and Head of Obstetrics and Gynaecology in the University of Edinburgh. Lately I have served as Vice-Dean of the Faculty of Medicine, and I am currently Chairman of the Academy of Royal Colleges and Faculties in Scotland.

Even if the PiggyBankKids Project was not supporting the charity Big Brothers & Sisters with this book, I would have no hesitation in identifying my own sister, Kathleen as the person who most influenced and inspired my career in medicine. The eldest of four children of a Scottish manse (I was the youngest) she preceded me by nine years at the Glasgow Medical School and during that time metamorphosed from a prim and proper studious and shy schoolgirl into a dynamic decisive and assertive young woman, who showed me that I could and should pursue a career in medicine and was an ideal role model. Although the first half of the twentieth century had seen the acceptance of women into medical careers, the 1960s were still a time when women were expected to subordinate their careers to those of their husbands and families. Kathleen devoted herself to her doctor husband, and both of their sons followed in their medical footsteps, but she remained always interested in the career development of her youngest brother.

She died in 2002 after many years of complex and harrowing illnesses and operations, during which she showed enormous courage and maintained a wonderful devotion to the needs of other people. Many teachers and professional colleagues have given me far more help that I ever deserved, but Kathleen was always the one who best understood me, advised me and encouraged me. She enjoyed and cherished life, not just her own but those of others, and I will never forget the impact she had on mine.

MY ADVICE: *Although entry to medical school now requires the highest levels of scholastic attainment, a successful and happy career in medicine requires a willingness to see beyond the narrow targets of passing examinations. Many of the most intellectually gifted colleagues I have known have been much less concerned with such narrow goals than with the need to have a broad tolerant and sympathetic understanding of the needs and failings of others. While the pursuit of personal happiness may seem selfish, an unhappy doctor is likely to be an ineffective one and the attainment of happiness lies much more in seeing improvements in the conditions of others, both in terms of health and professional progress than in monetary wealth and status, and above all we must try to keep a sense of humour.*

Dame Jill Ellison
Nursing Director, Birmingham Heartlands & Solihull NHS Trust

I was born in Wakefield, Yorkshire, and grew up travelling extensively due to my father being in the Armed Forces. Following nurse training I also spent two years in Israel, first on a kibbutz and then at the Hadassah Hospital in Jerusalem.

I undertook nurse training at the Middlesex Hospital in London, then specialised in general surgery and later intensive care, at the Charing Cross Hospital in Hammersmith. In 1980, I further qualified as a community-based Health Visitor working with several busy GP practices in a number of inner city areas.

In 1983, I moved into nurse management undertaking a variety of roles in the community, hospital and health authority settings. During this time I gained a Diploma in Management Studies at Birmingham Polytechnic and also a Health Economics Certificate from Aberdeen University. In 1990 I joined East Birmingham Hospital as the General Manager for Women's and Children's Services and also as Professional Head of Nursing. Since then the hospital has merged with Solihull Hospital and is now part of a large hospital teaching trust. I am now the Executive Nurse Director on the Trust Board. I also completed my MA in Human Resource Development in 2000, sit on a number of national forums and represent the West Midlands nurses on the National Nursing Leadership Project.

Miss Booth, my teacher at Skellfield school, was an unexpected source of inspiration. She had a big personality and would always find time to listen, and offer support and advice in a non-judgemental sort of way.

By the age of ten, as a services child, I had attended many schools both in England and abroad. So many new faces, so many fresh starts. This could not continue; something inside me realised that I needed educational stability. To my parents' horror, and after much nagging on my part, they reluctantly agreed to me attending boarding school in England. It was hard, very hard; parents living overseas, 11 years old and I didn't know a soul, homesick for all I knew and loved.

Miss Booth gave freely of her time, she spent many hours listening and talking with me. She gave me emotional security, strength, resilience and a thirst for achievement. She made me realise that only I could set my goals and achieve them.

In summary she was an incredibly caring person, who taught me a lot about the importance of the inner spirit and developed a belief in me that even when life was tough it wouldn't be like that indefinitely.

Ruth Evans
Health Sector and Consumer Affairs Champion, Chair of the Independent Inquiry into Drug Testing at Work

I worked for many years in the voluntary sector, running organisations which represent the interests of consumers, and now, in my 40s, work in the public and private sectors, mainly in health, in bringing my experience to a wide range of interesting commissions and inquiries.

After I left university, I first volunteered for Liberty, the civil rights charity, then became Director of the Maternity Alliance, then Deputy Director of the UK's leading mental health charity Mind, then General Secretary of War on Want, followed by a period as consultant to the National Rubella Council and the Department of Health. For seven years, I was the Director of the National Consumer Council representing the interests of consumers of goods and services, especially disadvantaged consumers. I served the maximum appointed term as Director there, and since 1998 have taken on a range of different interesting commitments including chairing an Inquiry into Paediatric Cardiac Services at the Royal Brompton and Harefield Hospitals Trust. My current appointments include Chair of the Independent Inquiry into Drug Testing at Work; Lay Member of the General Medical Council, Member of the Human Genetics Commission (and Chair of its Public Involvement Group); Member of the Medicines Commission and Member of the Independent Review Panel for the advertising of medicines for human use. I am also a non-executive Director of the Nationwide Building Society where I contribute my consumer expertise.

My Headteacher, Margaret Newton, was the single most influential individual outside of my family. I met her when I was 12, when I was sent away to school following the break-up of my parents' marriage. I had been extremely troubled as a result of the situation at home and, following my referral to a child psychiatrist, it was agreed that I should attend a boarding school in the wilds of Gloucestershire. It was a dreadful place, full of posh girls and weird teachers, unlike anything I had experienced at Willesden Comprehensive in North London! I was desperately unhappy and felt abandoned, stupid and unloved. Miraculously, my Headteacher, Margaret Newton, recognised my unhappiness and supported me through it over the years. She was always there to listen, to laugh, to empathise: she encouraged me to reflect on my feelings and to express what I felt in writing. It was profoundly affecting to come across someone who believed in me; she felt I had something to offer, made me feel valued and wanted me to succeed. She gave me hope and trust. It has stayed with me throughout my adult life.

Anne Jackson-Baker
Director, Royal College of Midwives, UK Board for England

I have been a midwife for over 30 years, practising initially in East Anglia and then the North West of England. I was a clinical midwife for 20 years and a midwife teacher for four years prior to joining the staff of the Royal College of Midwives (RCM) in 1992, initially as a Senior Professional Officer.

I have been the Director of the RCM UK Board for England for eight years. I am based in the Board office in Leeds, but my work takes me around the whole country. I am the senior manager of the staff that delivers employment relations and professional services to the 27,000 RCM members in England.

My role includes the professional lead for the College on English specific issues. Two pieces of work that I am currently delighted to be working on are the NHS Midwifery Leadership programme that has developed the Midwifery Leadership Competency Model and the Development Centre for Midwife Leaders and Birthrate Plus.

Both programmes will play a key role in improving maternity services for both midwives and the women and families they serve.

I first qualified as a midwife in 1971, and in 1984 was bringing up a family and working part-time on night duty. I wanted to return to full-time work and realised that to progress my career I would have to leave the camaraderie of my night staff colleagues and return to 'days'.

Jean Bracken, the Director of Midwifery Services and my senior manager, supported me in this and advised me to undertake the Advanced Diploma in Midwifery (ADM). Prior to midwifery degree courses the ADM was the route into career advancement and further education. Jean changed my life and career direction by saying yes to me at a time when the NHS culture was to say no. She boosted my sense of worth by taking an interest in me and by giving sound advice and encouragement.

The challenges sent by ADM and the people I met inspired me absolutely; they challenged my preconceptions and turned my thinking on its head. They opened up my mind and made me hungry for knowledge.

Eventually I became a midwife teacher and while in this job I was invited to contribute to a project that in turn contributed to the future of midwifery This introduced me to the movers and shakers, political and professional, and ultimately led to my working for the Royal College of Midwives in roles that have enabled me to influence the way in which midwives and the work they do are perceived and respected.

None of this would have happened without Jean, but it was the ADM that inspired me to move up a gear into midwifery leadership.

MY ADVICE: *A career is a journey that involves continual development and the need always to be looking round the next corner. Above all it is working with people to improve both the profession and the quality of midwifery services.*

David Kerr CBE
Rhodes Professor of Therapeutic Sciences and Clinical Pharmacology and Director, National Translational Cancer Research Network

'I want you to read a special book,' said his Auntie Anne. The wee boy squinted up at her, immediately curious. 'All these Sundays of us sitting reading and learning new words, well, this is why. The book's called *The Citadel* (by A. J. Cronin) and although there's some grown-up stuff in it, it's about justice, equality and being true to your roots. You're a clever wee oddity, Davy, and I want you to read this book and become the young doctor in it. That's the path for you to follow.'

'Aye,' said the wee boy.

Today, I work with my colleagues in Oxford to build a new Institute for Cancer Medicine. My own specialist area lies in the treatment of and research into colo-rectal cancer, and I am developing new approaches to cancer treatment which involve gene therapy. I have been fortunate to receive recognition for my work through the award of several international prizes, and the first Nye Bevan award for innovation. I have published more than 250 articles in medical journals and have contributed to many books on cancer. I work with other experts in the field as a member of the National Cancer Taskforce and of the Commission for Health Improvement. I am Chair of the Cancer Services Collaborative, a leading cancer pathway re-design project and the Editor-in-Chief of *Annals of Oncology*, Europe's premier medical oncology journal.

I also have a sense of rhythm and have appeared as drummer at revues at venues as varied as Ronnie Scott's and Symphony Hall in Birmingham.

MY ADVICE: *Be curious (not nosy).*
Ask questions (the right ones).
Don't give up (ever)!

Dr Ian Laing
Clinical Director, Neonatal Unit, Simpson Centre for Reproductive Health, Royal Infirmary of Edinburgh

I am a Consultant Neonatologist. My job involves caring for ill babies from the moment of their delivery until the time they are ready for home. I also teach undergraduates and postgraduates, and carry out research into the causes of illness in premature and mature infants. I have been invited to lecture on Newborn Medicine in many parts of the world, including Africa, Asia, Australia, USA and Canada.

. Born in Scotland, I attended Buckie High School and then Magdalen College School, Oxford. I was an undergraduate at the Universities of Cambridge and Edinburgh, and later was awarded a two-year Fellowship in the Joint Program in Neonatology, Harvard Medical School, Boston, Massachusetts. As a schoolboy I was a violinist in the National Youth Orchestra of Great Britain, and was its leader from 1967–70.

The Austrian violinist Fritz Kreisler (1875–1962) has been my constant inspiration. Fritz's father was a doctor, a native of Krakow, Poland, and an amateur violinist. Fritz required no formal violin instruction after the age of 12, and this allowed his genius to emerge in a truly instinctive way. I spent much of my childhood listening to recordings of Fritz Kreisler playing his own compositions – Caprice Viennois, Schön Rosmarin, Liebeslied. His tone and phrasing transcended anything I had ever heard.

It was my violin which took me to the National Youth Orchestra, thence to Oxford and Cambridge. Although I pursued a career in medicine, it was Kreisler who had opened up a path for a schoolboy from the north-east of Scotland. His influence is with me today. Every morning I play works by Bach and Kreisler before I leave for work at 7 a.m. My lovely Italian violin serves as an antidote to the stresses of newborn intensive care. On December 6th 1993, I attended a Neonatology conference in Washington D.C. and happened on Kreisler's Guarneri violin in the National Library of Congress. For two hours, the curator allowed me to play Kreisler's compositions on his own great instrument. Kreisler's music had given me a career in medicine, and Neonatology had brought me to Kreisler's Guarneri.

MY ADVICE: *Find something outside your working life which makes you fulfilled. Allow this fulfilment to infect your professional work. It is amazing how helpful previously-obstructive colleagues will be if you are cheerful and enthusiastic about your professional goals.*

Professor Averil Mansfield CBE
Professor of Surgery

I grew up in Blackpool and studied at the University of Liverpool. I worked as a Lecturer in Surgery and as a Consultant Surgeon at the Royal Liverpool Hospital. Since 1993 I have been Professor of Vascular Surgery at Imperial College School of Medicine at St Mary's Hospital, and was the first woman professor of surgery in the UK to become chairman of a department of surgery, a role I continued until 1999. I was a Consultant Vascular Surgeon at St Mary's Hospital, Great Ormond Street Children's Hospital and Hammersmith Hospital, all in London. I am also an Associate Medical Director with St Mary's NHS Trust. I was Vice President of the Royal College of Surgeons and also the Chairman of its Professional Standards Board. I was the founding chairman of the women in surgical training initiative of the college.

Edgar Parry is a gentle Welshman and a now-retired surgeon. I first met him when I was approaching finals in medicine at Liverpool University. He was then a consultant surgeon working at Broadgreen Hospital in Liverpool and he has been my surgical role model throughout my career. What was it about him that made him such a powerful influence on me?

He was about as far removed from the 'James Robertson Justice' model as you could wish to meet. Always a gentleman and always gentle, with patients, with staff, and with aspiring surgeons like me. Humiliation and intimidation had no part in his approach. Rather praise when justified and forgiveness when not. Like my father, his look of disappointment was a greater incentive to do better than any reprimand could ever have been.

He supported, encouraged and nurtured my career aspirations

in those crucial early years. My response has been to try to do likewise.

Doctor Tahir Mahmood
Consultant Obstetrician and Clinical Director

I completed my medical studies at King Edward Medical College in Lahore, Pakistan. I then completed my clinical training in Zambia and in Scotland. I worked as a junior doctor in Scotland at Forth Park Hospital in Kirkcaldy, Glasgow Royal Maternity Hospital, Bellshill Maternity Hospital, Raigmore, and Inverness and Aberdeen Maternity Hospital before taking up my present appointment as Consultant Obstetrician and Gynaecologist in Kirkcaldy, Fife. I hold clinical academic appointments at the Universities of Edinburgh, St Andrew's, Dundee and Aberdeen. I am actively involved in teaching medical students and junior doctors who are pursuing a career in women's healthcare.

As a young boy growing up in Pakistan, I was fortunate to be surrounded by a large, loving family. There was always plenty of free advice – some of it welcome, some unsolicited, much of it useful, some of dubious value – but all of it well meaning. I quickly learned to 'sift through the data' and decided for myself which of it to heed.

My teacher, Abdullah, was a wise man who influenced me greatly. His advice was always worth listening to. Often he would illustrate his point with a story to get his message across. I vividly remember sitting in our garden on a warm evening with my brothers while he told us the story of Robert the Bruce and the spider, and how, if at first you don't succeed, you must try, try and try again.

When I came to Scotland as a young doctor 20 years ago, there were exams to sit, job interviews with stiff competition, research projects to do (and get the results published) as well as coping with a different culture in a miserable climate and missing my friends and family. It was hard. My teacher's story about the Scottish king who refused to give up had stuck in my mind and kept me going through some tough times. I felt that King Robert's example was of particular relevance now that I was living and working in the exotic land of mist, castles and heather that my teacher had told me about all those years ago in our garden in Pakistan. My teacher taught me the importance of perseverance and hard work in achieving our goals and ambitions – universal principles equally valid today as in the fourteenth century.

MY ADVICE: *There is no higher goal in life than the acquisition of spirit to serve humanity. Medicine is a noble profession; develop a burning desire to be compassionate, kind, considerate, humble, courteous and generous, and nurture a commitment to serve fellow human beings.*

Never lose sight of your ultimate goal in life. Be passionate and persevere to achieve it. Your personal commitment and dedication are the keys to success.

Sarah Skelton
Director of Nursing & Midwifery, United Lincolnshire Hospitals NHS Trust

The person who inspired me in my career was Miss Elsie Clunes, the Head of Midwifery Service at Southlands Hospital, Shoreham by Sea, Sussex.

At school I was a failure, teachers continually advised me that I was not bright enough to achieve my ambition of becoming a vet, and I reacted by becoming disruptive and ended up leaving school at the age of 16 with no qualifications.

On leaving school, I entered the Cadet Nursing course at Lincoln, where I found the work interesting and began to feel valued and enjoyed being able to care for others.

However, when I decided I wanted to become a midwifery tutor in 1973 it was clear I needed to obtain a further academic qualification in order to be accepted. I applied to do the University of London Diploma in Nursing course at Brighton College, but my application was not considered as I had no GCSEs. Fortunately, Miss Clunes believed in my ability and gave me her total backing. She contacted the tutors at Brighton and persuaded them 'to take the risk' of allowing me to study for the Diploma. Her support and intervention were successful.

I started the course and found the work stimulating and

rewarding. It proved to be one of the most enjoyable periods of my career. I successfully completed the Diploma which enabled me to undertake the Midwifery Tutors Diploma at the Royal College of Midwives in London, qualifying in 1976. This proved to be the gateway to my career.

I worked as a midwifery tutor before entering nursing and midwifery management, allowing me to progress to my present post of Director of Nursing & Midwifery for United Lincolnshire Hospitals NHS Trust. This is an acute hospital trust covering the whole of Lincolnshire with approximately 1,900 beds and a financial turnover of over £200 million per year.

Not only did Miss Clunes believe in me, but more importantly she made me believe in myself and be confident in my ability to achieve my aim.

MY ADVICE: *To have a clear vision of what you want to do, be committed and confident; believe in your own ability and want to care for others.*

Dr Jane Zuckerman
Director, Academic Centre for Travel Medicine & Vaccines and The Royal Free Travel Health Centre, Royal Free & University College Medical School

I attended the Henrietta Barnet School in North London, and received my medical education at the Royal Free Hospital School of Medicine, University of London, graduating in 1987.

After junior posts in Medicine and Surgery, I was appointed a Senior Clinical Research Fellow and Honorary Consultant in 1995, and Head of the Academic Centre for Travel Medicine and Vaccines at the Royal Free Hospital School of Medicine. I was promoted to Senior Lecturer and Honorary Consultant at the Centre and the Royal Free Hospital in 1997 and 1998 respectively and also as Medical Director of the Royal Free Clinical Trials Centre, and subsequently the Royal Free Travel Health Centre.

I received the Special Achievement Award for European Clinical Research in 1999, and the UK Hospital Doctor Innovation Award in 2001. I was nominated as the UK Hospital Doctor of the Year in 2001. In December 2001, I was cited by the British Medical

Association in a published report as one of the 82 'pioneers in patient care: consultants leading change'.

I was inspired to be a high achiever by Mrs Birchall, a teacher at the Tea House, a nursery school preparing children for entry mainly to the Henrietta Barnet Junior School, in Hampstead Garden Suburb, London. Careful nurturing, stimulation and encouragement by Mrs Birchall led to the acceptance by the Royal Drawing Society of two of my paintings, *Tarzan in the Trees* and *The Clown*, for exhibition when I was nearly four years old. The exhibition was held in 1967. The paintings, incidentally, are still treasured by my parents.

Thus the guidance I received in early life in a welcoming and happy nursery school provided the inspiration to achievement throughout my school and academic life.

MY ADVICE: *Success in medicine is the result of absolute commitment to the profession based on dedication, a labour of love and not just hard work, resilience during many years of training, compassion and more than just a grain of ambition.*

emergency services

Sir John Stevens
Commissioner, Metropolitan Police

I have been in policing for 40 years, working my way from constable through every rank to commissioner in that time. Serving different forces and conducting investigations around the world, I have come into contact with many people who have had an enormously positive influence on me as well as those around me.

At the same time there have been a few who have taught me, through their ignorance, unprofessionalism and what can only be described as their self-centred approach, the way things should not be done.

The contrast between the two approaches has been a great education and influence in itself.

This influence, which is important, varies in impact depending on the job you are doing and where you are in the organisation, although it is interesting to see if there is consistency running through different levels of the police service. For example, do those who influence and lead at a junior level have any similarities with others who can create and shape a leadership and philosophy capable of dealing with the challenges at the most senior levels of policing?

Certainly, those I admired most as constables, detective constables and detective sergeants could be best described as task-orientated, having a high degree of professional ability and success, mainly related to the job immediately in front of them.

At its best, policing is about being proactive. For the successful detective it is about investigating and identifying those who have committed criminal offences. The principles are the same – whether it is a case of theft, violent assault, murder or terrorism – we are, after all, the agency of both first and last resort. As a result our success can be measured possibly by way of simple delivery, however difficult that can sometimes be.

There are two outstanding individuals who have particularly influenced me during the course of my service. The first was a detective inspector who went on to become a chief constable. He appeared calm in all situations, had an impressive appearance and was a very effective communicator. Added to that, he set high standards for himself and others to follow. If you maintained these standards you enjoyed his support.

He encouraged innovation and risk-taking – something that historically the police were not good at doing. Mistakes made in good faith were not criticised or attacked in a way that undermined those making them.

He could criticise constructively. On one occasion I saw him confront a senior officer in what can best be described as circumstances amounting to corruption. As a result of his intervention the corrupt approaches stopped. In another instance, in a pub, a conversation led to someone criticising a colleague and close friend. The thought went through my mind that with friends like that who needs enemies. The detective inspector told the critic that unless he stopped he would leave his drink on the bar and go. The man continued so he promptly left.

In short, he made me feel proud that he was a member of the police service and my senior officer. The qualities he displayed inspired our team to higher standards.

For me the influencing factors as a chief officer have to go beyond those exhibited by the detective inspector. The ability to influence needs to be more sophisticated. It is imperative that these top leaders succeed in both the operational and political environment.

One particular chief constable, who I greatly admired, influenced me immensely. Like the Detective Inspector, he had the ability to encourage innovation and was a man with impeccable standards. More importantly, he had a strong vision of the future.

Today, I suppose he would be described as a radical moderniser. However, his radicalism was rooted in common sense and an unparalleled professional knowledge.

His ability to influence his Police Authority was awesome. There were occasions when he had to stand his ground in extremely difficult circumstances. He always did this, even under provocation, in a controlled, polite and professional manner. A consummate diplomat when the need arose, he often showed both physical and moral courage.

I saw him in the art of persuading and influencing those who are our political masters. From him I learnt the reality that success for the police service could not be achieved without meaningful partnership and support from local and central government. I also learnt that it was important to support your colleagues at every level and that success could never be achieved unless morale was right within your own organisation.

He exemplified this in his determination not to be an 'absent landlord' as chief constable. Not for him weeks of absence pursuing other national policing business. In his own words he was determined to 'ensure that the home fires were kept burning', and the job for which he was paid, namely leading a large county force, was his primary responsibility and activity. This force became the most modern and probably the most effective of any at that time in the UK.

The detective inspector and the chief constable have, without doubt, had the most influence on my approach to policing. There were similarities and contrasts between them. They showed me how to succeed in difficult circumstances. I learnt the importance of resilience, which is so vital in the demanding and challenging job of policing.

Both of these impressive people were their own men. Good listeners and able to operate at every level of society, they had the ability to care for and relate to those who were less well advantaged in society.

They were men with a high sense of duty and a genuine love for policing and people. They epitomised the attitude 'don't do to others anything you do not want done to yourself'.

This philosophy underpins all that I do.

* * *

Janette Berry
Police Officer/ Chairman of the Police Federation of England and Wales

Whilst I am a serving police officer, I have been elected by my colleagues to represent them in our staff association. This is a full-time commitment where I speak on behalf of 129,000 police officers in England and Wales. I need to keep myself apprised of all issues affecting policing and seek to represent the views of my colleagues to influence constructive improvements to policing in England and Wales.

In a funny sort of way the main inspiration for my life (apart from my parents and husband) was my Headteacher from my primary school. At the age of 11 he deemed that I was not suitable for a grammar school education, despite having been in the top set throughout my primary school life.

The effect of this during the intervening years has made me very determined to fight injustice, be un-squashable and one who perseveres. I have sought to turn his negativity into a positive. The best advice given to me in recent years has been always to be honest with yourself and to look in the mirror in the morning and be comfortable with what you are doing and how you are doing it. Even though my life is very hectic I try to make time for people and I try to be a good listener.

MY ADVICE: *Know what you are good at, be honest with yourself, set yourself achievable targets and persevere. If at first you don't succeed try, try again.*

Hamish Campbell
Detective Superintendent, Race & Violent Crimes
Taskforce, Metropolitan Police

I am a Detective Superintendent in the Metropolitan Police. I joined the police service as a police cadet in 1974 straight from boarding school. I was attested as a Constable a year later, and transferred to the CID in 1979. I have worked in a variety of detective roles within the criminal investigation field, and this has included a number of CID offices across London, the Anti-Terrorist branch, the Criminal Intelligence section and the central London murder teams, including most recently the Jill Dando murder enquiry.

I am currently working within the Race & Violent Crimes Taskforce, which is responsible for re-investigating unsolved deaths. The investigation of murder has been my main interest and in which I have gained the widest experience during my career.

Inexplicably, and from an early age, I had always wanted to be a police officer. As a teenager I still maintained the wish, and in particular I wanted to join the CID. I had shelves of books on true crime cases and newspaper cuttings of current cases and I had an 'image' of the senior detectives and the role they played.

When I joined the Metropolitan Police I was equally determined to join the CID, but it was not as simple or as transparent a procedure as now. My public school background and difference was not the most appropriate fit.

My initial supporter and guide was Detective Chief Superintendent Basil Haddrell, now retired, who appeared to me as one of the 'gentlemen detectives' from my books. It was he who provided encouragement and advice, and interviewed me for entry into the CID. As a Detective Constable I worked as part of a team on murder investigations which he led. He displayed a calm and measured approach, and was able to help me, and had the time to explain how an enquiry worked.

He followed my career and provided support and steadiness, if only by letter, and even in retirement wrote to me during the difficult early days of the Jill Dando murder investigation.

Basil Haddrell, and a handful of senior detectives, have continued to provide inspiration as I proceeded through the CID ranks. Whilst on the central London murder squad, Detective Chief Superintendent Kenneth Woodward, also retired, provided similar support and mentoring. Such officers had a depth of investigative experience and knowledge, from which they were able to draw considerable strength and remain constantly unflustered by events.

Investigation of murder is a deeply serious and onerous responsibility and they showed me that experience was vital (hence my long years in the operational environment); and that a genuine patience and empathy with your own teams, as well as the victims, their families and the accused, is equally important.

full contributors list

Sir Andrew Turnbull
Simon Woolley

Jane Tewson CBE
Eileen Ware

Julian Richer
Roger Saul

Media   167
Introduced by Rebekah Wade,
former Editor, News of the World
  Dawn Airey
  Christiane Amanpour
  Jackie Ashley
  Lisa Aziz
  Floella Benjamin OBE
  John Bird
  Leslie Bunder
  Bill Campbell
  Peter Cox
  Susan Crosland
  Paul Dacre
  Greg Dyke
  Sir David Frost OBE
  Philip Graf
  Dylan Jones
  Diane Louise Jordan
  Mark Leishman
  Catherine MacLeod
  David Mansfield
  Terry Mansfield CBE
  Sir Trevor McDonald OBE
  Piers Morgan
  Cristina Odone
  Jeremy Paxman
  Raphael Rowe
  John Sergeant
  Jon Snow
  Carole Stone
  Parminder Vir
  Tina Weaver
  Caroline Westbrook

**Charity and Voluntary
Sector**   199
Introduced by Lord Victor
Adebowale, Chief Executive,
Turning Point
  Graeme Alexander
  Camila Batmanghelidjh
  Dorit Braun OBE
  Stephen Burke
  Beverly Cohen
  Dorothy Dalton
  Susan Daniels
  Stuart Etherington
  Pat Foxton
  Fiona Halton
  Avila Kilmurray
  Lucy Lake
  Anne Longfield
  Mary Marsh
  Richard McCarthy
  Daleep Mukarji
  Anne-Marie Piper
  David Robinson OBE
  Stephen Shields

Religion and Faith   225
Introduced by Rt Rev and Rt Hon
George Carey, former Archbishop
of Canterbury
  His Grace Bishop Angaelos
  Sister Rita Dawson
  Very Rev Andrew McLellan
  Very Rev John Miller
  Rabbi Julia Neuberger
  Archbishop Keith Patrick
    O'Brien
  Major John Thompson

**Human Rights and
Environment**   235
Introduced by Geoffrey Robertson
QC, Human Rights Lawyer
  Bob Alexander QC, Lord
    Alexander of Weedon
  Vicky Garner
  Anthony Hudson
  Professor Mike Hulme
  Lord Joel Joffe CBE
  Marilyn Mornington
  Leonor Stjepic

Farming and Countryside   249
Introduced by Michael Eavis,
Proprietor of Worthy Farm,
Somerset, and Founder and
Organiser of the Glastonbury
Festival
  Helen Browning OBE
  Ewen Cameron
  Ben Gill
  Jeannette Orrey
  Fiona Reynolds CBE

**Food, Restaurants and
Hotels**   257
Introduced by Perween Warsi,
Founder and Managing Director,
S&A Foods
  Loulla Astin
  Alan Bell
  Matthew Hooberman
  Fiona Leishman
  Paul Matteucci

Retail and Fashion   267
Introduced by Linda Bennett,
Founder and Managing Director,
L K Bennett
  Simon Burke
  Timothy Everest
  Johnny Grey
  Imtaz Khaliq
  Julia Ogilvy
  Victoria Richards

Cookery and Gardening   281
Introduced by Delia Smith, Chef
and Author
  Rocky Coles
  Mary Contini
  Rachel de Thame
  Loyd Grossman
  Janice Reilly
  Gary Rhodes
  Joe Swift
  Alan Titchmarsh MBE

Education and Science   293
Introduced by Sir John Sulston,
former Director of the Sanger
Centre founded by the Medical
Research Council and the
Wellcome Trust, Nobel Prize
winner and winner of the Mirror's
Pride of Britain Lifetime
Achievement Award for work to
sequence the human genome
  Sir Neil Chalmers
  Des Coffey
  Professor Roderick Floud
  Jenny Francis
  Baroness Susan Greenfield CBE
  Hyacinth Hall
  Keith Hewson
  Helen Hyde
  Joe Kusner MBE
  Sir Paul Nurse
  Wendy Parmley
  Sir Martin Rees FRS
  Julie Reilly
  Clare Nkweto Simmonds

The NHS and Medicine   315
Introduced by Sir Magdi Yacoub,
Heart Surgeon and Founder, The
Chain of Hope
  Professor Michael Adler CBE
  Andrew Calder
  Dame Jill Ellison
  Ruth Evans
  Anne Jackson-Baker
  David Kerr CBE
  Dr Ian Laing
  Tahir Mahmood
  Professor Averil Mansfield CBE
  Sarah Skelton
  Dr Jane Zuckerman

Emergency Services   331
Introduced by Sir John Stevens,
Commissioner, Metropolitan Police
  Janette Berry
  Hamish Campbell

index

**big brothers
& sisters**
give time change lives
www.mentoring.org.uk

What is Big Brothers & Sisters About?

It's About Time! At Big Brothers & Sisters we match adult mentors to children and young people from one-parent families. We don't ask for much from our mentors – only time (time for a careful assessment and screening, and weekly time for a child). But we know that giving time changes lives. So although we don't ask for much, we get a great deal for the children and mentors we match.

Big Brothers & Sisters is about people spending time together. Mentors spend a few hours each week with their 'mentee' doing everyday activities such as playing football, surfing the web, or simply having a chat over a milkshake. It's about friendship. It's about enriching and adding value to children's and mentors' lives. The result is about companionship and fun for both the mentor and mentee.

Why is Big Brothers & Sisters such a good thing?

Because . . . it's simple; it's special and it works!

It's Simple – We do not ask for much from our matches. We don't expect mentors to act as counsellors or behaviour therapists. We don't ask children to improve their conduct or their school grades. All we expect is that mentors and mentees will do things together that they like to do and that they talk about things they like to talk about. That's all.

It's Special – Anyone who volunteers to be a Big Brothers & Sisters mentor is matched with one child and only one. Only one mentor. Only one child. No competition. In a life when adults are so busy, the mentor commits a dedicated time each week to his or her mentee. Thus both the child and the mentor know that each week there will be time just for them: to learn about each other; to do what they want to do together. It makes them each feel special – each feels good about himself because someone likes him enough to spend time – one to one.

It Works! – Although the Big Brothers & Sisters Approach is still very new in the UK, we know it works. We know from testimonials from our first mentors and mentees here. And we know from experience and research in North America. For example, in one big American study[1], young people who had a 'Big Brother' or 'Big Sister' were found to be: 45.8 per cent less likely to initiate drug use; 36.6 per cent less likely to lie to their parent; 27.4 per cent less likely to initiate alcohol use; and 52.2 per cent less likely to truant.

How Big Brothers & Sisters started

In 1904 in Cincinnati, Irving Westheimer caught a young boy stealing from his business. When he made enquiries he found out that the boy didn't have a father. Westheimer wanted to help him and realised that more than money was needed. He gave the boy his time, encouragement and friendship. Within a short time, the boy was more confident, had greater self-esteem, stopped truanting and was generally much happier. Westheimer found the experience rewarding and decided to support more children in this way, so he founded Big Brothers, Big Sisters in America.

Where we are now

Big Brothers & Sisters is hugely successful in North America and has a very high profile, featuring in programmes such as *The Simpsons*, *ER*, *Seinfeld* and *Oprah*.

In 1998 Big Brothers, Big Sisters International was founded and Big Brothers & Sisters is now an international success story, represented in over 35 countries.

Big Brothers & Sisters UK has tailored the North American mentoring programme for this country. We launched our first local agencies in Bristol, Edinburgh, Glasgow, Birmingham and London.

We plan to expand in Wales and Northern Ireland and, within a few years, to have a network of agencies throughout the UK.

Our network of local agencies around the UK is supported by a central office in London which liaises with statutory and voluntary organisations as well as sponsors and funders and acts as the focal point for all operations, ensuring consistently high standards and keeping administrative costs to a minimum.

A mentoring agency manager, skilled in making and supporting successful mentoring matches, runs each local agency with the support of local volunteers. Mentors are recruited in partnership with local companies, other voluntary organisations and through advertising.

Big Brothers & Sisters UK has rigorous screening procedures which are integral to our mentor application and approval process. Screening and other effective measures to safeguard children on our programme are of the utmost importance and we have consulted widely with UK child protection specialists, and with experts from North America to ensure that best practice is incorporated.

How to get involved

If you want information on how to be a mentor, or to be a mentee, or to set up a local agency in your area, or to join the volunteer team, or to provide *pro bono* advice, or to be a funding partner, sponsor or donor, you can get all the relevant information from the website www.mentors.org.uk

---

[1]Public/Private Ventures (P/PV), an independent social research agency, undertook evaluation study over a period of 18 months. The research examined eight Big Brothers & Sisters mentoring programmes across the US.

PiggyBankKids

PiggyBankKids was established in 2002 by Sarah Brown to support charitable projects that create opportunities for children and young people. The charity, and its subsidiary company, PiggyBankKids Projects Limited, work on a number of specific initiatives chosen by the trustees to benefit the work of charities working in this way.

Moving On Up has been compiled and edited by Sarah Brown working with the PiggyBankKids team. The charity will receive all the royalties from the sales of this book and will be supporting Big Brothers & Sisters UK.

Contact:
Hugo Tagholm
Programme Director
PiggyBankKids Projects Limited
16 Lincoln's Inn Fields
London WC2A 3ED
Tel: 020 7936 1294
Fax: 020 7936 1299
www.piggybankkids.org

Sarah Brown is a Consultant to PR company Brunswick Arts, and President of the charity, PiggyBankKids. She is married to Gordon Brown, MP for Dunfermline East and Chancellor of the Exchequer. She is also the co-editor, with Gil McNeil, of two anthologies of short stories *Magic* and *Summer Magic* that benefit the charity, One Parent Families.